Praise

"When reading Monica Parker's *Oops! I Forgot to Save Money*, I laughed out loud then it gave me pause; HAD I forgot? I loved saving up my allowance as a child and consider myself fairly frugal, but did I even know now where my money was and exactly what it was doing?? We women are sometimes happy to let others take charge of finances as if it is something unseemly or, at best, unfeminine. OR, even worse, too complicated. Ms. Parker, with humor and charm (the Erma Bombeck of Bucks!) shows you that it's NEVER too late, and that taking even a TEENY TINY bit of control over your money will make a BIG difference in your life."

- **Jean Smart** – Mom, wife, actress (*Hacks, Mare of Easttown, Designing Women, Fargo, Watchmen,* and so much more…), Former Financial Wimp

"I laughed, I sighed and I giggled out loud reading Monica Parker's beautifully-written new book: *Oops! I Forgot to Save Money!* Monica is the sort of funny fueled by a life well and observantly lived. She has worked with many legendary talents – being one herself – but despite having a life most of us only dream about, she has remained a real human being. I am also abashed to admit that I assumed her having had an exponentially more successful and accomplished life than I have even dreamed of meant that she would not be heir to the same financial stupidity as I am just now learning to avoid. Nope, she had to learn how to deal with that most essential of commodities the hard way – just like everybody else (which I find quite comforting). Follow along as she shares stories of her amazing life, the people she's met – famous and ordinary – and in doing so, gifts us with her own hard-earned money wisdom. Practical, informative, and engaging – *Oops! I Forgot To Save Money!* will keep you hooked from the first word to the last. Do not miss this book!"

- **Maya Stiles Parsons Spier** – columnist and editor-in-chief, iPinionSyndicate.com

"*Oops! I Forgot to Save Money* is a fabulous revelatory, hilarious yet cautionary memoir. Parker has such a candid, unique and engaging voice – you fall in love with her mishaps and life journey. But it's also more than a wonderful romp of a read – it's an important book for women, most of whom, in my opinion, have been culturally handicapped to ignore their finances. As a game creator, I've always said that people 'learn best when they don't *know* they're learning.' The same applies to this book... you'll walk away with a smile on your face but an urging in your soul to take your head out of the sand!"

- **Laura Robinson** – Creator of the bestselling game *Balderdash*, inspiring motivational speaker, *Chicken Soup for the Soul* co-author, owner & executive producer of *Out & About Productions, LLC.*

"Monica Parker's amazing and courageously frank book "Oops! I Forgot to Save Money" lifts the cover on that most secret of topics… money. Whether you have it or live with the fear that you will never have enough to provide a safe landing, the subject of money is the last Taboo, and Monica believes we will all be better off if we can share our mistakes and lessons learned. She has made many, and so have many of the people who spoke with her. Their willingness to share will inspire and make you laugh out loud!"

- **Karen Tanz** – entrepreneur, producer of *Diana the Musical* on Broadway, Netflix Broadway investor of Tony Award and Olivier Winning Musical *Come From Away*, producer of upcoming Broadway musical *Almost Famous*

Also by Monica Parker:

OMG! How Children See God

Getting Waisted: A Survival Guide to Being Fat in a Society that Loves Thin

Oops! I Forgot to Save Money

And It Turns Out, I'm Not Alone!

by Monica Parker

Smart House Books

Copyright © 2021 by Monica Parker

All rights reserved. No part of this publication may be reproduced, distributed or transmitted in any form or by any means, without prior written permission.

Monica Parker is available to speak to your group with her witty, yet inspirational message that money woes are universal.
For more information, visit her website:
www.IamMonicaParker.com

Smart House Books
Toronto, On.
www.smarthousebooksandmedia.com

Front cover design – Michael Moore, www.michaelmoore.studio

Interior formatting and cover layout – Aaron Rachel Brown

ISBN 978-1-988980-13-3

Table of Contents

FOREWORD 11

CHAPTER 1 13
The Wolf Is At Our Door and He Has a Key

CHAPTER 2 21
Desperation and Delusion, a Recipe for Disaster

CHAPTER 3 31
Mom Bought a House and Dad Lost His Job

CHAPTER 4 45
The Badge of Not Having Money in the Age of Aquarius

CHAPTER 5 63
Investing Every Penny On Love

CHAPTER 6 77
The Price of Cinderella's Slipper

CHAPTER 7 95
Everyone Else is Thinner, Smarter, Better and Richer

CHAPTER 8 103
Whoever Has Most Stuff Gets to Worry About How To Keep It

CHAPTER 9 123
Denial is Definitely NOT Just a River in Egypt

CHAPTER 10 147
Smoke and Mirrors

CHAPTER 11 159
Trust Your Gut Not the Scam Artist!

CHAPTER 12 167
Having the Cojones to Face Up to Fear and Failure

CHAPTER 13 179
   Managing Money Was Harder Than I Thought it Would Be

CHAPTER 14 189
   Money VS Envy, Not Enough of One and Too Much of the Other

CHAPTER 15 199
   Security At Last, But Not Without Reading the Fine Print

CHAPTER 16 207
   The Unpardonable Sin of Getting Older in Hollywood

CHAPTER 17 231
   Changing the Past Requires Changing

CHAPTER 18 241
   Big Risk, Bigger Rewards

CHAPTER 19 253
   Even Squirrels Know It's Important to Store Their Nuts

CHAPTER 20 267
   People Cheat For It, Steal For It and Even Kill For It

EPILOGUE 277
   The Day the World Stopped

Acknowledgements 293

For everyone who has ever struggled with money issues.

Hello… I'm speaking to you!

FOREWORD

"I love money. I love everything about it. I bought some pretty good stuff. Got me a $300 pair of socks. Got a fur sink. An electric dog polisher. A gasoline powered turtleneck sweater. And, of course, I bought some dumb stuff, too."
– Steve Martin

OOPS! I Forgot to Save Money is my story. It's a book I had to write to understand myself. One grey hair and I knew I didn't have enough time to lean in. I had to dive in and change my story. I came to see how little I understood this very necessary commodity. I decided to see if I was alone. I interviewed 100 women about their relationship to money. It turns out it isn't just the currency we use to buy things; it's about wellbeing: mental, emotional, financial and even spiritual. It's the currency of survival. It gives us the ability to help others and fuel our own dreams, yet it's so rarely discussed in an open, honest manner. It carries with it a full spectrum of emotions: from shame, envy, greed, and resentment to joy, charity, opportunity, and generosity. There is no shortage of stories - the good, the bad and the best. I have made many money-mistakes but they have been the teaching tools I needed to wake up. As Richard Branson says, "At least when you fall on your face, you are still moving forward." Oops! I Forgot to Save Money is going to make you laugh and bang your head in recognition that much of me is you. I know I am not alone. I needed to take my shame, denial and above all fear and air it out loud. It hasn't happened overnight. It's a daily unwrapping. I believe it's not just about money; it goes deeper than that. It's about the value we place on our talents, our contributions, our abilities, ourselves. I wrote this book to help myself, and hopefully, help those who recognize themselves and their behavior in me. It's not a roadmap but a flashlight to help illuminate your own path.

CHAPTER 1

THE WOLF IS AT OUR DOOR AND HE HAS A KEY

The Cost: The stress that goes hand in hand with accumulating debt.

One day, in the middle of a morning when nothing interesting ever happens, the phone rang. I good humoredly answered it without thought. There was a clicking sound. I was about to hang up, thinking it was a wrong number when a tinny voice asked if Monica Parker was there. I responded, "Who is this?" The tinny voice became aggressive, making it clear that I'd better own up to being the lady of the house. I stammered that I was. The voice on the other end of the phone belligerently-announced that this was a collection agency assigned to deal with my long delinquent grocery store bill. I was in arrears in the amount of four hundred and thirty dollars. I was in shock. It was just for cheese and stuff. He continued that the amount would accrue interest every day that I didn't make good on this debt. I was indignant at such a threat. I didn't owe that store any money. Surely, this was a clerical error. The tinny voice abrasively said the next time the call would be handled by a supervisor. I hung up and sat at my desk, replaying the call. It made no sense. On my way to the kitchen to get an Advil and a chocolate milk chaser, I passed the 'drawer.' I opened it slowly. Envelopes tumbled out. I went pale.

I had totally forgotten about all the bills I had tossed in there meaning to deal with them at a later time... Was it forgetfulness or self-sabotage? I must have known a messy pile of unpaid bills filling the drawer of denial was going to be the thing that got me.

Money is not my natural siren call. If there were two doors, one marked "Money" and the other "Joy," without doubt, I would choose "Joy." As long as I had a roof over my head, along with some pretty things to look at on my walls and a fridge filled with enough food to throw a great dinner party, I was happy. *Probably not happy, but definitely able to coat myself in denial.* It was a very naive philosophy, given the wampum required to live a sensible life, made even worse in light of my propensity for living large. But I was a child of the seventies and I didn't care about being sensible or about saving money. I didn't really care about money. It was simply that necessary evil needed to live. Back then the middle-class was flourishing and everyone knew a few rich folk but being one of them wasn't a dominant fantasy.

Being unemployed was not unusual for me, or my husband, Gilles. As artists, we were used to living a feast or famine life. Usually one of us managed to hold down the fort, but we both had experienced a prolonged dry spell. When Gilles, an actor and designer, wasn't getting his usual big-ticket items, like voice over contracts or designing and making wedding dresses or leather anything, he shortened hems and let out seams. I too was an actor and a budding screenwriter. While I waited for my own projects to get picked up, I would fix other people's scripts and teach newbies how to pitch their projects. None of it brought in big money but it got us through. *Sometimes... clearly not this time.* I dug through every pocket, seat cushion and the loose change treasure chest under the seat in my car and I paid off that embarrassing outstanding grocery account, once again completely dismissing the other bills.

I spend a lot of time in fantasyland, but when I'm under attack, my already active imagination goes into overdrive. It's a quality that serves me well for writing and acting but could be devastating when unharnessed. As in, I'm more than a little obsessed with death - mine. I imagine how it will come about. It doesn't feel morbid, just a curiosity. It is, after all, a certainty. *Trust me, if there was a possibility that one could escape the inevitable, I would be working on that plan.* The glimpses can happen anywhere, anytime. While everyone is laying on their yoga mats drifting into the calm brought on by repetitive deep breaths, I will get a flash of me at a Bloomingdale's sale in a tussle with another woman who also wants the sixty-five percent off pearl grey cashmere shawl that I found first. The other competitive shopper hits me hard with her fake Dolce & Gabbana bag, yanking the scarf away from me. I fall, hitting my head on the corner of the display counter and I am dead. But just as I fade away, I see the woman in her fluorescent running shoes running into the crowd, paying next to nothing for that shawl and making it out of the store before anyone notices. The evening news makes much of the tragic death of an overweight woman so desperate to fill her arms with heavily discounted clothing that she got into a physical altercation with another customer. *So not fair. I saw it first.* I am grateful that while loading me into the coroner's van, nobody brings up the crumpled past due and maxed out credit card bills that *are* stuffed deep into my bag. *Even in a hallucination I am shopping with money I don't have.* This was a sign I should have paid attention to.

I knew I should have been solving the insolvency issue – having a yard sale, selling my body... *There's ten cents that won't do me any good.* But did I? No.

Instead, I wandered around straightening cushions and refolding the towels in the bathroom until they looked like they were display items. Our bed was tucked and pulled until it was Architectural Digest photo-ready. The side-effect of all that un-dealt-with financial stress was that our house, and anyone else's I came in contact with, benefitted from methodical picture straightening, unasked for spit-polished shine on all surfaces and a potential restocking of all books by size and color.

I was well past the cup of tea cure. A Xanax in chewable form would have been more helpful

I went back to being willfully ignorant that anything was amiss. Then the relentless phone calls started. *And this was before the safety net of call display.* One after another, like locusts, came the bill collectors and red lettered FINAL NOTICES delivered by registered mail.

The jig was up. We were in debt up to our eyeballs.

"How'd THAT happen?" Said sarcastically.

I became uncharacteristically quiet, but not in my brain. It was churning. I didn't know what to do. I walked past my husband, who appeared to be blithely sipping his third cup of coffee and reading "The Secret," or was it Deepak Chopra's "Creating Affluence." I knew if I got too close, whichever one it was would be ripped in half by me, before I hurled it from the balcony or bludgeoned him with it. I thought he should have been manifesting real work instead of hedging his bets on incantations and gobbledygook. I was fresh out of Ohmmms. *Namaste.*

I decided to go hiking amid the sycamores on one of the many hill trails that surround Los Angeles, not just to burn off stress but also to keep me far away from shopping temptation. *And from killing my husband.* I started speed walking, desperate to walk off the tension that was crushing me like a python. It wasn't working.

Is tension a component of depression? If so, I had that. I had the stiff neck and shoulders to prove it. I had hiked down the canyon. I was hungry, although I wasn't sure for what. I don't think it was just for food. I was hungry for salvation. I found myself standing in front of the smallest church I had ever seen, called The Little Brown Church, and there was something about the simplicity and lack of pretension that beckoned to me. Attending church is not a normal occurrence for me. My mother was a European Jew but had lost any desire to participate in religion. She could never come to terms with a God that would allow Hitler and his atrocities to have happened. My British father was raised in the United Church of England. He was quite clear that there was nothing united about it. Free of doctrine, I am a believer in Godliness. Remove a couple of letters, add an O and you get GOODNESS. That's a good enough belief system for me.

I sat alone in the tiny church and prayed. I prayed to understand how I could have allowed myself to get so far into debt. I knew all the reasons and had made all the excuses. None of them stood up. The real answer was simple and not pretty. We lived above our means! We had played Russian roulette with credit cards, shoving a full one to the back of the deck, pulling another with seemingly lots of room for spending to the fore and so it went. BAM! It happened in a blur. We were like so many Los Angeles newbies, so confident in our impending success that we lived 'as if'. We had slipped over the edge so quickly that we didn't see it happening. We hadn't succumbed to the 'look at what I drive' contest happening outside unaffordable restaurants where valets screeched up to the curbs in the newest Mercedes or Maserati. We were perfectly okay with our reliable, devoid of status vehicle. But it was the cumulative effect of all the small things: where we lived, what we ate. We had foolishly not adapted our spending to the life of uncertainty that we had chosen and loved. We weren't extravagant and did our best to keep costs down. Neither Gilles nor I cared about expensive things. Our disposable income, *(who has disposable income?)* was spent on larger shoes and soccer uniforms for our growing child. We likely spent too much on experiences because we saw it as another form of education. *And on occasional paintings to soothe my soul. Okay, maybe I liked some expensive things.* Hunting for and buying well-chosen gifts for friends was an indulgence I fed but should have been far stricter about. And of course, added in was the overpriced cappuccino addiction and buying real food instead of the chemicals in a cup variety. I had a flash of terror. Maybe I wasn't just depressed. Maybe I was schizophrenic, pinging from denial to shopping for luxury items. As a responsible adult, things had to change – meaning, I had to change.

I looked at the statue of Jesus and started to pray. He was well worn and chipped perhaps from the constant attentions of desperate supplicants. But his warm painted eyes invited me to unload my troubles. *I am well aware I am sort of, kind of Jew-ish but I was willing to ask for help from any deity out there.* I had talked to anyone and everyone else about good sex, bad sex, birth control, laughter-induced bladder leaks, bad bosses, crappy marriages, my many failures and I had even brought death out of the closet but here I was, needing to talk to Jesus about the B word. *Arrrgghh… Bankrupt.*

(He could keep a secret.)

It wasn't long before we found ourselves sitting with our heads down in a run-of-the-mill bankruptcy lawyer's office. He was a cold, beige, little man who droned on about things that really didn't interest me but that I recognized as hard, cold facts. Our credit was ruined. Our far-too-many credit cards were taken away. I imagined them being cut up into a million little pieces, then incinerated and finally buried deep in a concrete vault to guarantee that we couldn't dig them up no matter how desperately we might have wanted to. We would essentially be debt free but persona-non-grata in the eyes of creditors. "Good," I thought. I wanted to be invisible. Our drugstore card was even removed from my wallet. I felt as though I no longer existed. In a manner of speaking it was true. We would have to pay for everything with cash. I knew that meant we would be acquiring nothing new. *Who carries cash?*

My head hurt from the constant clanging of the alarm bell in my head. The expression, 'history repeats itself' was ringing loud and clear. We could no longer outrun the horrible, financial mess we had made. We were fresh out of boodle, clams, dinero and excuses. We were our parent's children, clearly exhibiting the sum total of our mutual fiscal upbringing: that is, none.

My mother invented the concept of 'fake it till you make it'.

My father had no ambition and the pocketbook to match.

My husband's mother was the family caretaker in a small farming community. She never had a pay cheque.

Gilles' father also grew up on a rural Quebec farm, but in a town his father had founded. His parents spoiled Louis. They both gave him money and each told him never to tell the other. Louis became an alcoholic at a very early age with a penchant for spending every day and night in the local pubs. He was exceedingly popular, no doubt because he would buy everyone their drinks. After his parents passed on, it took him no time at all to blow the family fortune.

Now, here WE were. The reasons were different, but the results were the same, made evident in our shared humiliation. We had to break the chain. It wouldn't be easy given our parental role models and our collective lifetimes of financial negligence. We had to talk about it. This was really hard for my hubby. He always has a broom and a rug to sweep all the unspeakable stuff under. *He should have married someone else. When I'm ready to get into it, I'm ready.* It occurred to me that Gilles and I had never had any kind of money talk before we married, or after. It had never occurred to us. Now, we sat cross-legged on the floor of our living room, neither of us speaking. I tried to make eye contact. I was ready to hurtle into an anxiety driven stump speech. He was in the room, sitting right across from me but he was not in his body. He had levitated to a quieter and safer place. I knew at that moment that I was alone in owning the mess we had made.

Note to Self: Lock this down. Never shop in high-end stores you can't afford, especially for groceries. Don't ever use a credit card for life's essentials. Buying a three hundred dollar purse and then having nothing to put in it is a lesson unto itself! Denial about one's circumstances is similar to a teenager who still sucks their thumb to soothe themselves. It doesn't. It just triggers expensive orthodontics. And to top it off, talk about what's going on. Suffering in silence will cripple you and prevent you from getting the help you need. Must remember to lift my head up, forgive myself and learn from my mistakes.

Recommended Medication: French Fries slathered in gravy and cheese curds; as if one or the other isn't enough. But it isn't. Fully loaded poutine is a perfect antidote for all aggravation.

CHAPTER 2

DESPERATION AND DELUSION, A RECIPE FOR DISASTER

The Cost: I thought we were rich until I discovered we weren't.

Why is it some people attract money? This is not a sour grapes question. I'm genuinely curious as to whether there is a definitive answer. I have asked myself this question often. I have shaken and looked into a Magic 8 Ball to see if an answer could be found deep within. Ouija boards and fortune-tellers have given me platitudes and hocus-pocus. There are theories galore, most of them colliding in inconsistency. It seems so effortless, and some of those people are not even particularly smart or imaginative. It just comes to them, not by inheritance but by being in the right place at the right time for some risky investment to pay off; perhaps a friend's board game company suddenly goes through the roof when the company is bought by an internet-startup. The game becomes a sensation, spewing a massive payout. Or they join a firm that is bought by a multinational company and those shares that came with their package, rocket skyward. There are thousands of examples. On the flip side, there are so many more people who do not appear to have the lucky money gene: children of the truly wealthy who have squandered away their family's fortunes, brilliant musical talents who never manage to catch a break, an inventor on the cusp of a Nobel prize-worthy discovery, only to be scooped by an unknown Icelandic wunderkind. There are endless stories of people worn down by walking on some endless money treadmill that takes them nowhere. My quest to answer the question made me look deeply into my psyche, examining my habits, my attraction to pleasure and my resistance to taking money seriously. "Do I not work hard enough?" Am I not good enough? Do I not pray enough? Is it because I'm not thin enough? *Really?* Why am I always pinging from feast to famine and why have I not built a solid bridge between them? Have I swallowed too much of my family's dismal financial struggles to know any other way?

My newly realized destitution forced me to think long and hard about my patterns of financial abuse and from whence those tendencies sprang.

Tenacity should have been my mother's first name*! It really works if said with a southern accent.* My mother - born Elsa but who, at an early age, took on the nom de plume Elizabeth, just like the Queen in more ways than just her name - was one of eight children. She was the most determined to break free, desperate to carve her own path in the world. As surely as cabbage borscht was a Friday night staple, she knew she was meant for better things. She left home as soon as she received her Master's certificate in dressmaking. Elizabeth was far more than a seamstress. She was a couturier, excelling in the design and making of one-of-a-kind garments, tailored exclusively to her clientele. *Never left unspoken, her true ambition was to be the clientele she served.*

Without experience or connections she stalwartly settled for making clothes for a less fashionable coterie but her top-shelf attitude remained intact. Keeping her mythology alive, she sourced only the finest fabrics, ribbons and lace trims. This mission led her right into the arms of a man who could sell breadsticks to a baker. Robert, a Czechoslovakian by birth, was only a year or two older than she was but he was a whole barrel of monkeys more determined to win over the dynamic powerhouse that was Erzy. (The Czech short form of Elizabeth). He didn't have to work too hard. Smitten by his patter and easy charm, the sexually inexperienced Erzy found herself pregnant. Robert and Erzy married before any loosening of belts would be needed. A few months later their exceptionally beautiful daughter Gerda came into the world followed only a year and half later by their twinkly-eyed son, Peter. For a very short time, all was well and wonderful. But then the Great Depression arrived, smiting everything profitable in its wake. Robert's haberdashery was soon a casualty. He tried to find a buyer for his collection of beautiful buttons and bows but everyone was in the same position, trying to unload their wares as fast as possible. In a last gasp of desperation he declared bankruptcy hoping to have something left with which to feed his family. He, along with so many others, was hauled before an unsympathetic court and sent to prison. He didn't know that in Austria bankruptcy was illegal.

After a few long weeks, Robert was released. Unfortunately, in spite of having grown up in Vienna with his family, he was then deported to his birthplace of Czechoslovakia, where he had to start over. Erzy and Robert's relationship wasn't able to survive the separation and hardship.

Life was tough for a single working mother of two. Elizabeth went back to her seamstress work. As her reputation grew, she made more and more money but spent less and less time mothering her two small children. She was trying to find her way in the world.

It was not long after that Elizabeth found bridge. Bridge appealed to her competitive nature. She took to it like Boris Spassky did to chess. It also landed her smack in the middle of a rarefied world of elite players, often with titles to match. Nothing was more potent than besting these power brokers at their own game. She became obsessed. Her children did their best at raising themselves. They made friends. They learned to cook or scavenge as Elizabeth was often not home to make their dinners.

The rumblings of war began to steadily thump towards reality. In what seemed like no time at all, Elizabeth lost client after client, some out of their fear of having a Jewish dressmaker, others because they were preparing their escape. Gerda came home from school one day sobbing that her friends no longer wanted to have anything to do with her. And the next day, both she and Peter were assigned armbands, emblazoned with bright yellow Jewish stars.

One of Elizabeth's bridge partners, a diplomat, offered her a visa to Nicaragua. Another, an Ambassador, could furnish her with papers for Scotland. She accepted the more familiar option. Unfortunately, she could only get one visa. She was faced with an impossible decision: take her children to Brussels, where most of her family had relocated after escaping Austria, and set up shop there, or go to Scotland and make a home for them to come to as soon as possible. Elizabeth knew full well that by the time the war ended, if they survived, they would have nothing left on which to live. Businesses along with families' bank accounts and possessions had been taken or destroyed. Very few had money to live on. And no one was having dresses custom-made while bombs were being dropped around them. With a heavy heart and her family's assurances that they would protect Peter and Gerda with their lives, she left for Scotland to set up a new life for her

Oops! I Forgot to Save Money

family. Little did they know they would not be able to keep their promise.

Elizabeth, now known as Elsie, a name that far better suited her circumstances even if her attitude didn't, hunted for a job in Glasgow. Any job. War levels many playing fields, sometimes disintegrating them. She got a job far below her aspirations working as a domestic: cooking, cleaning and sewing. She lived in a tiny room in a grand house on a tree-lined street. She loved the house, not the job, but wisely kept that to herself. But as always, she put one foot in front of the other, doing what had to be done.

The war raged on. All of Europe was now a hellhole. Borders were sealed. Letters to her children and family went unanswered. It was only as her English improved that she learned there was no postal service - no letters unless they were communiqués from the Red Cross. She had no idea that her son, Peter, then barely fifteen, was grabbed by the Gestapo, and that Gerda, hidden in a doorway, was a witness. She watched his terrified face getting smaller and smaller as the Nazi's car sped away. 'Elsie' wouldn't know what happened to her children for three years.

She lived in that small room and did without. She knew no one, had no relatives or connections, couldn't really speak the language, but she had that tenacity and determination. Her employer soon saw Elsie's sewing talents and put her to work, throwing in a bit more money here and there. It all went into a stocking. She was saving every penny to bring her kids to their new home. Elsa/Elizabeth/Elsie had survived so much heartache already. There was no way she was going to collapse under the weight of poverty. She had grander dreams than that. She studied English late at night and first thing in the morning. The lady of the house noticed how hard she worked to assimilate and opened

25

the door to her friends and soon Elsie had a small but devoted clientele. She made money remaking and re-envisioning the precious few dresses the ladies had managed to keep from before the war. She joined the Austrian Club, filled with refugees much like herself. Soon she was befriended by a wealthy émigré, Daisy, who had money, position and the ability to introduce Elsie into her well-heeled inner circle. That's when life changed.

She found her dream house just one street away from where she had worked as a maid. She cobbled together whatever money she had saved, sold some of her jewelry, and marched over to her neighborhood bank where, with her iron will and considerable charm, convinced the stodgy banker that in order to attract the kind of clients who would appreciate her services, she needed to appear successful. She was a force of nature; he couldn't refuse. The gamble paid off, handsomely. *If only she had known what to do with it.*

When the war was finally over, and communication to the continent restored, she found out the truth about her children and the horrors they had been through. She was sickened when she discovered Peter had been held in Auschwitz, one of the worst of the worst concentration camps. But guilt would not bring them back to her, so as always she just kept putting one foot in front of the other. Wading through the bureaucratic red tape associated with so many displaced persons was a nightmare. She quickly concluded that to get them into Scotland, she needed a fast pass, which meant finding a husband. She found one in Richard Watson Parker, a fifty year old, never-married Englishman. He had no money to speak of but he did have all his limbs and his papers. She chose to ignore their complete lack of chemistry and lack of common ground. He could walk and talk. He was perfect. As I have often been told by my mother, "We only did it once!" Then she would shudder, followed by a face that looked like it had swallowed a dead fly. I am here because of that dry and dusty coupling.

I was born into what appeared to be a well-feathered nest. *Little did I know those twigs and feathers were just illusions.* Overdale House, with its jaw-dropping marble reception hallway, impressive drawing room, eight bedrooms and bathrooms and formal garden, was practically given away for the ridiculous sum of one thousand pounds - a pittance for such a grand house, even post-war. Unfortunately, my parent's marriage was less than grand and ended before I had the ability to say Dada. My father, a mild, mannered, deeply repressed but dryly-funny figure was soon turfed back to whatever boarding house was available. Now that Mummy had her papers and an unexpected bundle, me, she set about building her business.

My mother's team of seamstresses and beaders toiled away in a vast workroom that took up an entire lower floor of our big house. Upstairs, in a large and beautifully appointed salon, our eye-rolling maid served my mother, dressmaker to the well-heeled, and her customers tea from a Sterling silver teapot that some other post-war survivor had pawned in order to eat. *These were the seeds that fertilized so many of my misconceptions about real life versus lifestyle. I thought we were rich!*

My father was the awkward tweedy stranger that came to visit me every second weekend. I looked forward to those visits because he brought me candy and kelp pills. He told me they were brain food. *I only cared about the candy.*

Living in that huge old gated house was a fantasyland that allowed my imagination to run wild. My mother's fire was stoked only by playing bridge and by becoming successful enough to become 'one of them.' My companions were Sheila, our irritable maid, and my mother's employees, all of whom I ensnared whenever they made a trip to the kitchen. No one paid much attention to me, except to sidle past my endless attention getting, performing-seal acts with a barely-there smattering of the acknowledgement I craved.

I tried a new tack. I advertised – big colorful crayon posters promoting my upcoming 'shows'. I swathed my body in yards and yards of silk and beads and invited all the neighborhood children to come see me in one play after another. I was the Lady-of-the-Manor in almost all of my plays. My stage was an enormous wooden window-shutter that had fallen to the ground. My props were pilfered from every room of the house. I sang. *Badly*. I danced. *Even worse*. I told stories and I charged every child whatever they had in their pockets if they wanted admittance to… "The Greatest Show on Glasgow's Leslie Road." I was eight! *Of course I became an actress and an entrepreneur. I had a lotta nerve.*

My glamorous grownup half-sister Gerda and my tattered, war-ravaged half-brother, Peter finally arrived in Glasgow, like the miracles they were. My mother was determined to lay down a perfect lawn to cover the psychological and physical torture my brother and sister had somehow survived. She stuffed them with every delicacy. New clothes appeared weekly. No expense was spared. And they didn't have to lift a finger. If she had thought to animate the singing bluebirds from Walt Disney's Snow White, they would have chirped relentlessly throughout our house. But there was nothing she could have done to erase Gerda and Peter's nightmares. She clung to her imaginary diamond encrusted life raft, determined to kick until she reached land. She spent money on the best of everything. It was money she didn't have.

I only cared that my audience had more than doubled. I was delirious at the possibilities.

Note to Self: Do not live in a fantasyland like my mother did. Do not be like Mom, spending money on the best of everything – money she didn't have. There's a huge price to pay for whitewashing the truth.

Recommended Medication: A slice of Mocha Torte would be perfect at this moment: delicious and dangerously high in calories but very comforting after an invasion of any kind.

CHAPTER 3

MOM BOUGHT A HOUSE AND DAD LOST HIS JOB

The Cost: Parents who get back together only to pay the mortgage do not make for a happy family.

For the first time, our big house didn't feel like it was too big. It was never quiet, with the constant comings and goings of these young adults trying to reclaim their lives. And then, everything changed when Gerda chose Philip, the doctor, to become her husband. They relocated to Toronto, Canada to begin their married life. Next in line, my brother was anointed as 'the get' in a sweepstakes to marry him off to the wealthiest of the few available single Jewish women in Glasgow. Peter was given little say in the brokering of this partnership. My mother desperately wanted him to feel safe and secure after the scorched earth he had somehow survived. Her very connected friend Daisy came through again, presenting as the winner her niece Susie, who was pretty but very heavy and not that attracted to my brother. Nor was he to her. None of that mattered. It was a misguided business deal birthed from Mummy's persistent guilt. Once Gerda and Peter were gone, our house felt sad and empty.

   A few lonely months later I came home from school one day to find my mother in my room. Most of my clothes, books and dolls were piled high on my bed. I stood silently watching her as she held up one dress after another, deciding whether to toss them onto the floor or into a huge trunk. I remained silent but accusatory. Was she throwing out my dresses because she knew I had gained weight? Or because I didn't put them away the way she liked me to hang them? She felt my agitation and turned.

I felt the steam rise in my body and I exploded, "Why are you in my room? Why are you throwing my things on the floor?" I could feel tears beginning to stack up. I tried to blink them away. My mother took my hand and pushed everything on the bed to the side. She hugged me hard. She took in a long breath and then smiled. She told me that she sold our house. She had a great offer from an order of nuns that wanted our house to become a convent. She saw my eyes blinking and she knew I was about to protest. She started talking very quickly that the house was too big now that everyone had left. I threw myself on top of my clothes as if to protect them from this disaster. I poked my head up and threatened to tell the nuns we were Jewish.

She laughed. That made me angry. I slept badly for the next few nights. I asked my mother where the nuns lived. I wanted to tell them our house was haunted with ghosts that liked to break things to scare them away from buying my house. Nothing I said changed her mind. It was a done deal and we were moving to Canada!

I needn't have worried. My normally very mild-mannered father threw a wrench into her plans. He made it very clear that he had rights and knew very well that she could not take his daughter out of the country unless he signed off on it. I think my mother was at first confused that my dad had an opinion. She had never heard him utter one before. After he assured her he was quite serious she fumed and paced, donning her full metal jacket along with some serious vocal firepower. "Rights! Since when

Oops! I Forgot to Save Money

has he had rights?" I could hear him squealing like a trapped mouse. I heard her at full volume driving over him in her bullet proof armored tank. Then there was quiet. A door slammed shut!

A letter from a barrister came for my mother. It stated in no uncertain terms that my father had no intention of letting me go to Canada. He was cannier than he appeared and had dug in his heels. I was proud of him. It took her two years to get him to agree and that was only if he was allowed to come too. My mother, the ultimate survivor agreed.

I didn't really know my Dad. I was now thirteen and this was the first time we would be living under the same roof and being 'a family'. It was and it wasn't the picture I craved.

Once in Canada, my mother and I, along with this odd stranger, my father, moved into a tiny apartment on the edge of the richest neighborhood my mother could find: Forest Hill, home to cliquish rich kids and their snobby parents. They reeked of privilege. Being fed the falsehood that we were wealthy and then finding out with no explanation that we were far from it left me without much trust. Gone was my stage, where I was the center of the universe. Gone was our big, beautiful stone castle. Gone was the place where I was the leader of the pack. And… Poof! Gone, banished shortly after our arrival, was my father. I wanted to believe that they really did try to be a couple. All the evidence said otherwise. My mother, who was rarely home, never seemed to even notice my father. And now his barely-there tenure was over. My parents were never meant to be.

Calm returned as my mother and I reclaimed being a duo. Forest Hill was a tough nut to crack and I was a half-Jewish immigrant child with a chubby body, a thick brogue, and to my utter shock, the realization that we were verging on poor! It was nowhere close to "Angela's Ashes" poverty but far from what I'd

33

been led to believe. *Money shouldn't be one's report card but in this neighborhood, I had an F.* I felt the first stabs of envy.

My mother continued her pursuit of the clientele that could afford her services and once again she overextended, borrowing money from a finance company so she could rent a boutique in the most fashionable area of town. She had no understanding of the heartless entrapment that goes with easily given money.

We had to move from the tiny apartment in that leafy high-end neighborhood because the apartment was too expensive. My mother found a house on a street in a brand new development at the northernmost tip of what was still considered Toronto. *To my mind it was as desolate as an Arctic outpost.* It was called Tangreen Village, but soon enough became known as Gangreen Village to my friends and me. When she found this suburban dream house, she reeled my hapless father back in to help pay for it. The house had cost a whopping nineteen thousand dollars and the mortgage was too steep for her alone. *Take that in. That same house today would be listed in the high eight hundred thousands but sell 'over asking' for a million and chump change.* The treeless streets were filled with identical semi-detached houses and they all had two cars in the driveway, except for ours. My mother didn't drive and neither did my father. *This was probably for the best as my father had no sense of direction and my mother had no regard for rules.* We lived together but somehow very apart. My mother was never a stay-at-home Mom like the other Moms. *Not even close, she was much more like a drop-in-Duchess.* She ran her new and very upscale midtown boutique six days a week and then she played bridge seven nights a week.

My father was the weakest link in a brood of nine in which he struggled to find his place. He was also the brightest of the pack but given his ongoing childhood battles with rheumatic fever, he

Oops! I Forgot to Save Money

became a Mama's boy. He had wanted to be an architect. She decided he needed something more practical. He became a tool and die maker, a job he loathed as it had him working the line with tougher men. Once again, he was made to feel he was the weakest link. My father was a quiet, book reading man with no competitive spirit. He never moved up the food chain, as he never asked to be moved. He remained an outsider, poor and overeducated his whole life. Dad did a nine to five stint at an airplane assembly plant and after his ritual egg and sausage dinners, he holed up in his room continuing his reading or puttering around taking exact measurements several times over before drawing up plans to perfectly hang something as mundane as our mailbox.

I was a regular guest at my friend Gerry's house. They lived in a large detached house on a pretty street just a few blocks away. Given the amount of time I spent with him, it would have been easy to think I was stalking him as a potential boyfriend. It wasn't him I was after. It was the whole enchilada - Gerry, his parents and his three rowdy siblings. They had a comfortable ease about them as they teased and wound each other up. There was always the smell of just baked bread or cookies coming from their fairly modest kitchen. But what I coveted most was the dinner hour. They all gathered at a beautiful old pine farmhouse table and ate and talked about nothing and everything and they laughed a lot. It was exactly how I imagined home should smell and sound. Mine smelled of lemon Pledge and emptiness.

My mother may have been a much in demand couturier but she was no businesswoman. Her rent was too high and her work labor intensive. From the time she took in a client's order along with a small deposit, adding in the time it took to find just the right fabric, have the dress cut, sewn, fitted, altered, refitted and ready to go, it was a very expensive process. Keeping her boat

35

afloat required a constant pumping out of product and pumping in of money. Naively, she was suckered by one loan shark after another. *I think I became an actress and a writer because from the time I was thirteen, I was pressed into action using one accent or another along with a variety of inventive ruses to rid my mother of these venomous snakes.*

My mother was rarely home and my father was sealed inside his room reading or writing perfectly parsed letters of complaint to the authorities in charge of all slights and annoyances. The only time my parents seemed to be in the same place was when my Mom's money worries bubbled over, automatically becoming my father's fault. He became the clay pigeon and she was the gun. They thought I couldn't hear their whispered fighting. It was the only thing I did hear. *It took me a long time to understand she was scared and that's why she lashed out.*

But the burbs weren't all bad. The sameness was comforting. No one was rich. It was a pretty even playing field and I became skilled in the art of making friends. I took on all comers and I was no longer lonely. *My standards were fairly loose. It was similar to shopping at a bulk store.* When it came time to go to high school, I knew I had to break free. I signed myself up at a big downtown school with a roster of far tougher kids but also a well-known art department stuffed full of all the freaks and geeks that my heart desired. I gave the school office a fake city address and I was in. It didn't matter to me that I had to get up an hour early every day just to catch the bus. I was so happy to have found my tribe. I took on my art classes as if I was a baboon in a banana tree. I felt free.

In spite of us not having any disposable income to speak of, I started high school with an enviable wardrobe. My mother made everything I asked for (although she always made adjustments to keep the outfit more to her liking than mine). I always said thank you and then I would pull out glue, scissors, staples and bits of

Oops! I Forgot to Save Money

fabric I took from her shop and set to work. If I couldn't be rich, I could be different. I reinvented every maxi-coat and mini-dress with cutouts and appliques of my own design. Each piece was perfect for a bohemian model – which I was definitely not. I was more of a grain-fed cover girl for a bratwurst magazine. A big boned, blonde of Mittel-European extraction with a need to be noticed. *I was desperate to be noticed. If this had been today, where tattoos are as commonplace as miniskirts were then, I'm sure I would now be a full on faded and wrinkled billboard in which all the inked birds have flown south.*

I had plenty of friends. My art school classes were all that I dreamed of. There was a boy I liked. *Fine, there was a boy I regularly stalked.* Our house looked nearly normal from the outside. There were a couple of pretty but slightly overgrown flowerbeds, lovely curtains in the windows and a pair of standard issue parents. I was feeling almost secure. I didn't yet understand my father, the seed that had made me, but I liked this weirdly eccentric man. I began to be on the receiving end of conspiratorial twinkles coming at me, whenever my mother looked his way, before giving off a perceptible shudder. But then the airplane factory where my father worked lost their contract and the entire operation closed. His financial contribution along with the stability of his well-vetted job was why my mother had wanted him back! With her slippery credit she needed his money and standing to get a mortgage. My mother became completely unhinged. She was like Rumpelstiltskin, hopping crazily from one foot to the other, wailing and worrying. My father, on the other hand, just shut down. He was a spectre, slowly drifting from the basement where he drew up more and more unnecessary plans, back to the vault known as his room.

37

Money worries are notorious for ruining relationships – Not that my parents were even in one. They were not abusive to each other in the traditional sense. *Is there traditional abuse?* But their intense dislike of each other seeped through the paint in our walls. The tension was always there, waiting for my mother's fast burn to reach the fury of a rocket-powered blast off. Whatever was at her fingertips would go flying, from an innocent slice of toast to the continuous crashing of every piece of her precious European silver flatware ricocheting to the ground. My father's response was to pull up the drawbridge and retreat behind the thick walls he had built up over time. He could sit so still, protected by his fortress of silence and he knew damn well that it would turn her fury even more combustible. It was his secret superpower. I came to believe he enjoyed knowing his stone-face caused her to become undone. I just wanted to find a bomb shelter or a storm drain to disappear into. In this regard I was far more like my father. I knew the power of not engaging.

Every family deals with money differently and many people live, as my family did, above their means. Sadly, I continued that tradition, but some children with that parental dynamic manage to break free, although not without cost. While digging into my history, I began listening to the stories of others and realized that even under similar circumstances there was a huge spectrum of responses… *often better than mine.*

∽

Maia is a young woman in her twenties. Both of her parents are nurses at a California hospital. They work hard, often to near exhaustion, to take care of their six children, one of them a special-needs young boy. Their monthly nut is overwhelming and stressful, especially with the amount of money that is needed to pay for their autistic son's medication, doctor's bills and

Oops! I Forgot to Save Money

childcare plus the care and feeding of the other four kids who are still at home. When their shifts are done, they come home to their large, boisterous and perpetually hungry family, often bringing about high anxiety for the overworked couple. They handle their stress in very different ways. Dad's tendency is to disappear into himself, ignoring the reality of their situation. He watches sports for hours on end like a zombie with no interest in helping around the house or interacting with his children. Zoning out is his default. (Much like my dad.) Mom, on the other hand, overcompensates in a thousand ways, the most obvious being her spending what little money they have on online shopping – and mostly on things none of them needs to improve the quality of their lives. The necessities, like food, are often forgotten, as their garage fills up with useless kitchen gadgets and clothing that is rejected by all of her children but never sent back to the retailers. Overcome by guilt and depression, the nightly calls from various creditors go unanswered.

Maia, their first born and the only true adult in the family, worries night after night that her parents could lose their one asset, their house! They have come perilously close on a couple of occasions. She herself is working two jobs to pay her own bills, including catching shifts as a waitress whenever she can. Maia is a theatre graduate and while taking on the additional job of caring for her brother, she started introducing some of her improvisational techniques to help him learn how to express himself. It was so successful, she has been inspired to start a small non-profit organization to teach autistic and other special-needs kids how to communicate through improvisation and writing. She has grand dreams of starting a real school that would be able to take on many more of these children. But she worries that if, or when, her parents' irresponsible ways leave *them and their kids homeless, she would become solely responsible for her young brother's welfare. She is already balancing so much. She talks a bit about denying herself any extras. She feels guilty if she even 'squanders' money on a cappuccino. As she told me about her life, I watched her eyes well up with tears. Maia pulled her shoulders back and settled herself knowing full well she is the real Mom of her dysfunctional family and there is nothing she can do to change that but say her nightly prayers. Maia's story breaks my heart.*

∽

My father's and my bond was about to strengthen, and not in a way I could have foreseen. It was my fifteenth birthday and I was feeling sorry for myself. I wanted... food. I wanted... love. I wanted... I wanted.

I left school almost right after the bell rang. I went to the nurse's office complaining of a stomach ache, a head ache and every other ache that would get me out of there. I set off by bus to a shopping mall near Forest Hill, the wealthy neighborhood where I had lived for a minute and had been shunned. I needed schoolbooks and I wanted Adler's – a particular kind of socks that all the rich kids were wearing. Even some of my school pals had them. They were expensive and coveted. I sat in a deli and ordered all my favorite carbohydrates. It was my birthday and I was going to enjoy it.

Almost sated - although I am rarely truly sated; there was too much 'wanting' churning through my body - I slipped through the door of a big and busy shoe store that I knew carried those socks. I wandered the aisles carrying two pair of those precious foot coverings as I examined pairs of shoes I would never wear. I asked the salesman to get me a pair of patent Queen Anne heels,

Oops! I Forgot to Save Money

to try on. He went off to hunt them down. I used the distraction to disappear the Adler's deep into my tote bag. When he returned, I thanked the salesman but the shoes were way too tight (as I had asked him to bring me a size too small). I left the shop feeling victorious as I had what I came in for. My next stop was the bookstore. I don't know what came over me but I was high from having pulled off my theft with such ease. I had never stolen anything before and now I was casing a bookstore for my next score. I had one geography book buried deep under the socks and my hands were reaching for an expensive history book when a balding man in a suit blocked my path. I knew immediately by the disgusted expression on his face that I had been caught.

With his hand firmly grasping my elbow, I was led up some stairs to a small storeroom with windows overlooking the entire store. He demanded my name and my parent's phone number. I was terrified. I could barely speak. Then he left me alone in that room. I heard the door lock. My imagination went into overdrive. I had visions of me locked up in a gulag with a dirty cement floor surrounded by bars with the sounds of crying and screaming all around me.

A hand on my shoulder interrupted my panicked breathing. It was my father. He looked so disappointed in me. I felt sick to my stomach. The store manager explained I'd have to go to court. He also said I couldn't come back into the store for six months. I had no intention of ever going back there.

On the bus back to our house, my father stroked my arm. I think it was the first time he had ever touched me. I threw my arms around him and started to cry. He assured me that this episode was between him and me. He had no intention of telling my mother. I think that was when I took my first real breath.

My mother brought home a birthday cake but I had no appetite. She said the school had called to say I had gone home sick. She didn't really believe that I had been sick until now. I never refused cake.

My Dad was right beside me at my hearing. I was scared stiff when my name was called. The judge said that because of my age there would be no jail time or even a fine. He then gave me a stern warning to never do anything like that again. He had nothing to worry about.

The evolving relationship between my Dad and me only seemed to escalate my Mother's frustrations. She was prickly all the time. I decided to escape into a summer job as a mother's helper at a resort called Crystal Beach. It was close to the US, on the north shore of Lake Erie, and far from the troubles going on in my house. I was ecstatic at the prospect of having a paying job looking after two young children. My nights would be free and their summer cottage was a stone's throw from the fabled Crystal Beach Amusement Park. I set about getting a whole new wardrobe from my mother's seamstresses, along with matching shoes that used up all my babysitting money. I wasn't worried. I was about to start earning a whole summer's worth of easy cash. It didn't take long for me to comprehend the expression, "Don't count your chickens before they've hatched." *Who am I kidding? It took years for that lesson to stick.*

Indentured servitude is what I soon came to understand was the full scope of my job. It was the parents who wanted to party. They had childcare and they were out of there. It was to be summer fun-times for them and none for me. I was left to manage the care and feeding of their children twenty-four seven. Day and night, I was to feed them, pick up after them and clean the house. I was scolded if I didn't get everything they demanded done. I did try, but they always had more for me to do. I wasn't a mother's helper; I was the mother, the maid and the cook. I could hear the happy yells from the roller coaster as it hurtled down across its wooden slats. I could smell candy floss. I just couldn't have any of it. The closest I got to the Crystal Beach Amusement Park was when I took both children to the kiddie rides. I was able to get ice cream but only if they wanted some. They hardly ever did. They wanted to go on the dragon whirligig for the tenth time, meaning I went on the dragon whirligig ten times. I lasted eleven days.

I was happy to come home…until I got there. The cold war between my parents was now Defcon 2 (the defense readiness condition). The next step, if they survived this one, would be nuclear war.

Note to Self: Be careful what you wish for. I wanted to escape, and I wanted to make some money. A job appeared out of nowhere and I jumped. There was no fine print to read but had I listened better, I would probably have passed on the offer of looking after three small children for the entire summer. Hello Cinderella. Know thyself.

Recommended Medication: Become a master in the art of homemade chocolate pudding. It's too rich and probably unhealthy but excellent for soothing a variety of disappointments.

CHAPTER 4

THE BADGE OF NOT HAVING MONEY IN THE AGE OF AQUARIUS

The Cost: There wasn't one... or so I thought. But I was young.

My high school years were thankfully behind me. I had been branded as one of those students with an attitude problem who was not living up to her potential. I felt quite smug in the knowledge that high school had nothing to do with my potential except to dampen it. I don't believe I was home school material but I would have thrived in a less formal system. I couldn't wait to get out of there and begin my life. I enrolled in a prestigious art college and they accepted me with my less than stellar marks and the accompanying damning transcript about my attitude problem. *What were they drinking?* When I discovered how rigorous the curriculum was however, I lost interest. I walked out and never went back. With this, both of my parents were in a rare moment of agreement. *Just as rare and unusual, they were actually in the same room.* They truly didn't care if I went to college or not. I had never learned discipline about anything and given that no value was placed on my education, it never occurred to them that having a solid education might prevent me from having the money worries they did. *If hindsight is twenty-twenty, foresight should be given double that value.* My hard working,

45

survivor mother believed in my talent and wanted me to come and work for her as a dress designer. My father wanted me to do whatever I wanted to. He had never been given that opportunity. All I wanted was to be loved. *My standards were loose.*

I found a job at a high-end fabric shop. I was making money, a whopping forty-five dollars a week. *That sounds crazy now but back then, it was enough to live on. It never occurred to me to put some of that money into a savings account.* I treasured showing those bolts of beautifully printed silks, the colorful stacks of featherweight wools and lace that floated through my fingers. Mostly I loved being in charge of my own life. It was time for me to move out of my parents' home. They didn't think so. My mother panicked, cornering me with the thousand reasons why I would fail out there on my own. In truth, she was terrified to be left alone with my father. He went on an actual hunger strike, possibly hoping he would die rather than be alone with my mother. After several false exits, I figured out a strategy. I simply pretended to stay with my best friend, Beverly, for a weekend, then two, then I threw a couple of weekdays into the mix. My parents never saw me actually pack anything. The clothes in my closet just gradually disappeared.

When it was all done, and I was fully ensconced in my new life and digs, there was some retro gnashing of teeth and wild threats about how I would flounder and beg to come home. With unwavering eye contact I responded, "I am home." There was a tense moment, which could have easily pushed my mother into battle-to-the-death mode. I pointed out that she wouldn't have to feed me, which could save her a bundle. I waited for a verbal blow to come my way. She surprised me by laughing.

That first apartment cost $150.00 a month, which was split between me and my beautiful and practical best friend Beverly, and our exotic but not exactly fiscally reliable friend Katya. It had charm, a small kitchen and bathroom and two living rooms. There were no real bedrooms but somehow that flat was perfect. We attracted an endlessly full house of suitors and friends that between the three of us, we could somehow afford to feed and entertain. I finally felt I had a family.

It was the Age of Aquarius. Most of us were quasi-hippies that had moved from the suburbs to downtown, a real world of falling-down houses and apartment buildings filled with guitar playing longhaired boys and lean, longhaired girls. From the back you could never tell which was which. *I was the exception. There was no lean on me.* Parents the world over lamented the fall of civilization as they knew it and struggled futilely to protect it. It was a post war world where the middle class mostly thrived. *Not my parents.* Suburbs popped up everywhere. Cars were big. Gas was cheap. Etiquette mattered. Men ruled and the ladies acquiesced. The baby boom children chafed at convention and rules and a global rebellion burst forth like sunflowers scattering their seeds. Flower power was in and a global youth-quake disruption from music to heartfelt idealism was felt, if not appreciated, by everyone. We had the desire to save the world with peace marches, commitment and loud music. Ideas and connection were our truest drumbeat. Money wasn't the holy grail of achievement in those days. It was, for most of my peers, viewed as the root of all evil. There was optimism that our generation would remain free of its clutches. *The irony doesn't escape me that we became the ones who ultimately shelled out more than a hundred bucks for the right pair of sneakers, and even more for the perfect jeans. We have only ourselves to blame for the four-buck cup of coffee with its ludicrous menu of add-ons. I'm not even going to get into the gluten-free obsession or the never-ending money grabbing diet promises.*

My mother's boutique sat smack-dab in the middle of it. The formerly uptight, pricey boutique world of Yorkville had become completely infested by draft-dodgers, musicians, hippies, beatniks, bikers and wide-eyed tourists. The high-priced shops were being taken over by mini-skirted and maxi-coat wearing fashionistas. Hand-painted bellbottom jeans began showing up on both young men and women along with clunky-heeled boots. Peace signs were proudly worn. It was all too much for the establishment. Being different scared the crap out of them. It wasn't tidy. It wasn't normal. Being at the heart of this counter culture wave was the gift I never expected. It was exciting. I was determined to create my story anew. In this new world order where the youth-stream ruled, I could be anyone I chose to be. I chose to pretend I came from money but that I didn't want anything to do with it. *That was some big-time insecurity. It was a weird form of protection born of growing up with none.*

I discovered a claw foot bathtub abandoned behind one of the formerly stately mansions, complete with a huge fluttering peace flag. The house was now home to as many as twenty hippie-kids. I painted my new bathtub purple and dragged it onto the sidewalk in front of my mother's shop, to her chagrin. I filled it with mountains of crepe paper flowers that I had made and was officially open for business. *Today it would be called a Pop Up Shop!* I sold hundreds of those flowers. I was making scads of money. I couldn't keep up with the demand. I had to pay a couple of girlfriends to make more and more of them. I bought endless amounts of crepe paper and wire. I threw my newfound money around on food and wine for friends and a parade of hungry hippies. Once again I was buying love from no one in particular. *It still felt like love.* My investment would never be recouped. After a couple of months of my lucrative side gig, I grew tired of making paper flowers. I felt chained to that purple bathtub. It was soon delivered to a scrapyard filled with other bathtubs and relics from another time. My purple one stood out as if to shout at me as I walked away that I was not just heartless but a fool for dumping a moneymaking enterprise. *This was a pattern I was to repeat far too often.*

It was then that my father landed a job as a janitor at a discount store. I was mortified. What if someone found out? I had contorted myself into being like all the other hippies, rich and poor, united in our disdain of pretension, but in truth, I was my mother's daughter. *It was the beginning of the big lie.* Whenever I was asked or it felt necessary, I pretended my father was still working for the Avro Air Company. I even managed to give him a promotion. He went from being a tool and die maker to now, a revered CEO. I had made it be about me, and how I would be judged having a father who worked as a janitor. *I still feel the shame at my pretension.* I was an affected git, posing as a hippie. Ugh! I should have been proud that my almost seventy-year old dad was willing to put his family first. If pushing a broom was the only way to keep a roof over our heads I should have showered him with praise not disdain. *I shudder still as I write this.*

Yorkville was paradise for the young. It consisted of only two streets smack in the heart of the city. It was as if a wild, never before seen circus landed on earth from some far off galaxy. Everyone who wanted to join was welcome. And everyone did want to join. And it was free. Being at the epicenter of this all day and every night party was akin to offering an unlimited supply of crack cocaine to a junkie. I was a people junkie and there was a full-on buffet from which I could choose. *I collected them like others collected teen magazines or baseball cards.* Everybody had a story, and I wanted to hear all of them. I was drunk on the possibilities. There was a kaleidoscope of musicians, artists, fashion models, and high school dropouts, suburbanites and hardcore bikers. Smoking dope and dropping acid. Coffee houses flourished. The Viet Nam war raged on but we were in Canada, only the stream of young draft dodgers joining our carnival gave us a glimmer of the horrors going on far away. It was hard to imagine all those boys my age fighting and dying for a war that was not even on their soil. They called themselves conscientious objectors. They somehow fit right in. These were the times of peace not war. I let a few of them camp out in my mother's shop as long as they were gone by nine in the morning, leaving no trace behind. This was also the beginning of the Yorkville music scene where future bold face stars came to try out their material. From Joni Mitchell, Cat Stevens, Robbie Robertson and The Band to David Clayton Thomas and Joe Cocker. There were at least ten underground clubs where they played with no cover charge. These music legends were still undiscovered and grateful to have an audience. *Oh, how times and ticket prices have changed. Few young people, and plenty of older ones too, can afford to go to a concert or a ball game today. Movies are stupidly expensive and don't get me started on the price of popcorn!* Out on the streets was an endless parade of color and sound always ready for whatever showed up. I fell in love at least once a week. I danced to my own drummer every night. I joined peace marches. I marched, I protested but I never joined in the drug scene. I was too scared and underneath the funky clothing I was more puritanical than I liked to admit. I was already high enough.

 My mother broke her lease on the prestigious Cumberland Avenue shop due to the endless loud music that now pumped out of every other boutique, and the growing parade of flagrantly 'underdressed' young people. *Her words not mine.* She moved a couple of blocks over to what she hoped would be a calmer, more exclusive venue from which to cater to her rich clients, but, to her horror, the baby boomers were everywhere, demanding a seat at every table, including in her new enclave. A large coffee shop opened its doors in the sprawling courtyard where my mother's shop was now ensconced, and soon became the watering hole for every young filmmaker, actor, actress, artist, and fashion designer, right alongside rogues, lawyers and a few of the establishment-wannabees. I wanted to be where the action was, so I finally accepted my mother's offer of a job. I also asked for and got a raise. I now earned the princely sum of sixty dollars a week - two hundred and forty dollars a month. I thought I was rich!

I was a fledgling dress designer with a gorgeous posse of models that became my unlikely Besties. As I travelled in their company, I came to understand that they were the bait that hauled in a catch of the good, the bad, and the very wealthy. Money was thrown at them to pay for the finest meals, cars, clothes and travel. I often got swept up in that net, not because I was beautiful but because I had access to those girls and they had access to my designs. I, too, became an 'It Girl' by association. To paint the picture with accuracy, I was pretty enough and I had a very friendly, possibly overly eager, tail-wagging personality. I was also forty pounds overweight. *That could be wishful thinking at work. It was more like fifty.* I found myself an unlikely boyfriend – a Dutch model fresh off a KLM flight. He had next to no command of the English language. I generously volunteered to show him around town. I just wanted to soak up his cologne as I followed in his impossibly handsome wake. He found me offbeat and funny. He also found me useful. I had a car. I was recruited to be his personal city-girl Sherpa - strong enough to cart around his wardrobe and collection of hair products - and his personal chauffeur. My hungry, love-seeking self felt the tradeoff was worth it. *When I see photographs of us then, I cannot connect to* that girl. I was always seated at his feet or walking ten paces behind him. Where the hell was I? I'm guessing, not yet born.

Carole, a leggy, gorgeous girl who worked in the men's clothing boutique next to my mother's, invited me to go on a road trip to New York. Carole could sell the overpriced leather jackets in her store back to the cows the hides originally came from. She was that good. She sold me on accompanying her. Not all the details were made clear. I decided to go with the intent of making my so-called boyfriend miss me. *I see now how laughable that sounds. The only thing he would miss would have been his 'do this, do that' Girl Friday.*

We boarded an eight P.M. Greyhound bus for the overnight ride to the mid-town Manhattan Port Authority bus terminal. Carole, who was much more sophisticated than I, got on board and popped on a black silk eye mask and went to sleep. That was my first disappointment. I didn't know her that well and I thought our bus time together would be an opportunity to change that. I couldn't sleep one wink. I was over the moon excited that I was going to be spending time in New York City. And not just any old time… Carole had a former boyfriend who was working as a page for The Johnny Carson Show. He had procured the very difficult to get tickets to watch a taping.

The bus had barely pulled in to the Port Authority terminal when Carole, fresh as a daisy compared to my groggy self, bounced off the bus. The luggage hold was opened and not one but two men helped retrieve her suitcase. I hauled mine out myself and we were off. We had sprung for one night at the Biltmore Hotel. We weren't going to the show until the next evening.

To my young eyes, the Biltmore was very glamorous. In the lobby, there was a very handsome gold gate with a big beautiful clock above it fronting the Palm Lounge bar and restaurant. Well-dressed men and women bustled in and out. I felt as though I was in a movie of my own making as a uniformed bus boy took my suitcase along with Carole's and placed it on a trolley. He gestured for us to follow him. The room was gorgeous. Carole's friend had got us a deal through the television station. Still, my share was twenty-five dollars, almost half of my weekly salary. I threw caution to the wind. I was, after all, in the Big Apple.

More than little bit exhausted, we hit the streets. I had never seen so many people jostling their way to wherever they were going. I felt a bit like a bowling pin desperately trying not to be knocked down. But I was delirious at all the possibilities. Saks Fifth Avenue took my breath away. Everything smelled beautiful and looked even more so. The price tags snapped me back to reality, but I couldn't resist. I wanted to have a Saks something… I bought a vivid pink lipstick and even it was way over my budget. Carole had warned me to hang on to my purse. I clutched it and my precious Saks bag with both hands as I exited the store. My head felt like it was on a swivel stick as I looked around in every direction for would-be thieves. I had both of our return bus tickets, some makeup and a less than full wallet. It would have been a very disappointing grab.

Exhausted and still going, we arrived back at the hotel. I decided that Carole must have lots of money. She didn't seem to care what the frothy Singapore Slings cost; she decided we had to have them to celebrate our fabulous lives. She saw me counting my money and waved it away as she picked up the tab. I knew then that I wanted to be flush enough to be that generous with my friends.

Rested and showered, we prepared for round two. Carole, a veteran New York visitor had our evening all planned. Bee-hived and hair-sprayed, we joined the endless throng that jammed the sidewalks heading in a hundred directions, all in a hurry. The relentless honking horns from the taxis trying to fight their way upstream in a gridlock that never seemed to end was just part of the night music of Manhattan. Carole let out a shrill whistle and in under a minute we were giggling in the back of our own taxi. When Carole said to take us to a bar called Maxwell's Plum, the Cabbie eyeballed us in the mirror. "You don't want to go there. You look like nice girls. Let me take you to German Town." Carole was insistent. So was the Cabbie. He was adamant that Maxwell's Plum was not a good place for good girls. I felt a wave of concern flush my face. Before I knew what was happening, she threw some cash into the front seat and we were out the car door and back to walking.

Maxwell's Plum was like no place I'd ever been. Stained glass and Tiffany lamps dominated the room. Huge brightly colored ceramic jungle creatures stared down from every pillar and crevice. I thought I was an urban Toronto girl who knew how to navigate the intricate dance steps required to have a fascinating social life. Maybe in Toronto, but in New York I did not. Jammed full of young, affluent men and women knocking back drink after drink, they checked each other out like sharks looking for a nighttime feeding. I thought the cabbie might have been right. I was out of my depth as much as Carole swam about in comfort. She flirted, laughed and moved on to the next. I, on the other hand, got cornered. Being too polite I didn't know how to shake one particularly slimy guy I had zero interest in. After being backed into a corner, I excused myself and went to the restroom where I stayed. I peeked out after a suitable amount of time and when the coast was clear I slipped back into one of the few unlit crevices where I waited for Carole to tire of being adored.

The next day was almost a mirror of the day before: endless walking while ogling the former mansions and ornate apartment buildings. Carole inducted me into the art of swanning through hotel lobbies as if we owned them just so we could make use of their beautiful and well-appointed bathrooms, then casually lounge on comfortable velvet settees, long enough to catch our breath. The trick was to act 'as if' - *Tips I still live by and encourage friends to take advantage of whenever traveling.*

The Carson show taped early. The plan was to go watch the show and then go out to dinner with Carole's friend and some of his friends, then go back to the hotel and get our stuff and head to the bus station for the one o'clock in the morning overnight journey home. I was feeling very proud of myself when I stopped in a drugstore to buy a faux-silk eye mask, almost like Carole's.

We pulled out all the stops getting ourselves ready. One might have thought we were going to be on camera instead of being part of the audience. Each of my eyelashes had been carefully and individually glued on. My makeup was intense, perhaps a bit drag queen-ish in its excess. It could have been the glittery eye shadow and heavy cat-eyed black eyeliner. I pulled on the beautiful hot-pink silk cocktail dress my mother had made me. *People actually dressed up in those days. Today, too many have a t-shirt with some overused witticism emblazoned on it for those rare special occasions.*

Andrew, Carole's ex, met us at the stage door. He seemed really nice. He and Carole were super excited to see each other. He led us down the aisle before the crowd was let in. Our seats were dead center, second row from the front. It was overwhelming to be that close to the stage, which was far smaller than I expected. It felt so intimate listening to these big stars talking to Johnny. Goldie Hawn and Burt Bacharach were the main guests. I loved them both. When the show ended, the ushers, including Andrew, herded everyone out and that's when everything stopped being fun. Carole was by my side as we made our way out and then she wasn't. I got swept up in the crush as the audience pushed their way out. I was suddenly alone. I looked everywhere but the whole area went from being a chaotic zoo to becoming a ghost town. I managed to find my way back stage and saw Mr. Carson being led to an exit where he got into a limo and he too was gone. No ushers. No Carole. I felt a wave of panic. I finally found one of the pages as he was heading out. I asked him if he had seen Andrew. His response, "I saw him and some girl heading out right after the show was done." I was stunned. I was on my own. *There were no cell phones. No way to text my fury at having been dumped.*

Overdressed and overtired, I headed back to the hotel. Gripping my purse tightly, I walked as fast as my platform shoes would allow. Every shadow caused a sharp intake of breath. I knew Carole was capricious but I didn't think she was thoughtless. I reminded myself I didn't really know her at all. I let out my panicked breath as I walked through the doors of the Biltmore. The big beautiful clock chimed nine P.M. I made my way to the banquette beneath it and assessed my situation. The bus back to Toronto was leaving at one in the morning. We had checked out before we left for the show. I needed to change into travelling clothes; cocktail attire on a Greyhound bus was way too weird. I went to the front desk and asked if I could retrieve my suitcase from the holding area. The girl behind the desk asked for my claim ticket. I opened my purse, and then remembered Carole had them. I had the bus tickets. The desk clerk was adamant that I could not get my bag back without the appropriate claim ticket. I begged. I over-explained again and again. Her icy expression made it clear, there would be no bag. I was close to bursting into tears. I didn't know what to do. I went back to my

Oops! I Forgot to Save Money

station on the banquette. I tried to think my way through this conundrum as I alternated minute to minute from sanguine to completely agitated. Eventually, a man in a grey suit appeared directly in front of me. He was youngish, maybe in his early thirties. He looked pleasant enough but in an ordinary way. "I was in the bar and I could see you struggling to stay calm as you talked to the desk clerk. And then when you sat down, you appeared even more upset. Is there anything I can do to help?" I told him my story. He held his hand up, smiled and told me to sit tight. I watched him have a few words with that same girl behind the desk. He didn't raise his voice. I saw him hold out his room key, not a wand. In what appeared to be next to no time at all, he was walking toward me holding my suitcase.

Gavin invited me to come and have a drink in the bar. "You need to calm down. Nothing is ever as bad as you think." I gratefully accepted. He was a teacher from Columbus, Ohio on a two-day teacher's convention. He said he wanted to get on the school principal track. We made small talk for over an hour. Gavin seemed exactly as advertised, a nice man with a good job, from a good family. He was a little bit nerdy but kind. After I had told him my entire tale of travelling with Carole, he offed the opinion that she sounded like a self-centered girl who used people to get what she wanted. I sadly agreed.

When he offered me the opportunity to come up to his room to watch the opening monologue from the Carson show, possibly catch seeing myself on TV and still have plenty of time to get to the bus, I gratefully followed him to the elevator. I was in his bathroom pulling on my travelling clothes. I could hear the familiar theme for the show. I was feeling better and was more than a little excited at the notion of seeing myself.

I stepped out of the bathroom and Gavin was lying on his bed watching Johnny doing his monologue. I headed for a comfortable

57

chair in the corner. Gavin patted the bed next to him and said I should join him. I shook my head and went for the chair. He insisted. I again shook my head. It took no more than a second for him to be off the bed. He grabbed me roughly by my arm and yanked me up from the chair. *So much for his pretending to be the kind and helpful teacher. God, how could I have been so stupid?* He was far stronger than I was. He kicked the chair out of the way and dragged me towards the bed. I fought back with all I had. I heard the bedside lamp crash to the floor. He was on top of me. I kicked and clawed at his face. He yelled and let go. That moment gave me enough time to get upright and somehow over to the door. It was chained but it opened enough. In one of those miraculous moments that can't be explained, the elevator door opened at exactly the same time. In those days, there was an elevator operator. I shouted for him to hold the elevator! I heard him say, "Are you alright, Miss?" Gavin was right behind me. He knew I would scream. He backed away and said in a voice so chilling I can still hear its tone. "If you tell anyone about this, I will find you and kill you!" My hands were trembling really hard but I got the chain off the door. I grabbed my bag and stepped out into the hallway and onto that magic elevator.

    The girl behind the desk took one look at me and knew. She called for the manager, a dyed-in-the-wool New Yorker. In silent admonition, he shook his head over and over as I recounted what had happened. Gravel voiced, I heard him say what I had already said to myself, "Didn't your mother teach you about going to hotel rooms with strangers?" I tried to fight back the lump in my throat and keep it from turning into tears. I heard that clock in the lobby chime midnight. What had I been thinking? I should have known I would never get to the bus in time. That was the final straw. The tears came fast and I couldn't stop crying. In that moment I knew I could have been not just raped but murdered. I felt so stupid and so angry with myself. Then I realized I didn't have enough money to spend another night and the next bus wasn't until morning.

It turned out the manager was really a softie, his crustiness the armor that came from battling his whole life to survive amid the endless swarm. He gave me a tiny room on the top floor and told me to bolt the door. He was going to 'take care of that son-of-a-bitch teacher'. The police were already on their way. I didn't sleep a wink. I lay against the pillows holding my slim pink razor in my hands... as if that would keep me safe.

In the morning I boarded that Greyhound with a flood of relief. I spent the entire journey sitting next to a garlicky smelling Ukrainian woman who generously shared her lunch with me. She kept patting my hand as if she knew everything I had been though. Three days later Carole, completely oblivious to what she had put me though, bounced into my mother's shop with the intention of sharing her New York adventure with me. I made it very clear I wasn't interested. She seemed confused.

My so-called boyfriend didn't seem to get the seriousness of what I'd been through either. He echoed what I already knew... I had miscalculated. *Understatement.* And ... and... It was my fault. That was the extent of his concern. He needed me to focus, so we could figure out his schedule and my ability to service it as his chauffeur. I was stunned when I realized that I had just had back-to-back encounters with two full-blown narcissists. I swore I would not let that happen again. I found the courage to dump my Dutch far-from-model boyfriend, even though I was more than a little obsessed with having him on my arm. Or was it that he dumped me for a better car and a more arm-candy worthy driver? I cried. I moved on. *Finding pretty people to latch on to is easy when one is in their early twenties. Nearly everyone is a rose.* I drove him to the airport to make sure neither of us changed our mind.

After a day of tears, as I threw away hundreds of pictures of him posing - in a tree, or against a lamp post or his very favorite, a double vision *Selfie* gazing deeply into a mirror - I was free. *I remember worrying I'd never find another great-looking boyfriend that would enhance my status. Ugh... This is something I actually worried about.* It was a shock to discover how little I missed him.

It would take months before I really felt safe again. I was obsessing on what might have befallen me given my bad judgment. *That could have been about both Carole and the all-about-him-jerk I had wasted so much time on.* It was in fact about my near-miss-rapist.

A completely unexpected encounter with an actor friend shifted my energy back to my optimistic self. He suggested I go and meet the head honcho of a new television station. "They are looking for outside-the-box ideas. I have one for you! I know no other big girl who is as flexible as you. You should do an exercise show." We all have opportunities in our lives that come out of nowhere. For me, this one was like a deeply felt 'AHA' that I needed to listen to. It wasn't that I was unhappy with my chosen fashion design career. It was something else. An internal ringing bell was insisting that I pay attention. I did. It was the moment that completely changed my life. I went through those doors with a confidence I didn't know I possessed. But I was possessed with the deep knowledge that it was a meant to be. People were suddenly buying what I didn't know I was selling... Me!

Note to Self – Part 1: Making smarter choices earlier on might have paved the way to a more solid financial future. *(And kept me* *out of a compete stranger's hotel room!)* I wish I had been shown how. As a parent, it's important to make money mean something and to teach children the value of a dollar. *Teach* them that results don't come from just working toward goals but actually completing them.

Note to Self – Part 2: Being with people who toss money around to make themselves feel important creates insecurity and worse, envy. Finding your own self worth takes time but is ultimately more rewarding. It's not about what you have but who you are.

Recommended Medication: Irish coffee with Bailey's whipped cream. After a hard day and night of playing a hippie, it is the gift that keeps on giving.

CHAPTER 5

INVESTING EVERY PENNY ON LOVE

The Cost: Choosing to invest in love versus a long-term savings plan.

Yowsa! In what appeared to be the beginning of something big, I had landed my very own exercise show at a brand-new television station in Toronto, where I had the nerve to do backbends and every other showy-off move I could think of, all while cracking jokes. *I was very flexible. I was young.* Being a fat girl with chutzpah got me a lot of press. I happily showed up at the zoo that was this upstart television station, filled with young people who knew full well they had won the lottery. We loved our jobs and the opportunities that sprang up everywhere. Having a sense of humor got me noticed. *Okay... so did wearing a leotard on my less than svelte body.* My show was a hit. Dan Ayckroyd got his first job as my announcer. Gilda Radner was a close friend. She used to come on the show once in awhile and exercise with me, because she thought she was fat and I didn't seem able to convince her differently. City Television also became an instant success. No one had ever seen programming like we put on the air. *I realize now how ahead of the curve we were. I was comfortably outrageous but I didn't yet understand the potency of my every-woman relate-ability.* The press coverage I got was all positive and affirming. It ego-proofed my formerly body-shaming, insecure self. The dividend I received was that my family stopped being disappointed with my failure to lose weight. I was a celebrity and by association, so were they.

Most people believe that everyone who appears on the TV screens in their living rooms must earn big bucks. I did, too. I learned, but only after I'd done the job, that being a success on a small cable station, especially back in those days, did not come with the imagined big paycheck. I had a contract. *I just didn't bother to read it. It was all "forthwith and in the case of..." mumbo jumbo legalese to me.* The top tier executives owned the programs. They made the big bucks. We, the talent, were never going to see any big money - not then, and not for a long while. The money I made from my exercise show was a pittance, but it didn't matter. We weren't any the wiser and we didn't need that much to live on. Soon I had a bucketful of notoriety and a bit of money in the bank. I was filled with gratitude for having the opportunity and the visibility, along with the joy of spending time with a magnificent tribe of hard working, fun-loving compadres. As soon as I was done filming my first season, I stashed my meager but meaningful earnings away in my first bank account.

I checked its balance every day to make sure it was still there.

Not long after, a highly respected touring theater group, Young People's Theater, invited me to join their company and I jumped at the chance. I had somehow become an actress but I had no legitimacy. It had been serendipity, not training, that had launched my new career. I wanted to be better; I wanted to feel less illegitimate. The rehearsals were long, sometimes hard but once again I was smack in the middle of a readymade family. We ate together, spent every day together. I likened it to a dog park filled with lots of alpha personalities as well as the peacemakers, the comedians and the rebels. I think I was a mix of cheerleader,

Oops! I Forgot to Save Money

peacemaker and rebel with a hint of alpha. Our director was desperate to retain his designated top dog role. He almost always blew it with his failure to control the pack by raising his voice and stamping his feet. As a group, we were uncontrollable. I almost felt sorry for him. It was worse than trying to corral lion cubs. I loved it. I was learning. We travelled to small towns all over Northern Ontario, staying in cheap motels and eating in cheaper restaurants. We were a pack. Love affairs began and ended but the friendships continued, for many to this day. And many of our troupe went on to become very successful actors, writers, and producers while some left the business. Sidebar: The theater was and remains one of the toughest careers in which to make a living.

Once the theater tour was done, I returned to my mother's shop, designing dresses for the rich and famous. They wanted the best of everything but didn't always want to pay for it. *It was from that experience I learned that most people do not appreciate the value of the time spent in making a one-of-a-kind garment, a piece of handcrafted furniture, or a hand blown glass bowl and on and on.* Many would bargain over the price of a button. My mother found the relentless nickel-and-dime-ing uncomfortable and exhausting. Inevitably she would throw in the towel and allow herself to take far less than she deserved. Even then, many of her clients would take far too long to pay. There was always an end of the month struggle for her to have enough money to pay her bills. I wanted her to have a clearly listed set of prices but apparently that was not the way it was done. *Weirdly, I was the more practical one.* Each client was handled with kid gloves and catered to depending on their whims. There was too much competition to alienate any of them.

Being in the most fashionable neighborhood as well as the hotbed of Toronto's baby boomers' cultural disruption was thrilling. However, it wasn't good for my mother's business. Young people didn't want to have their clothes custom made, unless it was for an elaborate wedding gown. The pop revolution in Britain, represented by fashion upstart Mary Quant, and the booming music scene there meant that most young people were now heavily influenced by what was 'in' on London's Carnaby Street. The barely-there dresses and clunky-heeled boots scandalized nearly everyone over thirty-five. *That might have been the point.* And it may have been the beginning of the affordable fashion-for-the-masses movement. I too had a trendy wardrobe but mine cost me nothing. That didn't stop me from having more than a touch of attitude. I was perilously close to putting on a British accent. *If I had met me today, I would have laughed at this deeply insecure and pretentious girl. But I didn't know me then to warn me about how transparent I was.*

Once again, serendipity struck when a stunning, pouty-lipped, leggy, blonde model, who I vaguely remember being Estonian, Austrian or Carpathian stepped into my mother's shop. Her name was Tiiu. *Throw a stick at whichever country it was and you'd have hit at least fifty of them and their names all rhymed with Shih Tzu.* This swan-on-stilts brought a filmmaker friend with her. He was making his first movie and needed dresses for his actresses. I told him I would give him the dresses but then jokingly demanded a leading role as payment. For a moment I thought he took my request seriously. It seemed as if a wand had been waved as he nodded yes. Panic set in. What did I know about being the lead in a movie? NOTHING! I came thudding back to earth as I heard him say I couldn't have the lead but I could have a small part. He said it would be significant. I happily, and with some relief, handed over the dresses. *My apologies to all those who paid big money to study the Stanislavsky method or attend RADA; I got my big acting break by supplying wardrobe. I played a hooker. The director, Ivan Reitman went on to make so many bold-named movies. One of the*

Oops! I Forgot to Save Money

biggest was Ghostbusters! The guy who served coffee on the set was none other than Eugene Levy of Schitt's Creek fame.

A commercial came next. It was for Scotch tape. I was strapped into an old fashioned treadmill with all that was behind me, vibrating hour after hour. I didn't understand why that had anything to do with sticky tape. It certainly wasn't used to hold my jiggling thighs in place but it paid. A guest appearance on a police drama followed on the commercial's heels. I went out and bought an answering machine to contain all of my auditions and potential job offers. I decided it was time to take my new career seriously, which meant telling my mother/my boss that I was leaving. She wasn't thrilled about losing me as her in-house designer, but I think she liked having a daughter who was on television. It gave her bragging rights at her never-ending bridge games.

I had walked out on my paying steady job sure that a tidal wave of acting work would keep on coming. It didn't. I wasn't prepared for the lull. My savings were slim and getting slimmer. If only stress had the same effect on me. *Oh how easy it was to be fooled that a freelance life offered financial security.*

I couldn't help but think about other actors I knew: the ones who were totally committed to their art, and the ones who gave up too easily. When the going got tough, they didn't have the grit or the belief in themselves. Talent is a necessary requirement but one must have passion and determination to ride out the tough times. I am reminded of Jeanne Beker, one of my touring theater pack who went on to become a world famous fashion journalist and style icon. We both got our big breaks at City TV. Her path proved to be far more meteoric than most.

Jeanne came into this world with big dreams and chutzpah. Chutzpah is Yiddish for 'having the balls to go for what you want.' It wasn't that she was fearless; it was her willingness to go for it despite her fear that propelled her to take on every opportunity with gusto. She also has the innate understanding of her power to convince people that they should take a chance on her.

Jeanne's boyfriend had been offered a post-graduate fellowship at a university in Newfoundland. He convinced her to come with him. Jeanne was a trained mime artist at the time, but since there was little demand for that particular expertise in Newfoundland, Jeanne decided she'd try to go back to using her voice. She approached the local CBC radio station. She convinced the producer of their consumer show to hire her as an arts reporter, suggesting that she could cover the arts scene there from a consumer's point of view. After three successful years on the job, she and her then husband moved back to Toronto. Armed with a stash of audio-tapes, she approached every radio station in town, calling several many times a day, until she got an outright "NO!" Determined to get hold of the program director at the number one hit station at the time, she called his office relentlessly, ten times a day, every day for about a week until she finally got hold of him.

Impressed by her determination, he called her in for an audition, not even sure if there was a position available, but he liked her young sounding voice and the fact that she had all that experience in a smaller market. So he created a regular spot for her lifestyle reports within the daily newscasts.

Jeanne worked her ass off and people took notice. There was also the serendipitous timing in that the very same radio station

Oops! I Forgot to Save Money

had just acquired a hip, maverick cable TV station, where I had, coincidentally, done my exercise show. *By the following year the radio station wanted to cross promote some of their radio stars, and Jeanne was camera ready. MTV hadn't been invented yet, there was a plan in the works at City TV for a music magazine show that would get up close and personal with rock stars. Jeanne was hired as the ground-breaking show's co-star and with "The New Music," got to go on the road and interview everyone from Paul McCartney and Keith Richards to Elton John, The Who, Blondie, Robert Plant, Frank Zappa and on it went. Those interviews took place on smoky tour buses, bizarre, drug and booze filled hotel rooms and backstage. Naturally curious, always prepared and unafraid, Jeanne was a hit.*

After a few years she wanted something fresh and more challenging. There was a super-star collision of sorts happening globally - a synergy between the haute and the hot. Rock stars had started hanging out with fashion designers: Madonna and Jean Paul Gaultier, Elton John and Vercace, David Bowie and Thierry Mugler. No one had really covered the fashion world as entertainment before. The young producer in charge of the new show-to-be wanted to cast a model to be sort of a fashion Veejay. Jeanne decided to throw her hat in the ring and convinced management to give her a shot as the show's host. Jeanne took "Fashion Television" into the stratosphere and went right there with it, hosting the show for its entire twenty-seven year run. She never looked back.

∽

It was easy to compare myself to Jeanne as we had both been in the same theatre company and both worked at the same indie TV station. We had both moved between acting and TV hosting.

69

Jeanne had much more experience as an actress that I did and already had done several acting gigs by the time I arrived in Canada from Scotland. And, by her admission, Jeanne had always wanted to be famous. But it wasn't just about fame. It was also about having the security from the money that came with it. That was her lodestar. Fame was never on my radar. But, neither was money. *Tell us something we don't know.* 'Experts' are always promoting the success that comes with creating vision boards; reminders of goals set, visuals front and center to remind you of your wants and desires. I have always had multiple visions. *Not the Jesuskind.* I loved being a designer but I also loved entertaining people; being an actress and most definitely spinning stories was all part of the mix. They each took top position at different times, making it more tentacled, rather than following a single path. *Variety is the spice of life... Lots of balls in the air... or perhaps, a seriously short attention span.* The one thing that I love above all others is the doing. I have often likened myself to a Clydesdale: one of those huge horses that front the Budweiser wagons. Pushing or pulling beer wagons might be a bit of a stretch. But pushing and pulling in some form or another was what I was meant to do, more with my mental capacity rather than the physical. I have worked since I was a kid. As long as my curiosity is piqued, my attention held, I am a willing and happy participant.

Just as I was ready to crawl my way back into working for my mother, I landed a part in a movie called Keep It In the Family, as the best friend to a ridiculously gorgeous girl. I was thrilled – not necessarily about my art imitating my life but about landing such a big role that paid well. I was excited to be heading to beautiful Montreal where the movie was going to be shot.

Oops! I Forgot to Save Money

As soon as the first day of filming was done, my nerves settled. The director was very welcoming as were all the other actors. The hours were long but they flew by. The hotel where all of the actors were staying was gorgeous with a gracious, old-world charm. My room overlooked a small but perfectly manicured park, made more beautiful by a dusting of fresh snow. Room service was a brand new experience and soon the very snobby and cranky bellman began to soften. I had no idea what was expected, so out of the fear that I might not be doing it right, I handed him a twenty from my rapidly diminishing envelope of something called per diem (a whack of cash to cover expenses) with every delivery he brought. *I only found out later that I was insanely over-tipping him.*

On my second day of filming, one of the actors, an imposing looking and very enthusiastic young man was to pretend to knock me out by hitting me with a realistic looking but break-a-way chair. In the heat of his moment, he grabbed the wrong chair - a heavy wood one. He swung hard towards my shoulder. The blow knocked me out for real. After I came to, apologies came at me from every corner. A doctor came to check me out. I kept saying I was fine. Scenes were rearranged and I was sent back to my hotel to rest up.

After sleeping off the pain, I had an unexpected day off. I was eager to explore the city. None of my newest friends, the other actors, were around, so with no makeup and unwashed hair I ventured out. I walked for what seemed hours. All the stores had their Christmas decorations up. I marveled at how pulled together everyone looked, including the men. Everyone wore scarves, twisted and tied with such understated elegance. I caught my reflection in one of the windows and instantly looked away. I was far from pulled together. *Upon reflection, I think I looked like a homeless bag lady without the bags.* I was hungry and cold. I stopped at a little café and found

71

a table far in the back. I was minding my own business, alternating between making sense of the all-French menu and watching the perfect, runway-ready crowd, when a gorgeous Frenchman crashed my private reverie. The restaurant was crowded and he too was hungry. He gestured a 'did I mind if he could share my table?' Hell yes! I minded. I looked like week-old cheese. He spoke very little English, which was fine, as I wanted to remain hidden behind the incomprehensible menu. He knew exactly what he wanted. *So did I. HIM! But that seemed like a man-in-the-moon reach.* Before the very attentive waitress could leave, he tapped my arm softly to ask if I needed help. *Understatement alert.* I stayed hidden as best as I could. He moved the menu away from my face and asked again in a combination of French and sign language if he might help. I couldn't help but laugh. It took only a second, and then he was laughing too. Of course he couldn't help. He barely spoke English. The waitress, who was not part of our shared moment, huffed and turned on her heel leaving us to laugh even more. I chose toast with 'jambon'. I didn't want anything that could drip, drop or splatter, or leave visible evidence on my teeth. He didn't understand half of what I was saying and yet he seemed to enjoy my blatant flirting. He said his name was Gilles. I stammered out my name, blushed and took cover once again behind the menu.

I was madly, deeply and truly in love. Insane, given that I had spent no more than a total of an hour and a half in his company, which was when I excused myself to calm my beating heart. In the interim I called my mother. I told her I had met the man I was going to marry. She thought I had gone crazy. Me too. When I returned to the table, he was still there. A good sign...

To this day, I'm not sure how or why he chose to spend nearly all my free time with me. I had no eye-of-newt or hypnosis-inducing potion. I prayed and I wished relentlessly. He would appear as if out of nowhere, over and over. I was besotted with this magical man. He was also somewhat slippery. It was obvious that I made him laugh but that seemed to be all. And much like a male Cinderella, every night around midnight he vanished. Somehow he would keep reappearing, sometime early in the morning bearing croissants and perfect lattes. Other times the hotel lobby phone would ring. He'd be waiting to show me a favorite but obscure part of his Montreal. There was laughter and a definite chemistry but no hint of anything physical. I was beginning to feel like a fat cricket in heat. I couldn't say anything real that might lead to a crippling rejection. I was left feeling on edge, twitching and lusting but pretending I felt no more than a buddy-like sense of camaraderie. Ugh, my heart ached with unrequited yearning. My time on the film was over. Gilles walked me to the train station. He carried my suitcase. I carried a sense of doom as this man, whom I was convinced was intended to be my forever-man, was hugging me good-bye as romantically as if it was a scene from Casablanca.

 I sat on the train reliving that farewell moment, looking for even a tiny clue that he felt as I did. When his arm encircled my back as he helped me up onto the train, didn't I feel an extra squeeze of deep regret as his hand seemed to press harder into my back? *No kissing... just hugging.* A clap of vivid clarity came flashing across my brain. He's gay! Yes, he wants to hang out with me but just as a friend. I'm his buddy…like one of those clingy breeds, a retriever of some kind. I paddled backwards over every nuance, every moment of deep eye contact. Nope. Not gay. Shy? Emotionally paralyzed? He's a hermaphrodite? The train rattled by one small farm town after another. He's scared of me! I'm a lot to handle. YES! That must be it.

 Once I was back home, I knew that we needed more time together. I had made more money on this movie than I had ever made in my life and it was time to roll the dice. I waited for a few days. My stomach was in knots and my heart in a fragile state. I called him and told him I unexpectedly got another week on the movie. He seemed delighted that I would be back in Montreal. I checked back into the very expensive hotel that had been completely paid for while I was shooting the film. I was convinced this was a necessary ruse, in order to have enough time to convince Gilles I was the only woman for him.

Once in Montreal, I would disappear every day under the pretense that I was on set shooting new scenes for the film. I was mostly hiding out in the central library, catching up on the classics I had never intended to read. We spent every evening and weekend day together but just like that damn Cinderella, before the clock would strike midnight, he'd be gone. A sweet kiss, but that was it… and possibly a ruffle of my hair, like one would give to a favorite pet. No glass slipper, no clues to where or why he was going. He never made excuses or gave any explanation. I was on the verge of following him but I thought he might catch sight of my largish shadow under the streetlights and then I'd be toast.

My money had run out and I still hadn't made a dent with this elusive man. I dipped into my precious savings and gave myself six more days. I was aware this was not a smart-money move. If I didn't win his heart, I'd be heading home with no guy and only half of this month's rent money.

It was the last day of my gamble. I knew I had to take that huge leap into potential heartbreak. I asked him where he went every night. I held my breath waiting to hear him say to his girlfriend's house. He lifted his head and looked into my eyes and said. "I go away from you." I didn't understand. "What does that mean? Why? Don't you want to be with me?" I was afraid to look at him. I was hurt or maybe I was scared. I felt his hand under my chin. He lifted my face up towards his. His eyes and his nose were so close to my face they were melding into one another. But then his lips were on mine.

The next morning, I couldn't even luxuriate in what was now our bed. I had to pack! There was no way I could afford to miss my checkout time. I was happy, terrified and confused. What was that? Why did it have to happen on my last night? Like a relentless earworm, the replay in my head kept repeating "I go away from you."

Rarely am I quiet, but that's exactly what I was as we shared breakfast at a café in the train station. Gilles was patient. He didn't ask. I looked at the clock. The train was just moments away. I sucked up my courage and faced him. "Why did you say you go away from me?" Gilles took both my hands in his and looked at me with those deep ocean eyes. "You don't like no. I am not fast in response like you. I needed to be sure I was going to be a yes in my heart." The train whistle was getting closer. It took me a moment to make some sense of his words. When they sank in. I was all over him like that sticky tape I had shilled for. "You have a yes in your heart for me!" Gilles laughed and kissed me hard.

Note to Self: Always read your contracts, even if they are numbingly boring. It's our job to understand the fine print. If you really want to protect money, it should be put into a savings plan with a penalty for early withdrawal. But the question for me remained, was spending that money folly or was my chance at true love the best investment I could have made?

Recommended Medication: Champagne Cake. When love comes along (even if a small amount of manipulation is involved) Celebrate!

CHAPTER 6

THE PRICE OF CINDERELLA'S SLIPPER

The Cost: Giving money no respect made us waste it instead of empowering it and ourselves.

I was behaving like a southern belle with my very own fainting couch. My heart fluttered, seeming to skip a beat every time I thought of Gilles. I wanted to rent a sky plane that carried a banner proclaiming our love for everyone to see…especially for those who had rejected me in the past. *Okay, it wasn't my finest moment but it was honest.* Gilles and I spoke every night. It was a true mash-up of French, English and a form of lovesick mooniness, mostly on my part. I believe I begged him to come to see me about twenty times a call. In a truly unexpected moment, he said yes!

The dusting and vacuuming Olympics were on. Everything that could be scrubbed and deloused was attacked with full force. New bed linens unwrapped, casually subtle sexy lingerie bought; the fridge was stocked with all the French food I could carry. Receipts were hidden even from myself. Romance didn't come cheap. I called my mother to tell her my exciting news. My boyfriend Gilles was coming! I almost passed out from having used the boyfriend word. She was happy for me but oddly distant. My mother usually wanted to extrude every detail of my life. Her distracted demeanor was clearly a red flag. I immediately asked her what my father had done to upset her. She actually said he did nothing wrong. Okay... Now, I knew trouble was afoot. I grilled her some more. Soon the truth escaped in a rush of tears and anguish. Her business was in trouble. Big trouble.

My mother was desperately trying to keep her couture business from going under. All her costs were going up; her rent had recently been raised due to the demand from outsiders wanting in on the now hip and happening area, her longtime staff's salaries were up for a bump and her supplier's prices had also gone significantly skyward. She was tired. She was almost seventy and she no longer had the energy needed to charm or fight her foes. Instead, she dug herself an even deeper hole by naively borrowing money from not just one but two very skilled loan sharks; experts in flimflamming those in dire straits. These slick hustlers with soothing demeanors promised easy cash to put an end to financial troubles overnight. My worldly but financially clueless mother had zero understanding of the punitive contracts she had all too eagerly signed. It wasn't long before the inevitable happened; her debt load became overwhelming. The loan sharks circled and then bit down hard. Exorbitant compounding interest, buried deep in the fine print, was activated. Her only shot at getting out from under was to declare bankruptcy... and lose almost everything. She managed to get her prized cutting table, a couple of sewing machines and some imported wools into storage before it was all taken. Her beautiful boutique went to her creditors – and with it, the very core of her existence.

She bade tearful farewells to her longtime staff. And as sad as it was to see all those gorgeous imported silks and hand-embroidered fabrics being sold off, along with a herd of mannequins and several costly sewing machines, there was a sense of relief that she was free.

Oops! I Forgot to Save Money

I had so wanted to show Gilles my mother's shop and the Yorkville scene that had given me so much, including my start as an actress. It was now an empty shell; the "For Lease" sign was already gone, replaced with one that said, "Rented." A wave of nostalgia and sadness swept over me.

I took Gilles home to meet my parents; two people who had stuck it out, sharing a house, not a home, because they needed each other to patch up their very different leaky life rafts. The long-held image in my head as I imagined my mother meeting my father, was as if the Titanic had smacked hard into an ice cube.

To my shock, my father was withering just like the last few leaves that hadn't yet succumbed to the night frost. He had begun to show signs of early dementia. His eyes that used to glitter with humor were flat. Almost overnight, he had become an old and frail man. My mother, in spite of her misfortune, was, as always, able to put on a show. She was dressed in something she had made. It was beautiful and refined, showing her impeccable taste and skill. One look at the very handsome Gilles and that well honed, deeply ingrained spark from a former femme fatale flashed to the surface. The good china came out, as did a never before seen overt flirtatiousness. I was concerned that if she batted her eyelashes any faster she would ascend to the ceiling like a human helicopter. They hit it off like a clapboard house on fire. He genuinely was interested in all that she had to say. His mother was also a dressmaker, albeit not with a fancy-ass shop like my mother used to have. Sigh… He had learned the trade from watching her. He was also an actor. He worked a lot in film and theatre in France and Quebec where he spoke the language. He told her that to make extra money, he started doing alterations for friends and soon he was much in demand. *What was up with me and the clothes makers? It must have been one of those higher*

79

power moments reaching out, knowing I was far from an off-the rack-size and would always need a dressmaker in my life. Just as we were saying our good byes, my father stepped forward to ask who we were.

His rapid decline was alarming. He was rarely here. He had travelled back in time. His British accent became more pronounced. He spoke to me as if I was his older sister, asking over and over about his Ovaltine. I knew it was some kind of warm drink he liked when he was a boy. We didn't have any. I made him tea and that made him uncharacteristically angry. He waved his fist at me. "That's not Ovaltine." I was taken aback by his fury. He had always been so meek, and always sweet to me. Out of nowhere he flipped a switch, deciding he wanted me to accompany him to his drawing class. I took a breath and said I would. I don't remember him ever having been to one. He thankfully fell asleep. It was easy to see he needed more care than my mother could give. *Caring for my father had never been her priority.*

My mother began feverishly looking up elder care homes in the yellow pages. Anything she hit on that vaguely sounded like it dealt with something old or rusty got a call. Used car dealerships and an auction house specializing in antiquities almost got possession of my father. I stepped up and found him a placement in a very nice, formerly grand house fronted by beautiful gardens. He lasted less than two months; he was too far-gone for the minimal care they provided. We scrambled to get him into a private memory care facility but they were all prohibitively expensive. Neither of my parents had thought to plan for their sunset years. After scouring every possible old age home as best as we could, we finally found a supposedly good facility that was somewhat affordable.

Amid all the drama and pain my parents were going through, Gilles gave me unconditional support... with a little coaxing from my end. *Understatement!* My most recent roommate had been a neurotic hot mess of an actress who specialized in endless self-examination. "Are my eyes too close together?" "Do I come across as someone who is too self-involved? I don't do I? I just want to be true to my essence. I think I present as a person that people want to be friends with. Don't you?" I was exhausted after every interaction. But she had just given me notice and was soon heading to The Esalen Institute in California to work on her personal growth. I couldn't have been happier. It wasn't because she was moving on, which was great news, but the better news was that Gilles was moving in. The timing was perfect. He packed up his life in Montreal and moved in with me in Toronto. As a French Canadian who had spent the last several years in Paris, his English needed work but I was more than willing to be his very personal teacher.

Making a living in English Canada turned out to be much more of a challenge for Gilles than we anticipated. Here, I was the one with the bigger career and many more connections. His would take time. But this man was no slouch. Gilles had a great eye and an enormous talent for making beautiful clothes for both men and women. Unfortunately, charging any real money for the magic he made was not in his toolkit. He seemed to have a disconnect regarding the value of what he was good at. He simply wanted to make people happy. *And he skates on water. Who is this guy?* What if we decided to have a family, *(oops leaping way ahead)* how was that going to work if money is so meaningless? I felt a wave of panic creep into my throat.

Two artists who live together and love each other is a beautiful thing but far from practical. *Alert: Any artist who chooses this path to make money needs to do a deep dive into the stats that say otherwise. To be an artist is a way of life that reels one in because it's something we must do. It's not a choice.* We moved in together exactly at the time when my television series came to an end. Without many pennies to his name, Gilles bought me the most beautiful pink rose quartz ring. And I, *newly unemployed,* bought him a stupidly expensive but gorgeous handmade Irish cable-knit sweater. And that was just because it was Tuesday and the sun was shining. We both believed that money was for spending and sharing. *Hah! It never even occurred to us that saving was a thing... We were young and there was still time to hope that we would add saving into that mix.*

Waking up to greet the day is normally a joyful time. Promises are made to exercise, eat healthfully, make big strides in knocking off all those things that fill my to do list. By noon many of my promises have gone to hell in a hand-basket. Life has intervened. Mornings can also be treacherous.

The sun was streaming through our picture window. Gilles and I were peacefully reading the morning paper, coffee close by. Croissants half eaten. The doorbell rang. It was a police officer asking to speak to me. At that time, I was a fairly well known actress. My exercise show had garnered a lot of press. Who didn't want to know about a fat girl in leotards, who could do backbends while eating a doughnut from the cruller decorated Christmas tree that I had dragged onto my set? I had no idea why he was at our house at seven in the morning. I invited him in to join us for coffee. I assumed he was there to ask that I buy tickets to some police function. No. He was there to take me to jail.

I unknowingly, or more likely indifferently, had amassed more than six hundred dollars in parking tickets. Some delirious part of me must have believed that by not acknowledging their existence, they would no longer exist. Officer Emery politely told me that was not the case. He also told me he had to take me in. *"In?"* I laughed and cracked a couple of felon jokes, still sure

Oops! I Forgot to Save Money

that I could somehow talk my way out of this. Officer Emery was a really nice man. He suggested, I get out of my pajamas and put on some clothes and he would then drop Gilles off at the bank to pick up my bail money. *"What! I'm going to jail?"* Officer Emery knew me from TV, so he made the assumption that I wasn't a stone cold killer and let me ride up in the front of the police cruiser enroute to drop Gilles off at his bank. My final word to him was "Hurry!" Gilles was notorious for becoming sidetracked by anything and everything that caught his fancy. If I went to the store to get milk, I would be back in twenty minutes. I told my personal police escort that for Gilles, a milk run could mean long enough for a missing person's report to be filed. Emery laughed and said, "I hope not. The food is awful at that jail." Gilles assured me he would be quick. We headed off to the police station, where I would be processed. *Processed*! As we entered the building I walked by his side, chatting as if we were pals. I didn't want anyone to think I was his prisoner. Soon we were back in his squad car but this time he had me ride in the back like a common prisoner. *It was parking tickets. I didn't cold cock anyone!* He was taking me in to the notorious Don Jail. I was now officially terrified. He drove under an archway and I was in another world: dark, ominous and heavily barred. Lovely officer Emery said his good-byes and handed me off to a steel-haired genderless officer from central casting. She led me through a windowless tunnel into an even scarier central booking area. The Don Jail was well into its second century. It was quarry stone and dank. I was then handed off to the pleasant looking matron who admitted every female prisoner. She immediately recognized me from my television series. She was quite chatty. For a moment I thought this warm and engaging fan might let me slip out some secret passage. A loud buzzer interrupted the

83

moment. The matron listened to a call and immediately hustled me into her office. "I got a couple of tough ones coming in. Stay in here!" "Uh okay…" The gate swung open and a pair of brawling bitches kicked and cussed their way in. My sweet chatty matron, turned into 'Elsa the She Wolf' as she cuffed them and hauled them away.

I knew then that I never wanted to do anything illegal ever again. The matron was back and now it was my turn to be admitted. Fan, or not, she was taking me up to a holding cell. On the way, I had a clear view of some seriously badass women prisoners who were doing time for a variety of crimes, including murder. I could tell how long they had been in, by the length of their roots.

The good times were over as my chatty matron handed me off to a far less interested officer who, without a word, put me in a holding cell. Think of an old fashioned zoo where the primates were kept. Only I had no bars to swing on, just the kind to keep me locked up.

And now I waited and waited. I prayed Gilles would not be lured by anything curious or appealing. It could be something in a thrift shop window or some medical marvel he spotted on his way to bail me out. I got even more nervous when an officer doing his rounds inquired how many were in for lunch. I squeaked out a "not me." And went back to praying.

Suddenly I heard my name called. Another officer unlocked my cell and I was out. I walked out through those huge metal doors and an officer who had no idea I had only been there two hours or why patted my arm on my way out. "Good luck on the outside." I smiled and said thanks. Gilles was waiting. He laughed and said that because of 'time served', my fine had been reduced by half. Over a good and expensive celebratory lunch, I soberly said I would never

Oops! I Forgot to Save Money

do that again. Getting parking tickets was stupid enough. Not paying them was even stupider.

It seemed that overnight many of our friends were speaking a whole new language. Their conversations were sprinkled with words like 'mortgages', 'RRSPs', 'life insurance' and babies. We listened for a bit, then turned our backs and focused on far more pleasing pursuits like romantic picnics, tap-dancing classes or staying home and cooking for friends, while dressed in our finest identical coats of denial.

We consciously chose to remain unconscious without any understanding that the future comes along at the speed of a bullet train. The 'why' lay buried for many more years before being unearthed. Consciousness apparently has its own schedule.

In a freelance world like ours, it's always feast or famine. Gilles and I were so in love and happy while we continued wearing horse-blinders about all things practical. We coasted on whatever the tide washed in.

My girlfriend Joanie recently told me a story about an experience she went through back in the days when so many friends seemed to be getting serious about investing or buying a home. Joanie was single. She worked occasionally as an actress but began to get involved in editing films, mostly because she didn't want to be a waitress/actress. Joanie loved travelling and living life to the fullest almost as much as I did. When money ran out, she would hit up her contacts and pick up some more editing jobs, gradually becoming incredibly successful at it. She was happy living exactly as she was until a mutual friend of ours, Martyn, took her to task. They were out for coffee one afternoon when he began chiding her on her irresponsible life. She was more than a little irritated by his attack. He looked at her hard and asked her if she had any savings. Joanie could barely look at him when she replied no. Martyn fixed his eyes on hers and told her in no uncertain terms that if she continued on this path, she would one day find herself unable to 'grab a job here and there' and still be able to afford her peripatetic life. He continued berating her with talk that she could end up homeless and eating cat food. Defensively she shouted at him that her life was her business. She grabbed her coat to leave but not before exclaiming that she didn't even have a cat!

Joanie looked at me and laughed as she related this story to me but then added that Martyn had scared her so much that after her next couple of jobs, instead of running off to Europe or the far east, she had cobbled together as much money as she could and with the help of a realtor friend bought a small house in what was at that time an unfashionable neighborhood. She put a down payment on it and did some minor touchups to make it attractive. She rented it out almost immediately. She added that she had never felt so proud and solidly independent as she had in that moment. She now owns two rental properties and jokingly calls herself a land baroness.

At a recent dinner party, I was seated next to my friend Martyn. I asked, "Why didn't you scare the crap out of me too?" His response, "I thought you were smart enough to know that stuff already."

I sighed. I wasn't.

∽

My employment scarcity came to an end with an offer to host a "how-to" show. It came about from a dinner party I impulsively hosted which should have been disastrous but surprisingly became

Oops! I Forgot to Save Money

fortuitous. It started out as a small gathering of four people but then someone dropped by with a friend. Then another and another called and I asked them to join us. Soon we were ten with enough food for the original four and a table that barely sat three. I pulled everything we had out of the fridge and managed to make a vegetarian chili. Some stale bread soaked in milk, raisins (plucked out of a breakfast cereal) and a found-stash of walnuts became the inspiration for some amazing maple syrup soaked bread pudding. I asked Gilles to drag our headboard from behind our bed into the living room. A white bed-sheet made a great tablecloth along with a gathering of candles stuck in wine bottles, jam jars and even on a soap dish. It looked magical. One of the guests was a fledgling television producer. She was inspired. A few weeks later, she asked if I would like to host a show called Any Woman Can.

With next to no planning and not enough preparation, I was thrust in front of a camera; the premise being that I would have a guest come on the show who was an expert in flooring, or tiling, table-making, plumbing, wall-papering and on and on. If I could learn the task the guest of that specific show would teach me, then any woman could. It was a great idea, possibly well ahead of its time but the show was put together so quickly, it could have been so much better. There was not much research, and there wasn't always enough time to get the best guests.

They came from all walks of life. The Italian bricklayer was to show me how to easily put down a stone walkway. His English was almost non-existent but he had charm, a sweet disposition and great skills that made the whole show informative, with me trying to translate from his broken English/Italian into something more comprehensible. I had never spent that much time bent over,

87

other than reaching for food from the bottom of my fridge. *My back may still hurt.*

I had one guest, a shop teacher plucked from a local high school, who was to show me how to install dry wall. He was not just shy but terrified whenever he saw the red light on the camera blink, meaning we had started. First he twitched nervously and began clearing his throat... nothing came out. Not one word. He truly was a deer in the headlights. I tried chatting as if we were sitting across a table from each other in a coffee shop. "How is your day going?" I got nothing. I tried talking about the subject he was here to teach me that he supposedly was an expert in and I was not. I was making stuff up. "I gather drywall can be made of gypsum?" No response. Without commercials I had twenty-four minutes to fill and I knew nothing about dry walling and the shop teacher was still frozen. I punted. I took out a measuring tape and walked over to the area that had been designated our drywall installation zone. I measured. I recited the dimensions for no reason other than to fill time. I pointed out how much more serviceable and attractive an ugly old unfinished basement would look with new walls. It would enhance not just one's daily life but also the resale price. I smiled hopefully at my supposed mentor. He was still catatonic. I felt a slight flush of panic wash over me. What do I do now? I grabbed the sheet of dry wall that he was supposed to show me how to affix to the struts. I babbled about how light it was. How smooth. *Oh God, help me out here.* I picked up a nail gun, not having a clue what to do next and more than a little afraid of its power to become a potential weapon. I was hoping I would have the strength not to shoot him in the leg just to wake him up. Something snapped in the shop teacher when he saw me wielding that nail gun. He grabbed it out of my hand, almost shouting, "That's not how you use that!" Whew... We were off to the races. He was finally all about the business at hand.

Oops! I Forgot to Save Money

The show was shot in blocks, which meant we taped five episodes a day for thirteen days making for a total of sixty-five shows. By the time we were done, my fingers felt like stumps and my brain was malfunctioning like a street lamp with a short.

At the time, I believed I was being paid fairly well, especially when multiplied by sixty-five. In next to no time, I had made close to twenty five thousand dollars. It was a fortune to me. What I didn't know was that I had signed a contract that paid me in full with no provision for royalties, also known as a 'buy out'. "Any Woman Can" played in several English-speaking countries for many years after but I never received another penny. I had no recourse, as I naively hadn't known any better at the time.

The show was barely in the can when we made plans to go to the Bahamas for a week of R & R to celebrate and to recover from the craziness of that unrelenting schedule. *It didn't occur to us to invest some of that money.* We hadn't even had a chance to pack, when the call came that my father had died. I was broken-hearted - strangely less about his death than about having never really known him in life. And now I never would. His English stiff upper lip had always made him keep his feelings under lock and key. He had been that slightly befuddled man who came to visit me every other weekend when I was growing up. He never talked about his family or life, just about all the books he had read and the ones he deemed good for me at appropriate times. He pointed out the names of every plant and tree species on our many walks. I knew my father had precious few loves; there was me, then reading, nature, and the masses of obscure trivia he liked to throw out when the silences got too quiet. "Did you know zebras' black and white stripes may be an evolutionary feature to fend off bugs?" "You probably think that a blink is just something you do to keep your eyes moist or keep dust out of them. They are as useful as a micro-nap which are thought to help our attention span." I blinked back a tear from my eyes and thought about all the dinners we never shared. Whenever he was invited back into our lives, he still behaved like a boarder who took all his meals in the privacy of his room. There were no family gatherings that I ever remember him participating in. He was somehow always hovering around the sidelines, never quite sure if he was welcome or not. But yet, he could be bitingly funny when he muttered his observations regarding people's behavior, describing them like an anthropologist observing a zoo. I wished for a do-over… One dinner, one meal … I would play the interviewer with a hundred questions about his life, his dreams. Did he have dreams? I'd ask him about what he wished he had done… Then I would find a way to make whatever it was happen.

Many years later through an ancestry search, I found out that my father, whom I thought might have had one sister, turned out to be one of nine! There were so many people who had claimed him once but now they were all scattered in the wind like seeds. Hopefully they had a chance to flower and do this family thing better than he had done.

    My father's death led to a difficult period with my mother. She carried weighted sacks filled with equal measures of guilt and denial. The loss of my father was mine to carry, not hers. She couldn't go there. She was still grieving for her lost business. Every interaction between us was loaded with defensiveness or an explosion ready to detonate. Gilles was the bridge that somehow kept us from snapping each other's heads off. He was now family but because he wasn't born of our blood he wasn't activated at the cellular level. He maintained his calm demeanor through simple acts of caring for both of us, by making sure there was always a ready meal or a pot of coffee to get us through most of it. *Oh God, I hope Gilles and I aren't related! Given the diaspora that characterized my Dad's family, there were actual possibilities. I shook that nightmare off...*

My mother decided she needed a fresh start. We convinced her to put her house up for sale. It was a way to pay off her creditors and to be able to sleep at night. I helped find her a very nice and affordable apartment in the neighborhood she was most comfortable. Our healing transpired as we picked our way through the house, deciding what should go with her and what should be tossed or donated. Every object seemed to elicit a story that brought us to tears or to fits of laughter. The expensive pinkish blonde bouffant wig my brother, sister and I had bought for her one Mother's Day, just to help make her busy life simpler, had turned her into an Austro/Hungarian banshee hopping from one foot to the other, accusing us of always having hated her hair. The fact that we had never mentioned her own always-sprayed helmet of hair was how she knew. She had thrown the offending wig into the dark recesses of a closet, never to be seen again until this moment. We convulsed in laughter and syncopated hiccups, making it even funnier in the remembering. Spending so much time together, getting to know each other in a non parent/daughter way, but more as friends who could also drive each other crazy as only family can, was worth every hour.

In a soon to be time honored ritual whenever I had some money or windfall, I spent it on friends, family or on whatever whimsy struck my fancy. I wanted to give my mother a break from the jolt of losing so much. I happily splurged on a trip with some of the money I had earned, so she could join some of her bridge-playing friends in Daytona Beach. *There was more than a little ego involved in playing fairy godmother.* We soon realized we had not taken our Bahamian vacation because of my father's death. We had an unused airfare credit. On a whim, we decided to surprise her in Daytona before heading to Nassau.

My mother and her bridge partners were in mid argument, each one more adamant than the other that they were right about some obscure bidding convention. Their conviction was so loud they didn't notice us standing in the doorway of the hotel games room. One of the ladies slammed down her cards on the table so hard that a bowl of nuts flew into the air, scattering its contents everywhere. That's when the shouting became really loud. I couldn't help but laugh. I had seen some form of this behavior enacted my whole life; shouting, chairs scraping, handbags clutched to chests as they headed for the exits, not speaking until they gathered for the next game as if nothing had ever happened. Gilles moved in and began picking up Brazil nuts and pistachios from the floor. That's when my mother noticed we were there. She beamed with joy, more at Gilles than me. Her lipstick suddenly appeared as she less than subtly rouged her mouth. I shook my head in wonder.

We spent two days with her doing everything Daytona had to offer. Then we left her back at the card table where we had found her. All the ladies were fussing over Gilles while my mother beamed. He was so completely charming and kind that I was totally forgotten. I didn't mind. I was leaving with him. They weren't.

We finally caught a flight to Nassau for our long awaited holiday. As a blond fair-haired girl, I should have known better than to lay out next to the pool soaking up hours of sun, but no one wore sunscreen back then. The smell of baby oil permeated the air. Row upon row of sun worshippers baked on chaise lounges. Many, including me, held a foil covered cardboard under our faces, just to make sure we fried. To any other species

Oops! I Forgot to Save Money

we must have looked like the roasting rotisserie chickens in the supermarket that twirled around and around under the glare of weird infrared rays. It didn't take long. My skin became crispy and flame red. Gilles was a golden brown. *Of course!* I was miserable and in pain. We tried yogurt, cold cream, wet towels. Nothing worked. A little butter and some parsley would have been better. I could have fed a hungry mob. Instead, I spent my long awaited vacation slathered in some local remedy that looked like chicken fat but smelled like medicated sludge. I was isolated - unable to touch or be touched by my hunky boyfriend. Even the room service staff just knocked, placed the tray outside our room and then bolted. "I have a sunburn, not typhoid!" Not only did I pay dearly for attempting to tan my pale pink sun-resistant skin, but the hotel was also an irrational overpriced folly. It wasn't Gilles who chose it. I did. I hid the price from him and pretty much from myself, until that bill stared me straight in the face. Gilles had also seen it. He was upset. I knew immediately it was because he didn't have the money to pay for it. I didn't care. It didn't matter to me. But I had to work hard to make it okay for him. *I had already pretended to make it okay for me.*

Back at home, the ennui set in. My father was gone. My career was once again AWOL. I was at loose ends, which was never a good place for me to be. I grazed on anything and everything as I tried to figure out where I could land to get some financial security. My brain hurt from over-thinking. Ideas sprung forth but most of them didn't survive a day. Some were impossibly complex, like the time I corralled two of my friends into helping me bring to life The Company Picnic Company – a catering business that serviced all the offices in the midtown area where most of us hung-out. We would dress 'adorably' in heels and mini-dresses. *I clearly forgot I had legs better suited to maxi dresses.* We'd wear little gingham aprons and deliver sandwiches and drinks from coolers to the masses of office

93

workers. There were so many things wrong with this idea. *Let's start with the heels, then the aprons*... Not that delivering food was a bad idea; it was a great one, just not one that could be carried out by my two blonde model pals and me. We knew nothing about sourcing food at the wholesale level. Our attempt at making a hundred sandwiches from a non-commercial kitchen was a disaster. We didn't particularly like all that shopping, cutting, dicing and slicing then wrapping. We made cute labels and got coolers but we were three blondes and... Well, the jokes write themselves. We had done no research as to whether anyone stayed in to eat, how many offices we were 'catering' to, or if we had competition. We did.

Then there were the just plain pointless ideas...an electric ashtray? Or even worse, good ideas but not thought out enough to become viable. I was saved from spinning my wheels by a totally unexpected offer to participate in a televised evening of standup comedy, something I had never done and was terrified to do. I couldn't afford to say no.

Note to Self: Get this into my head once and for all – Take money seriously. Don't spend money you don't have! Always do what's necessary to insure that bills can be paid, that there's a roof over your head and food on the table, before buying anything frivolous. Put away what you can even if it's a small amount. There are rewards in behaving responsibly. It's called solvency. And learn to understand contracts, leases or any deals presented on paper.

Recommended Medication: Over-the-top nachos – a yummy protective coating well suited to unexpected life smack-downs.

CHAPTER 7

EVERYONE IS SMARTER, THINNER, BETTER AND RICHER

The Cost: Temporary insanity, separation anxiety, and the end of life as I knew it.

The only night I took to the stage to do standup comedy remains a blur. But the terrifying fear is still a far too vivid memory. From the minute I walked into Yuk-Yuks, the comedy club, I was greeted by many of the other comics with hostility. I was not one of them. I was on television. I was an interloper. This was the same club that gave birth to Howie Mandel. As I mounted the steps to the stage, I felt much like Mary Queen of Scots must have felt on the way to her execution. Flop sweat and fear filled every pore of my being. The bright lights blinded me. Words did pour from my mouth. I do remember speaking in various accents as I described the enactment of sex around the world. For the Latin countries, I samba'd, lisped and breathed lustily. For the northern-most countries, I shivered and shrunk back whenever touched. I can't quite remember what I did for Germany, but it wasn't pretty. It was easy to mimic what I thought my very British father must have been like during his one and only tryst with my mother. "Dust blew all around his tweedy barely unzipped self. His eyes were tightly shut, his face grimacing as he climaxed with barely a whimper." I followed with my impression of my Austrian accented mother, her dirndl askew, her eyes even more tightly shut, praying that this mildew-y moment would be soon over and done with. And when it was, I made the face of someone who had just eaten something moldy.

What I do remember in vivid surround sound is the massive applause when I was done! Stunned, I walked off that stage not sure what had just occurred but I didn't have much time to think about any of it. My thoughts were interrupted by two men, approaching me with an offer of a job in Los Angeles. What? This must be a joke! It wasn't. They were bona fide producers and they wanted me to be part of a writing team for a Helen Reddy television special.

I sat on the plane heading to the land of movie stars and all things glossy and I felt a wave of excitement about stepping into this unknown. I took in a breath at having been chosen to go on this adventure. That moment of exhilaration was followed by a bigger wave of panic, building to thoughts of leaping out of my seat and pushing that jet door open and jumping into the relief of nothingness. A wall of doubt overcame me. I really couldn't understand why I had been chosen. I had never written for television before. *The stuff that comes out of your mouth when you are ad-libbing is the beginning of actual writing.* I was a dress designer; I was an actress by happenstance. I had made people laugh when I did exercises on TV. I did write a standup comedy routine one time and here I was... *Yes, it's called freaking out.* The man next to me kept looking at me and I could feel he wanted to ring some emergency buzzer or throw me out of the plane himself. And the worst part of all, I was consumed by the fact that I didn't know how to type. Pecking at a computer was not typing. How would I survive in a writer's room full of the real deal? I wasn't even sure I wanted to go to LA. It was too big, too risky.

A shaggy haired, overly tanned boy/man in shorts and work boots stood at the base of the escalator at LAX holding up a sign with my name on it. He was my driver. *I had a driver...* His name was Keith and he welcomed me to Los Angeles. He handed me a large manila envelope filled with money – my per diem. There was a lot of it. Wheehoo! I couldn't wait to throw it away. Keith held the door of my limo open. *I had a limo...* We drove out of the airport directly into a smog-filled sunset. The palm trees had an orange tinge, as did the strange, metal, pecking dinosaurs dotted through the dry and dusty hillside. Keith explained they were oilrigs that spewed money day after day, year after year. He pulled up in front of a tall building behind what appeared to be every tropical plant in existence. I thanked him for being such a great tour guide. He said you're welcome in what I learned was the traditional California manner. "Uh huh…" And then he sped off.

My suite was done in every shade of grey known to mankind. It was elegant in the anonymous way that all rentals are for their temporary inhabitants. I was starving. The fridge was empty but then I saw a bowl of ruby red apples. I took one and bit into it, only to discover it was a fake. *I was about to see a great deal of that soon enough.* Besides the unexpected money, the envelope contained directions to my office. *My office.* Directions I would never need, as it also said I would be picked up and driven home by my new buddy, Keith, my personal driver for the duration.

Keith picked me up promptly at nine in the morning. I barely had a chance to absorb the thrill of seeing Universal Studios, Disney and Warner Brothers as the car entered the freeway at a death-defying pace in order to compete with all the other speed demons. Literally seven minutes later we arrived at an anonymous brick building. Keith wished me good luck as he held my door open. I was as nervous as a fourteen-year-old heading into her first day of high school, still panicking that I couldn't type as I walked through the glass doors into the writer's room. Within a few minutes my fears evaporated. I had landed in the middle of junior high with all the kids that spent most of their time in detention. It was smart-ass central. As for worrying about typing, there were two eye-rolling secretaries who could give as good as they got, and did all that transcribing and typing. My job, it turned out, was to spitball ideas with the team and duck the tossed donuts that these writer-delinquents threw at each other when they weren't engaged in a full on Nerf gun war. I was deeply embedded in a fruitcake factory filled with nerdy, wild haired reprobates from far-flung, Midwest outposts.

Once again I found myself falling in love with this make-shift family of writers who took me in and made it their mission to watch me head to the ladies room for fear of wetting myself with uncontrollable laughter. The practical jokes that came my way were a test to see if this new girl was worthy. Yet writing comedy was serious work that required discipline and long hours and a lot of recreational spirits, among other things, to keep on going. It was the early eighties and cocaine was on the daily meal plan. It seemed to be everywhere. Massive sums were spent on getting a fix. Lots of showbiz people blew their savings on the stuff, but so did everyone else, even dentists and realtors. They lost their homes to it and often their health from the excess that became a full-blown addiction. I gratefully have no tolerance for any-mind-altering substance. An Advil makes me see visions. My drug of choice is and has always been sinfully dark chocolate with a heaping side of potato-anything.

I felt the way I imagine Alice felt when she fell down the rabbit hole. Consumption was rampant and wealth was suddenly aspirational. This was the Dallas and Dynasty TV era. When Joan Collins swaggered onto the screen in full fur and fury - that was *acting* rich. *All that 80's flash and trash set the stage for today's must-have designer bags and sky-high-heels. The arrival of 'reality' television in this millennium brought a new cast of breast-enhanced, trouty-pouty unreal women onto the scene and materialism became 'a thing.' The fully blown envy-icons of this epoch are the KKK – Kim, Kourtney, and Khloe. I hold that 3-D-lipped trio responsible for making the old nouveau riche look positively homeless by comparison. I hold all of the 'reality TV' clones responsible for the millions of glossy pretenders who live above their means just to appear faux rich. It has officially spawned a rampant plague of must have-itis. The fetishizing of clothing and objects that represent the cool factor is not new. It's always been a way to separate the rich from those who are not. Who else can spend hundreds of dollars on designer ripped jeans that look like packs of wolves dismembered them?* But today, there are some creative ways of getting what you want.

Through family friends I have come to know a lovely young woman who holds a responsible position, managing money for more than a few of her investment company's high-value clients. Vanessa is twenty-seven and along with her posse of like-minded girlfriends is an avid television watcher of shows like The Bachelor and The Real Housewives of Everywhere. She comes from a family fully loaded with equally lovely but on-trend sisters as well as a pair of happy-to-indulge parents. Vanessa is kind and smart but belongs to the tribe that needs the very latest of everything. That being said, she is newly married to a very handsome, but much more fiscally conscientious analyst. His salary is a pretty good one but not in the bracket that can afford a life of 'lifestyle'. I asked Vanessa if she would be able to cut back on her desires to own the latest 'must have' accessories. She looked at me directly and completely candidly said, "No. I think I should be able to have the things I want." She added that she had no desire to make her husband feel bad that they haven't got that kind of money, but then she smiled conspiratorially and said her birthday was coming up in a few weeks, so she had sent out a crowd-funding notice to her girlfriends, so she could get the seventeen hundred dollars she would need to buy the red-soled Christian Louboutin boots she desperately wanted.

∽

Everything in LA seemed to be on steroids. The scale was outsized from the boobs to the boulevards. It was as if the whole city was on a spending bender. The money that was tossed around on cars, houses, big-boy toys and high-end tequila, along with just-flown-in-from-Japan Kobe steaks was obscene. I was stunned by the shift from the simple life that we flower children had created, fought for and so wanted. We were now the ones we had despised. We had become them. The price of even the simplest pair of sneakers was over the top. Of course the words simple and Los Angeles never appeared anywhere near one another. But most striking was the hustle that never stopped. Everyone was always angling for their next gig, the next opportunity, the next way they could stand out from the pack and get noticed.

My bosses asked me to stay on and become part of the team that went on to create and write Friday's, the TV series. One of the newbie writers was none other than Larry David, who went on to create and star in Curb Your Enthusiasm. Here I was being offered a slice of that most coveted pie. People killed to get an offer like this. Why was I hesitating? The truth is I liked being a big enough fish in the gentle stream I was already navigating. I was afraid of the sharp teeth and turbulent water that came with such an ambitious territory as LA.

I flew back home with an even greater panic attack. Was I insane? I had just turned down an offer to work in Hollywood. I was so happy to be met at the airport by my amazing partner. Gilles reassured me in his mystical way that it was not my time to be there and when it was, the opportunity would appear. I nodded, like one of those dogs that sat on the dashboard of a car, perpetually bouncing their heads up and down. We slipped back into the rhythm that was our life. Gilles was appearing in a very successful French Canadian play and loving the intense commitment. With my LA success, I had no trouble finding work in Toronto but the money was a far cry from what was possible in LA. I reminded myself endlessly that I chose this. It felt simpler and less challenging. That's what was bothering me. *The truth was, the cutthroat competitiveness terrified me.*

Note to Self: The words in our heads are the script we live by. But we can't let fear dictate our choices. Believing you are not good enough to be paid well or not worthy comes from the same source that says you are too fat, not tall enough or not pretty enough. It's in your head, not in anyone else's. The same can be said for thinking you are better than others. Life is hard. Get a helmet. But in order to make clear and informed choices it often means asking for help and advice. Do it.

Recommended Medication: A double chocolate mocha trifle is something less than light to suit any and all fearful episodes that life throws at you.

CHAPTER 8

WHOEVER HAS THE MOST STUFF GETS TO WORRY ABOUT HOW TO KEEP IT

The Cost: Spending money to soothe anxiety is the same as an alcoholic walking into a bar to feel better. It doesn't.

I was consumed with finding a way to convince Gilles that marrying me would make our lives even better. He assured me, very gently, that our lives were practically perfect just as they were. I instantly hit on the word, 'practically'. Gilles quickly recalibrated and said, he meant our lives were perfect just as they were. He then trotted out that favorite male excuse that marriage is just a piece of paper and it wasn't one that our union needed. *Said him – never me!* I needed that paper! I needed to belong in the most official and conventional way. *As a card-carrying bohemian, I do blanche at the memory of being so needy. I got over it. I decided I could be both bohemian and conventional. Oh, how we redraw the lines when necessary.* I pulled out every reason I could think of. Our taxes would be cheaper. We would use far less laundry detergent. He would have the right to unplug me if I ever became terminal. I added I would unplug him if he didn't marry me. I could see the flush spread across his face, suddenly wary of the crazy girlfriend sitting so close with such a determined look in her eyes. After a far too long period of silence, he asked me why I wanted this so much. I flippantly responded it would be one thing off my bucket list. He pulled the car over and asked me again why it mattered so much to me, again explaining he was one hundred percent committed to our relationship. I took a breath as if I was thinking. I knew the answer. "My finger needs a ring on it, because even though I know you are all in, I need the whole world to know that this is real! And I need my mother to believe that you love me enough to make it real!" Gilles smiled, nodded and said okay, "If it's to make your mother happy, I will do it". I knew he was teasing, but I also knew we were going to be married. I exhaled as if I had been holding my breath for most of my life. That's how much I needed to be wanted. *It's impossible now to imagine that I was ever that insecure.*

My mother was beyond happy with our news. She was wing-flapping, bonkers at the thought of me tying the knot. I wouldn't be languishing on her doorstep, alone and unattached. *Maybe that thought was mine.* My marrying Saint Gilles would enhance her status with her bridge-playing pals. They all adored my boyfriend, now fiancé. I believe if she hadn't been so financially strapped, she would have arranged a parade with fireworks and floats, with her and Gilles at the forefront and me hovering somewhere nearby.

My mother took charge, pinging between ringmaster and a Mama-Bridezilla. Both Gilles and I felt like spectators instead of participants. It was similar to watching a runaway train that desperately needed to have the switch pulled. If anxiety was contagious we shared it in equal doses as we were grilled on our cake preferences - there were dozens to taste. The sugar frenzy was eye-popping. A full Versailles garden's worth of flower choices. Place cards, rented wine goblets… A graphologist's nightmare of signature styles to pick from for our keepsake matchbooks.

Oops! I Forgot to Save Money

Singlehandedly my mother snuffed out all romantic notions of what I believed a wedding should be. I put it down to her need for excess after all her wartime stress and rationing. The end came when she brought out the beaded French lace swatches along with a long held secret book filled with pasted in possible venues, several dozen wedding dress pictures and their matchy-matchy parade of hand-maid's dresses. The wedding gown clippings rivaled anything any of the Real Housewives of Dubai would have worn. I had a momentary flash of an ample sized me blocking the aisle in my overly bejeweled Macy's Thanksgiving Day balloon-sized dress as I pushed my way to stand before my hysterically laughing future husband.

On a return trip from visiting Gilles' family, he came up with the idea of telling her we had pulled off a quickie wedding at the registrar's office in his hometown while assuring me that we would tie the knot but in a simple ceremony that belonged to us, not to the world. I was totally on board.

At first, my mother wasn't sure if she believed us but it turned out that Gilles was a really good actor and very convincing. She congratulated us even though she was bereft at not having had the opportunity to send in the wedding clowns and more. We thought we were safe. The next day, the announcement of our 'marriage' appeared in both daily papers, followed by invitations sent out to everyone she could think of to come celebrate our marriage at the wedding-palooza she was throwing the following weekend. My mother was not one to be denied. Once again, I stared into the mirror of money being spent that she didn't really have, in conflict with her desire to give! It was always in conflict with her desire to be the Queen of Largess.

With our secret safe and the over-the-top party now behind us, (complete with my mother's Kabuki make up and

105

shimmery party dress) we went back to reality. Out of the blue, we received a chain letter invitation in the mail. We recognized several of the names, so we figured it was sanctioned by people we knew, if only slightly. It had a set of instructions that asked us to send two checks, each for thirty-seven dollars and fifty cents to the first two people on the list that were under our names. Once done, we were to put those names at the bottom of the list. There was also a request not to break the chain or we would ruin the outcome for others. The letter promised that soon we'd be receiving endless checks for that same amount as this letter spread far and wide to friends and friends of friends. I thought it sounded like fun and we immediately did as the letter asked. Soon, I began to receive money in the mail and it would come almost every day, thirty-seven-dollars and fifty-cent checks. Gilles never received a single check. This meant that someone on his string of names broke the chain. I felt terrible for him as I was counting up my bonanza. I felt so badly, that I sent him a check in that amount as if to somehow kick-start his windfall. It didn't.

The money letter became so popular that people on our list decided to throw a dinner party so we could all meet each other. It was a raucous and celebratory evening. We met many wonderful people, most of whom were from the arts, from National Ballet dancers to painters, writers, and actors. The gathering of creative people made sense given that these types of chain letters get passed from one recommended friend to another and another, and this was our tribe. One of the people I met that night, a theater director, had been an early buy in. With his loot, he had made enough to buy a small plane. Apparently those at the top of the chain stood to make the most money and those near the bottom often lost their investment as the group exhausted its circle of names to send to. My take was modest but enough to buy us a great dinner out and a pair of semi-pricey shoes for me. That was it. Gilles got nothing

Oops! I Forgot to Save Money

except the check I had sent him. The unexpected bonus from that dinner was that I met my soon-to-be writing partner between the hors d'oeuvres and dessert. *It was years later that I found out that money-soliciting chain letters of this nature were one hundred percent illegal.*

I was thrilled to have a writing partner and soon he and I were spending every weekday together hatching screenplays and television series. Evan was a psychologist-turned-writer so therapy, often unasked-for, came with the package. My antennae were sending signals to my brain that I was jumping into this relationship too quickly but I dismissed my inner consiglieri because I wanted a partner to share in the burden of writing. We were enjoying the process between arguments. It didn't take long for us to find some early success when we sold a TV episode to a production company with a hit show. Around the same time, the Los Angeles producers I had worked with came calling, wanting me to come back and write another show for them.

Gilles and I were deep into a weeks-long discussion of whether moving to LA was a good idea or not. I felt that life in Toronto offered plenty of opportunities and I liked being a big fish in a smaller pond. I was about to expand on that metaphor when Gilles interrupted. He offered up that he thought I was pulling back from the opportunity because I was scared. I immediately became defensive, bordering on shrill. *I do believe he struck a nerve.* I continued laying out my case. I didn't want to rock the boat. I knew that my Mom would be bereft if we moved away, not that she'd stop us. It was just a feeling that it was important to be there for her. She had gone through such a tough time and needed me.

It turned out it wasn't anything I would have to worry about. One week later my mother suffered a brain aneurism while playing bridge. *The irony did not go unnoticed.* We got the call, rather

107

than my half-sister or brother, as we lived closest to the bridge game where she was stricken. Having the painful and surreal gift of being able to comfort my mother as she slipped in and out of consciousness was like no feeling I could have ever imagined. This complicated, fierce warrior of a woman who had survived so much was dying. I held her hand and stroked her back all the while praying for a reprieve. There was still so much I wanted to share with her. For a brief moment, I felt the hairs on my arm stand up as she came to. Her eyes twitched through the extreme pain in her head – I felt her will them open. Pure love radiated towards me. She squeezed my hand, then her eyes closed and she was no more. But she would always be…

A couple of months passed. The space that my mother had so overwhelmingly occupied would never be filled. She was one of a kind. With Gilles' constant love and support, I began to heal. I knew, because my sense of humor returned. I kidded that my bridge-playing mother must have had a bad hand. She must have been a sore loser. That's why she checked out. I could see the horrified faces on some of my family and mother's friends. Making jokes allowed me to keep her front and center without showing all the emotional pain that was no one else's business.

My mother's estate… *It was laughable to even call it that.* Much like my Dad's, it was a sad indictment on their lack of financial wherewithal. My mother's precious bridge trophies and some silverware were divided amongst my half-brother and sister and me. I took her Chanel Number 5 as it was her scent and I needed to have it. One whiff and she was right beside me. With both my parents gone, Gilles and I decided that the opportunity that had come knocking may never come our way again. It was time to head west - to prospect just like the thousands of gold digging prospectors had done before us. Our gold was buried deep in the hands and minds of Hollywood's power brokers. We held a mammoth garage sale that doubled as a farewell party.

With a little trepidation and very few belongings, we headed west to our new life. A close friend who had recently moved to Los Angeles from Canada invited us to come and stay until we found a place of our own. Lynn was not only beautiful but also warm and generous, unlike her soon-to-be fiancé who was possessive, territorial and selfish and those are the kindest things I can say about him. *The smart thing would be not to name him but I feel a burst of pleasure at busting him.* Charles, as he sonorously corrected anyone who called him Charlie, was the single most pompous person I had ever met. Both Gilles and I felt a twinge of angst at the idea of staying too long at this isolated mountain top house which, he was quick to point out, belonged to him and not Lynn.

Lynn, Gilles and I spent many an evening in the outdoor Jacuzzi overlooking the glittering lights of Hollywood, sharing stories and laughter. But we should have trusted that twinge. Charles became increasingly resentful of our bond. His habitual jealously devolved into unwarranted, mean spirited attacks on Lynn and hostile mutterings directed at us. Visions of a crossbow aimed in our direction did cross my mind more than once. My lovely friend Lynn's horrible partner, in a fit of his own making, pointed his finger in my face, declaring, "Do you know what your problem is?" I felt my body tighten and held my breath knowing the answer was forthcoming. "All you ever want to have is a good time!" I momentarily stifled a laugh as relief washed over me on hearing what my problem was. I knew I would be poking the bear but it was worth it. "Thank you for pointing this out. You are right. I'm guilty. You are safe. This is a crime no one will ever accuse you of!" I headed inside before he could blow up! He wasn't wrong. Having a good time was mandatory to my soul. It required no effort. I do have a talent for living with gusto. I believe with all my heart that it's one of the ways I can show gratitude for having been given life. That being said, it was becoming all too clear that we had overstayed our welcome and it wasn't even a week. Out of thin air, we were saved. A friend who knew our predicament called to say she was moving in with her boyfriend and thought we should take over the lease on her house. We didn't care what part of town it was in or even if it had running water. We just wanted to run.

We moved from the top of Nichols Canyon, which was similar to driving up the Matterhorn every day, to living in a sweet, blue shuttered cottage on Beverly Glen, a canyon road which was home to hippies, reluctant celebrities, deer and their sworn enemies, coyotes. We couldn't have been happier.

Gilles got another job in Toronto, a prestigious Michel Tremblay play, which meant he would be away for a couple of months. *Plays don't pay. But they do add cachet to a resume, especially in LA. It means you are a real actor, not just another pretty face.* I knew I would miss him terribly but I happily took on the outfitting of our new home. In order to make our cross border move simple, we had brought very little with us: our clothes, some of our artwork, my jewelry and a pair of beautiful inherited carpets. We also brought our vacuum cleaner and of course, our very hairy, endlessly shedding Chowchow, Seya. We knew it would be easier to buy whatever appliances and electronics we needed. We couldn't wait to hit up the garage sales and flea markets to find our furniture. We had more money in the bank than we had ever had - Thirty seven thousand dollars. Not that much today but back then, we could have used it as a sizable down payment on a modest but nice starter house. The money was mostly a combination of what I had earned on my

Oops! I Forgot to Save Money

TV series back in Toronto and from my first LA writing gig. *Having never had any sizeable amount of money before, I was like a Mother Hen, checking on its survival at every opportunity.* Our biggest expense was our need to purchase a car. It's almost impossible to live in LA without one. A friend of ours knew someone who was about to trade in his five year old Audi for something far more impressive. *I soon discovered that in LA, you are what you drive. First impressions make for lasting ones in this company town that reveres the trappings of success.* We were excited to buy that Audi for far less than if we had gone to a dealer, so excited that we neglected to take it to a mechanic to make sure it was in running order. And I totally forgot to factor in car insurance and the registration costs. Along with the car, we needed all the essentials, from a bed, to bed sheets. On one of my forays to pick up some basic kitchen necessities, I fell in love with a beautiful, huge painting in the gallery next door. It cost more than our already pricey rent so I walked away. It called me back. Throwing caution and common sense to the wind, it was soon hanging in our living room. I could feel an unasked for defense springing into action. The painting was an expenditure that would make our house look and feel like a welcoming and successful home. I rationalized that having beautiful things was as important to my wellbeing as food and water. *That may have been true. Those follies took me years to recognize as far from sensible.* My nest egg was disappearing at an alarming rate. I just shook my blonde hair, choosing to bet on my unknown future earnings. Evan and I continued to work on our screenplay. Our long distance phone bills were astronomical but I justified it as an investment.

Our charming little cottage was unfortunately situated on a freeway of sorts. Beverly Glen was a beautiful pass that crossed

111

a mountain from one side of town to the other. It was also a shortcut that was well known to those who worked in the many film studios in the valley. Speeding cars seemed to be the only way the road in the canyon was travelled. But, the sun was shining as it did every day and it was January. I took a moment to bow down in gratitude. I put our dog Seya on her leash and headed out to walk her, taking great pleasure in greeting the gardeners in my newly learned but broken Spanish. Seya snarled and bared her teeth, perhaps intuitively. There were no sidewalks on Beverly Glen so any walking was treacherous. *People don't walk in LA! They hike.* Neither Seya nor I enjoyed our stroll pressed up so close to fences and flowering hedges in order to not get sideswiped by the speeding parade of Mercedes and BMW's.

Exhausted from our perilous outing, we returned through our gate. Strangely the gardeners were already gone but had left their tools behind. I guessed they had gone for a lunch break. Wrong. They had stolen my mother's silver cutlery, most of her Sterling silver bridge trophies, my jewelry and every new piece of electronic equipment we had just bought. The appliances meant nothing. But those bridge trophies were my mother's legacy. They meant so much to me because they held the essence of her.

Two gun-wearing policemen came, but reluctantly. Burglaries were so commonplace in Los Angeles that they were practically non-events. I told them the gardeners were absolutely the thieves. They had left in a hurry, with the grass only half cut, and they had left their tools. I suggested they sweep for fingerprints. They both laughed instantly and derisively. The gruffer one stopped laughing. "You have seen too many cop shows! Even if we did check for fingerprints, it would be a waste of time. These guys are most likely undocumented, and will be long gone with your valuables. If they can be melted or sold, it will be done fast

Oops! I Forgot to Save Money

leaving no trace. You're a grain of sand in a damn beach-full." I felt overwhelmed. All reason left me. I snapped at the cavalier cops that they had no idea how much money we had spent on all those appliances and we weren't insured. We had just moved in. I had no idea how I was going to afford to replace everything! I stopped shouting, overcome with emotion. It was the loss of my mother that had suddenly landed. The gruff cop tempered his voice, becoming disarmingly calm, surmising that he might be dealing with a very unstable woman. "I hate to tell you, this won't be the last time you are robbed. Be happy that's all it was". They were out the door. My imagination went into hyper-drive. What could that mean? *Whatever it meant, the robbery was simply a preview of the havoc to come.*

    I knew very few people in LA and they all lived far away in other canyon enclaves so I spent a lot of time alone. The howls from prowling coyotes were guaranteed to keep me from having restful nights. I was also so unfamiliar with the enormousness of this sprawling city. With Gilles still away, I drove to work at the big shot producer's giant mansion, which was oddly not far from our funky little cottage. Even though it would have been impossible to get lost given that it was a straight shot up the hill from our little cottage, it was nonetheless a white-knuckle drive as everyone in LA was very important and always in a hurry. They impatiently honked, then when a bare sliver of opportunity appeared, whipped by me in German sport-cars better suited to racing at Le Mans. It was a short drive but a whole world away. Everything they owned seemed to be on display. It was designed for maximum show and tell impact. I admit I didn't understand the appeal of an outsized blown-glass bowl containing a dozen gilded ostrich eggs. The possession of shiny objects is a symbol of belonging, and some people go to extreme lengths to be in the club.

Monica Parker

∽

In her youth Jennifer was a charismatic and charming go-getter with looks and a determination to prove herself. She needed to escape the small town of her childhood where everyone seemed perfectly happy with the status quo. No one there dreamt big. So, Jennifer moved to San Francisco and set her sights on real estate. She learned the ropes and soon, through the force of her personality and ballsiness, she landed in a corporate real estate firm. This was the perfect place to meet wealthy men.

Her first husband was twenty years older than she was and loved the attention she showered on him. In less than a year, they were married and after three years they were divorced but by California law, Jennifer was entitled to half of everything they had acquired during their marriage. She had collected a lot of very expensive art and furnishings and was entitled as well to half the money from the sale of their very high-end condo. Jennifer was set.

Cavalier and opportunistic, she did well in business and with lovers but she always found some reason to trade up to the next level. Her biggest shortcoming was that she was inherently lazy. She lacked follow through in her work and even more so in her personal life. If someone didn't take care of her needs, she moved on leaving her messes for others to clean up. The downside being that whenever Jennifer did move on, she shoved all that she had obtained into storage, and she moved on a lot.

Jennifer is now in her mid-sixties, alone and almost broke. Having left every relationship in tatters along with many, many thousands of dollars of 'valuable' item's she just had to have - from antique Biedermeier tables to expensive art and designer labels - for others to dispose of, or gathering mold in basements

Oops! I Forgot to Save Money

and storage units, simply because the inconvenience of taking care of her own business was left to minions to look after. It's hard to feel sorry for someone who felt so entitled. She can't understand what happened to her life. We can.

∽

Back on Beverly Glen, my only other outing, besides work, was to the grocery store and back. This required navigating yet another winding canyon road with people speeding in both directions. The prize, once I got there, was the gaggle of movie stars that shopped at that particular Gelsons (given that it was near to many of the gated, movie star encampments). I practically stalked Warren Beatty to see what he put in his cart. I can definitively say no one ever looked at the prices. I, however, was in constant sticker shock. But I kept going back. That rarified air filled me with possibility, and a false sense of calm.

On yet another perpetual hot and sunny afternoon, I was sitting outside brushing Seya when I noticed a young woman coming out of the cottage next door. I was excited to see a human being. I walked over to the fence to introduce myself. Lena was very friendly and was also an actress. I discovered soon enough, that everyone in LA was somehow part of the show business world. *It was a company town. If it had been Detroit, all one's neighbors would have been connected to the auto industry.* Lena was giving me a bit more understanding of the lay of the land when I heard the screeching of tires…The vision of a giant water delivery truck came suddenly into view as it crashed through my fence, right through a grove of bamboo trees, coming to a stop inches from where I was standing. The shock I felt was like nothing I had ever experienced. Instinctually I prayed Seya was not under that truck. She was wide-eyed but safe laying in the

115

shade of our picnic table. A dazed looking mess of a man climbed out of his truck. He had taken the curve too fast and had come careening into my yard as he tried to stop. There was an 18-foot gash where the fence once stood, bamboo trees were broken and bent. But we were all okay. Again the police were called. The driver was handcuffed and led away. He was drunk. A tow truck hauled away his rig.

My landlord, a soulless, penny pincher, resisted my pleas to get the fence repaired. He actually tried to make a case that the house had more curb appeal without a fence. My nights were now even more traumatic as I thought with the fence down, serial killers and coyotes would definitely find their way to my bedroom. Charles Manson made nightly appearances in my sweat-induced nightmares. I knew that Gilles was coming back soon. I hoped having him by my side would calm my nerves. I also knew he would find a way to get that fence repaired, with the landlord's help or not. There was no way we could afford to pay for a new one.

Before Gilles returned, I welcomed a visiting friend who arrived from Toronto. I was happy to have company. Bill was also thinking of moving to LA and had come to check out job possibilities. He was a commercial editor but wanted to open the door to broader challenges. He very sweetly offered to help try to restore the garden. While clearing the broken trees, he unearthed a beehive. From in the kitchen, I heard his screams. I reactively ran outside. I saw the swirl of angry bees circling about his head. I screamed! They must have heard me. *I wondered if bees had ears. They most certainly had sensors!* In a flash they were on me. Some were tangled in my hair, amplifying their menacing buzzing in my ears. I think both Bill and I were in a state of shock.

I was now convinced our sweet looking little house was a magnet for trouble.

We agreed we should get to a hospital, given we shared a hundred stings. Unfamiliar with its location and long before Google maps, we called for directions. We were told the closest hospital was not far from us, on the UCLA campus that I had seen many times on my drive to work. Unfortunately it was a massive area with several entrances. The bee stings that covered so much of our heads and arms were now red and radiating pain. Bill was becoming anxious that we could be allergic and go into anaphylactic shock and die. I tried to calm him by telling him that if that were the case, we probably would be dead already. More than an hour had passed since our own personal horror movie moment had taken place.

As we pulled into the hospital parking lot, we heard an ominous whirring and then a clunk. Bill took a cursory look under the hood and gave the car a quick once over. He concluded that we had probably dragged something and it had just released. I hastily accepted his response, as I was desperate to get some pain relief from those pulsating stings and I didn't want to entertain the creeping panic that the car we had bought so blithely was unsound. I knew whatever it was, would be expensive to repair.

Once the hospital staff realized how long we had been driving since the time of the swarm attack, they shoved the crash cart back out into the hallway (emergency over) and asked us if we wanted our Benadryl to be taken orally or as a salve to be applied externally. I was ready to go for the liquid but Bill, now knowing he was going to live, had other ideas. He answered for both of us, "Topically please. We don't want to get drowsy." I looked at him quizzically but he avoided my eyes. The soothing gel was applied to our arms, faces and wherever they could get through our hair. The most amazing part of that entire experience was, no one asked for our

I.D.'s, or for payment of any kind. This was the early eighties and no one was using computers. Giving help was what nurses and doctors did. There was nobody holding back treatment unless proof of insurance or cash was supplied.

I am reminded of all the people I have either heard about or actually known who were refused treatment because they couldn't provide insurance or enough money to pay their outrageously inflated bills. I know people who spent all their savings and then borrowed from friends and family to keep life saving options available to ill loved ones, and some who died because they couldn't afford treatment.

I had barely climbed into my car, when Bill said, "I think a visit to Tijuana is necessary. When this gel wears off we are in for a rude awakening. It doesn't matter that we have a jumbo tube of the stuff. It barely makes a dent. We need to drown our pain with some seriously potent tequila." For a girl who doesn't drink much I somehow agreed this was a good idea…

All gassed up, we hit the road. There was next to no traffic and we got close to the border in just under two hours. Not close enough. The clunking sound from somewhere deep inside the belly of the beast had returned. Then the car quietly stopped. We were luckily on a slight grade and Bill put the car into neutral, guiding it off to the side of the freeway. We both got out to take a look. *An ambitious notion on my part as I know nothing about cars beyond driving them.* Bill was about to open the hood, when he noticed that the cable connecting the gas pedal to its mechanism had snapped. I was close to tears at the idea of being so far from home, and that the Benadryl was wearing off. Bill somehow managed to jerry rig the two cables back together and we were off, but not before passing along the dire information that to get this fixed properly could be expensive. For reasons that can only be explained by the volume of unexpected crazy that the entire day had presented, I began laughing - almost hysterically.

Back then the border was, if not exactly a warm and fuzzy experience, a pretty easy glancing once-over accompanied by a couple of questions as to where we lived. Passports weren't needed. A quick flash of a driver's license was all that was required. And with a wave of a hand, we were through and in Mexico.

The Benadryl had definitely worn off. The bee-stings were inflamed, growing in size and they hurt. Bill pushed open the swinging doors of the first bar we came upon. Heads raised, dark eyes landed on us. Oh oh… Had we stumbled into No-Gringo territory? This was no tourist bar. It boasted a dirt floor and a snake-eyed bartender along with some very wary Mexicans. Bill asked for shots of tequila. We were handed a bottle filled with a nearly clear liquid that had a worm sprawled across the bottom. I could hear snickers. One of the guys in the bar got up and shuffled over to our table. He stared at us willing us to bolt. I would have but Bill held his gaze. The guy then laughed and hit Bill on his back. In reasonably good English, he explained that Mescal had magical properties. He said we should each keep swigging it and whichever one of us got the worm would have their wish granted. Bill was all in. He hoisted back the bottle and took a long pull of the throat-burning liquid and then handed it to me. I desperately wanted Gilles to walk through those doors and rescue me from this potential nightmare but he was more than three thousand miles away. I could feel everyone silently betting I would pass. I tipped the bottle back and drank, all the while praying I wouldn't get that disgusting worm. After about three sips of Mescal, I didn't care whether I swallowed the worm. I didn't care about having been stung by a whole hive's worth of bees. I couldn't feel anything, including my legs. I have no idea if either of us got that worm or if we even finished that bottle. We were experiencing a true altered space. I must have forgotten I could get a near hallucinogenic reaction just from knocking back a single Tylenol.

Suddenly starving, we realized we hadn't eaten for hours. We stumbled out into the street desperate to find food. About a dozen churros later, we were 'slightly' more sober. I remember buying giant sombreros and Bill bought a box of fireworks. It was late, even for Tijuana, a town that partied late. We walked for what seemed hours. We applied more antihistamine and got back in the car and headed for the border. We were sober and right back in pain-land.

Leaving Mexico was not as simple as entering it. The US border agent was about to wave us through when he noticed a tangerine on the dashboard. He ordered us out of the car. The look on his face made it seem we were packing an AK-47. We didn't understand the problem. We explained we had brought two tangerines into Mexico. We had eaten one and this one was to be shared on the trip home. We were ushered inside the customs building as our car was about to be searched. We were exhausted, probably hung over and in agony. We must have looked pathetic. The two agents inside both indicated chairs where we could sit. I asked why a single tangerine was such a huge offence. One of them actually laughed and explained there was something called a Medfly infestation and the US was very strict about no fruit coming into the country as it had reached epidemic proportions. There was going to be aerial spraying and a ban on all imported types of fruits as they didn't know which country the med fly was coming from. The border guard that stopped us came through the door. He was holding our box of fireworks. He was a completely changed man, almost mellow. He announced to the other officers that there had only been one tangerine and it had been tossed. We were cleared to go. Almost as an afterthought, he tapped on the box of fireworks and in a relaxed voice he told us, we couldn't bring these into the US either. Bill casually asked if we turned around and went back into Mexico, could we have them back. They looked at each other and shrugged.

Five minutes later we pulled over, once again on the Mexican side of the customs area. I had no idea what Bill was up to until he got out of the car. He then held the door open for me. We stuck every one of those fireworks into the soft ground. Bill told me to stand back. He lit them.

From the safety of the car, we watched Roman Candles, pinwheels and colorful eye popping starbursts light up the sky. We could hear the applause and 'oohs' and 'aahs' from not just the people coming through both sides of the border but from the Mexican and US inspectors too. We were given a huge round of applause as we crossed back into California. For a full fifteen minutes we forgot about the pain we were in. We were giddy from the whole crazy experience.

Note to Self: The money I spent on that painting to make myself feel better was a temporary buzz. It could have been used in a hundred other ways. It could have been the seeds that would have grown into a down payment on a house and that would have no doubt made me feel much better. Our Tijuana experience may not have been without pain but it cost almost nothing and was a memory that would live on forever.

Recommended Medication: Cinnamon sugar-coated churros, perfect for snacking and recovering from all traumas.

CHAPTER 9

DENIAL IS DEFINITELY NOT JUST A RIVER IN EGYPT

The Cost: Not doing the homework on any business venture is living to regret it.

We had been in Los Angeles for almost two years. We had come to love the openness not just of LA's enormous expanse but also the sense of opportunity that was out there. LA is where people had come for decades to make their dreams a reality. Between the glittering ocean and the fairy tale look of the whimsical houses with their turrets, or the many Italian villas and their improbably lush gardens that dotted Hollywood, it did seem one could manifest anything. One simply had to close one's eyes to the low rent districts where those dreams came to crash and burn after a few years of constant rejection. That was not possible for me. Eyes wide open. *"There but for the grace of God…"* kept me from ever getting complacent.

We had discovered the outsized Canadian creative community that had given us access to a world of people like us who fit in effortlessly with those born in America. We Canadians were continuously being good naturedly teased for our willingness to apologize even when someone else was standing on our toes. We soon had no shortage of friends from the global village of actors, writers, producers and directors who, like us, had been seduced by the lure of success. Gilles found himself much in demand not just as an actor but also as a clothing designer. He had one young client who came from huge industrial wealth. He was forever losing and then gaining weight. He would toss out all his skinny clothes when he got fat, order new ones, then lose the weight and toss out the fat clothes and order a slew of new skinny ones. We joked that he was our human cash machine... until he had gastric bypass surgery. He finally achieved weight stability and we lost our easy money.

My writing partner and his wife decided to roll the dice and finally move west. Our scripts had gotten us noticed and we now had a good agent who felt that we needed to be in the same city if we wanted a shot at the big time. Evan had barely arrived and already our Filofaxes were filled with meetings at Warner Brothers, Universal Studios, and MGM etc. *For those born in the tech age, Filofaxes were much-prized organizers and appointment books that we carried with us everywhere, much like our precious cell phones of today.* We were both beyond excited by the response to our movie pitches, until everything came to a crushing halt. With our Writer's Guild union cards having just arrived in the mail, we were now on strike!

We had barely dipped our big toes in Hollywood's rarefied water and we were now walking the picket line with a full gamut of writers. There were the bold names, like Neil Simon, marching alongside the yet to be discovered's like Jon Stewart and Adam Sandler. At first the strike was, for me, an opportunity to meet and network with others like us, as well as those who were rich and famous. It was all camaraderie and access to a gold mine of connections. The commonality was all about the issues. But after a couple of weeks, the optimism devolved into a gripe-fest of personal issues. The studios had unlimited resources and thought they could outlast the writers. It was war! The writer's union was galvanized to stay in for the long haul. The writers knew that producers couldn't continue to make product without scripts! We wanted a fair share of the revenues from the people and the corporations that profited from our creativity. Our residuals were at stake as the studios wanted to roll them back, along with escalating the amount that needed to be earned annually in order to be eligible for health care. The strike was long and ultimately terrifying and it changed the business forever.

After experiencing that devastating strike and then a further three-month lockout by the actors' union, we were hit with another work stoppage from the Writers Guild that was willing to go back and fight for more. We were feeling skittish about our future, as was our whole industry. We had little money put aside for emergencies or unexpected life hazards. I chose to wear blinders and convince myself everything would be fine. The voices in my head were telling me differently. But I shut them down and kept doing the same thing I had always done. I chose to wrap myself in the comfort of denial. *We all know how that goes – not well!*

Being competitive is ingrained in every aspect of show business and we all accepted that. Gilles' niche had been playing the handsome Frenchman, from maître d' to diplomat. My salt-of-the-earth body and Labrador-retriever-friendly but somewhat bossy nature had given me the edge playing everything from best friends to therapists and a long string of hookers, maids, and madams. But after that awful and protracted strike, the competition for jobs made us feel like guppies in a pool of piranhas. These were desperate times. We had enjoyed a good run of guest-starring roles but now the parts that seemed perfect for us were going to those who had bigger star power or better connections. Gilles and I were lucky in a way, as we had work opportunities back in Canada that we were very grateful for, but it meant that we were shuttling back and forth to Toronto, which was exhausting and expensive. It was also harrowing. We were as yet not officially permanent residents. This meant every time we did get a job, the producers had to prove we were the best choice for the part over any American. In order for that to happen, it first needed to be determined that we had real credibility in our own country. I had a folder filled with press clippings and letters from all the networks and famous people I had worked with as proof of my 'superior' talent. The studios, with their deep pockets, had a battery of lawyers who could make it happen in no time at all. When we booked jobs without the protection of the wealthy production entities, we had to spend big money for a personal immigration lawyer who knew how to get it done. Crossing the border from Canada into the US always required a deep intake of breath and a prayer we would not be denied entry.

I had just wrapped a really good movie role in Toronto, called Improper Channels, starring Alan Arkin, I was heading back to my new home, where Gilles and our dog were eagerly waiting at the airport to surprise me. A very officious customs agent began interrogating me as to my purpose in going to Los Angeles. I met his gaze and said as I had been told to do, "Visiting friends". He asked me. "Who? Where? How long will you be staying?" I had never been grilled like this before. As he waved my ticket in my face, I flushed. Friends had warned me about never using a one-way ticket but I had forgotten their advice. The agent then asked to see my wallet. I was confused but gave it to him. He went through every photograph and there were lots, especially of me and Gilles entwined in each other's arms. He looked at them

Oops! I Forgot to Save Money

carefully and pulled one free. "Who is this?" I stammered but didn't lie. "My husband." He flipped it over. The date was visible. It had been taken only a month before. He said. "I see you and your husband are under a palm tree beside what is obviously the Pacific Ocean. So… I think you are living there illegally. You are not going." He closed my passport and handed it back to me with cold eyes. I was panicked but pulled myself together. I took a deep breath. "May I speak to your supervisor please?" The customs agent glared at me. "No. He isn't going to say anything different." I felt the line behind me becoming impatient. But I had to get home. I asked again. "May I speak to your supervisor please?" I wasn't going to let it go. Neither was he. Just then another customs agent approached to find out what the holdup was. Officer Meany told him. The other agent motioned for me to follow him. I had a small moment of panic but somehow I knew that changing the guard at the gate was my only hope.

I sat in what was the supervising agent's office, understanding he held my fate in his hands. He listened as I explained, that yes, I did live in California and yes I had told a lie. But I explained there was no way I could work there unless a permit was agreed to and paid for and that's only after it's proven I'm the best person for the job. His face was a mask of inscrutability. My heart was in my mouth. My husband was in LA with our dog and I was here, possibly forever.

I inhaled and then asked him what he would do if he were in my shoes. He made eye contact and gave me a small smile. I knew in that second he was letting me go. He stood up, shook my hand and said, "I was young once. Good luck. We will know if you take a job without going through the right channels." I let out a long breath and thought about hugging him, but instead, I shook his hand and thanked him, probably excessively. I did take a small amount of pleasure as I sailed past Officer Meany, appearing even surlier as he watched my back going through the gate.

All that back and forth travel came to an end, when I received my long awaited Green Card. I was ready to take the world by storm. But as the saying goes, "What does God do when we make plans? She laughs." "Shazam!" I was pregnant. It was exhilarating and worrying. How would we take care of this child given our rootless and impractical ways? Gilles attempted to calm my hysteria by reminding me that I was the one who believed things work as they're supposed to. *What the hell did that mean? I never said that. Did I? He was the one afflicted with blind faith. I believed that worry was like an overweight shoulder-sitting demon, there to remind one to do better.*

As my tummy grew bigger, so did our circle of friends. I spread the word about Gilles' amazing talents as if I were Gypsy Rose Lee's mother selling her daughter's strip-tease act. But Gilles, the true artist, again refused to charge anything close to what his designing and clothes-making skills were worth. *Perhaps, Doctor, he wasn't quite up to speed on his own value.* Gilles' good looks, easy charm and skills made him appear to be a sure candidate for success. Doors opened, people stepped aside to let him in but he had no desire to go there. He got that I wanted so much more and was only too happy to stand back and support all of my dreams. *Why couldn't I accept that he is not me?*

I spent the wee small hours of the night interrupting my panic induced nightmares by dreaming up get-rich-quick schemes from the practical to the ridiculous. There was the 14 carrot *(sic)* gold necklace, which I had a jeweler friend of mine make as a prototype, with fourteen perfect little gold carrots hanging from a gold chain. It was charming. *Haha!* I called a couple of jeweler connections but they passed. I had no idea what to do next, so I abandoned it as if it never existed, in spite of the evidence to the contrary. One would have thought as an actor I would have understood that being rejected once didn't mean I wouldn't land the next audition. *It was too soon for me to understand that rejection is part of every artist and entrepreneur's path.* Perhaps, this would have been a good moment to get to the bottom of why both Gilles and I kept operating from a tried and true place that wasn't working. It might have required investing in some therapy but we weren't ready for that. We were too busy inventing excuses that would have been transparent to everyone but us.

I read about a huge Chocolate Show coming to town. I asked my long-time best friend and partner in so many crimes and capers to come with me. Arlene was the perfect companion. We were both up for just about any adventure. She was Ethel to my Lucy even though she was the one with red hair. I wanted to suss out the products on display to see if I had any competition for my next BIG idea. *Yes that, and sample a lot of tasty chocolate. Who wouldn't want to go to a chocolate show?* My idea involved two of my favorite things – chocolate and art. I had struggled making the prototype for this one. In my head, the process of making copies of some of the best known sculptures in chocolate seemed pretty simple. I had a friend who was coming from Paris buy me small replicas of the Venus de Milo and Michelangelo's David and for those modernists, a composite version of a Henry Moore bronze, from the Louvre Museum's well stocked gift shop. I tried repeatedly making plaster molds of the three very recognizable statues that I could then fill with chocolate. But each time, they either slumped or gained bumps, making them look more like mini hunchbacks or humpbacked whales. I decided to just dunk the real statues in dark melted chocolate. They looked great. I just

129

prayed no one would try to bite into them or they'd be toothless and I would be sued.

I'm no longer sure which one of us came up with the idea to pretend we were journalists covering the show, so that we could not just get in free but so that we could be sure to get in there early before all the samples were gone. We actually had the gall to make bogus press passes from the imaginary Sunset Times, which we wore with equally bogus confidence on brightly colored lanyards around our neck. Arlene and I roamed the aisles looking at what chocolate best sellers were flying of the shelves, our mouths and pockets constantly replenished with silky smooth chocolate samples. I carried my chocolate covered statues lovingly wrapped in cellophane, in a small, red, ice-filled cooler. I was nervous they would melt, or crack. My panic must have shown on my face as more than one person asked me if I was carrying a heart or liver. *"Yup, I'm a doctor. I thought a stop in at the chocolate show on my way to the hospital to do an organ transplant might be fun... Seriously?"* They must have somehow missed my press pass – possibly because it was now smeared with chocolate. I was thrilled to see I had no competition for my EAT YOUR ART OUT gift biz. *(Anyone reading this who is connected to the chocolate business and gets that this is a good idea, let me know.)* My purse was stuffed with chocolates and business cards for follow up meetings.

After a couple of hours Arlene and I were on an out of control sugar high as huge as meth addicts driving toward oncoming traffic in a stolen police car. I believe our resemblance to whirling dervishes was noticed as we spun past many a pointed finger, accompanied by loud laughter as we headed for the exit. Talking fast and lurching, we tried to remember where we had parked the car. When we finally found it, I was completely discombobulated.

Oops! I Forgot to Save Money

I put the cooler carefully on the floor of the back seat, I got in and started the car, but I couldn't see the cooler so I got out to see if I had lost it or left it on the ground. I looked through the back seat window and heaved a sigh of relief. But then I realized I had locked the keys inside with the engine running. The sun was beating down and all I could think about was David's melting chocolate penis. In a moment of sugar-induced insanity, I called 911. I believe I said, "My baby is locked inside my car!" They promised to come right away. At this, Arlene became even more agitated than she already was, stepping right up in my face, telling me what I had done was a felony. It took a moment for me to understand she wasn't talking about the cooler and me saying I was a heart surgeon. Once I understood, I begged her to call 911 back and say she had a file thingy and had got the baby out but Arlene bolted. *Coward!*

A few minutes later, a tow truck pulled up and a big bruiser of a guy got out. I was sweating and nervously trying to plead my case. He didn't understand a word I said. He was either Mexican or Moravian and didn't care. He jimmied the lock in a nanosecond and then headed back to his truck. I stuffed twenty bucks and a pile of sticky chocolates into his surprised hands. I quickly got into the car and blasted the air conditioning. Arlene stepped out from behind a large dumpster and got in the car. We convulsed in near hysterical relief.

I was convinced I had found my Pet Rock. *In the eighties, somebody had the idea to market a rock in a box as a pet. The sheer stupidity propelled it to become a million dollar seller.*

I diligently set up appointments with all the chocolate companies in Los Angeles. I dressed in my best business attire, which for most of LA is expensive jeans and a high-end t-shirt, worn with diamond accessories. *Every day in LA is Casual Friday.* I went

131

for something basic and black, accompanied by my perfectly fake diamonds. I even printed out a nondisclosure form so no one could rip me off. *Maybe I'll get a few inserted into the back of the book for y'all to sign.*

The first meeting was with a fairly well known chocolate company situated four freeways and one very confusing, maze-like industrial park hell zone away. The person I met with wouldn't even consider signing my nondisclosure after asking me just one question. "Is this item for a novelty chocolate idea?" I of course answered yes. She held the door to her office open so she could walk me out explaining they were in the business of bars and cups. I tossed off, "I'm guessing you mean chocolate not booze." She did her best not to grimace too obviously, clearly having heard that one before. I was outside in the parking lot of the hell zone in less than seven minutes and without a single chocolate drop for my trouble. I should have told them I was pregnant and needed sustenance.

My next meeting was with the very famous Kron Chocolatier Company. They were lovely and willing to listen. It didn't hurt that a mutual friend had made the introduction. They soon explained that they specialized in their own novelty line of chocolate: legs (life size), as well as bunnies, bears, frogs, golf balls, numbers and letters, chocolate dog bones and even a female chocolate torso. I was excited, seeing as they were already in the business of making chocolate molds. Not so fast – they thought I had a great product idea but they didn't need to buy outside ideas. They warmly wished me luck. I left licking my wounds and some delicious samples.

I struck out with a couple more companies. Each time, I ran an internal monologue as soon as I was alone in my car as to how these companies were missing a great opportunity, that they had no vision. Not once did I do an internal check to see if perhaps the problem was coming from my end. Eventually I met with the CEO of a large chocolate and candy manufacturer in yet another industrial region requiring faith and locked car doors to ensure that I wouldn't be car-jacked. I was met with an open and welcoming mind. I made my pitch with all the exuberance of a true believer. I delicately removed the tissue and showed off my three chocolate prototypes. The CEO looked at them briefly before properly schooling me on what would be required to take my little piggies to market. He inquired if I had a business plan. Had I thought of packaging that would stand up to FDA standards as chocolate was in danger of melting? Did I have access to refrigerated trucks for delivery? What kind of output was I thinking of? Had I worked out my budget for all of the above? The hammer hit me hard. *Aaaaarrrgggh! I had not done my homework.* I was so excited about my idea that I thought savvy candy manufacturers would jump up and down at the prospect of paying me a huge sum of money for my idea and then they would take on all that research and work. I suppose that can happen but only if that same company makes most of the profits for having taken the risk. *Shark Tank was not yet in existence. If it had been, they would have verbally smacked me down for my lack of preparation and I would have been made to do the perp walk off that show with my head handed to me.* Mortified, I walked to my car, knocking back the bag of chocolate covered something that he had given me as a parting gift. It was more than I deserved.

∽

Sonja Picard is a successful and award-winning jewelry designer who specializes in creating empowering symbols using ancient symbols and mantras. She is much more than a jewelry designer;

she is an alchemist and artist who creates adornments and art to inspire our lives. But it was a long journey to arrive at her success today. Sonja had been a professional full-time artist since 1990, the first few years as a sculptor. She threw herself into her vision of creating large-scale sculpture which got her noticed with an invitation for a solo exhibit in a prestigious gallery. Sonja worked for four months to produce 22 large-scale sculptures, endless days and nights spent creating her dream exhibit. But the show was a bust, due to the gallery moving from a high-traffic location two weeks before the show.

Devastated, exhausted and financially drained, every penny now had to be considered for food or gas in her car. Her family tried to dissuade her from continuing in her artistic pursuit and move back into another more financially secure 'job'. This added fuel to the feelings of defeat. Against all odds she remained determined to make this work – her personal mantra by Joseph Campbell 'follow your bliss' was her guiding force, knowing if she stuck to it, the money would follow. The lesson she learned was that diversifying her creativity was the key to success. She went back to Studio ceramics and by chance a piece she had been commissioned to make for a friend created a frenzy of orders. Her business grew to 80 stores in 2 years, which caught the attention of a leading giftware company who purchased her designs and hired her as a designer for a few years.

But now Sonja wanted to shift her career to jewelry. Starting over with an art journal full of ideas in a new industry had her investing all the financial resources she had... because what bank would make a loan to a woman who is an artist to start on an unknown path? Sonja knew she had to invest in herself to make her dream a reality. She started her line in silver creating a name for herself in Vancouver. She opened a gallery in the

Oops! I Forgot to Save Money

heartbeat of the city and realized halfway into her lease she was not happy or cut out to be in retail. Sonja had to make a huge decision to let ALL her hard work go just as she was now seeing good financial rewards. Not only did she manage to let the gallery go, she let go most of her silver line and began creating high-end couture pieces. Her life and career changed yet again and she was invited to trunk shows in prestigious spas and galleries all over the U.S. Today, Sonja looks back at the fear of others who allowed their dreams to evaporate. She turned her fears into rocket fuel, which in turn just gave her power to create her limitless possibilities towards success and financial freedom. She succeeded beyond her expectations because she 'believed' and took a chance on herself to 'follow her bliss'.

 Courage and saying no to failure appears to be the true alchemy for success.

∽

What Sonja had that I didn't was a clearly defined sense of her own destiny, and the knowledge that the risk and the hard work were worth the potential reward. I was still too scared and scattered, and unsure of what I wanted my future to look like. I'm an idea person, often awake at three in the morning, my brain on its own acid trip. Fast moving colors and fragments swirl around as if in a kaleidoscope, coming into focus in a fully formed idea that in that moment I think is born of pure genius … until about nine in the morning, after coffee, when I try to drill into my head to extract said brilliant idea. Sometimes they remain good, often they either have vaporized or they are made of nonsense like the electric ashtray that plugs into a wall. Why? No idea. Not all ideas die because they are bad or nonsensical, some die because they are too unwieldy or because I am no longer excited by them or

135

Monica Parker

because, and most likely, I don't have the skills or patience to see them through. In spite of these huge failings, I somehow must have convinced some people in high places that my creative instincts were worthy. In one of those bolts out of the blue moments, my phone rang and the CEO of Playtex, who was a friend, suggested I join a team that was being assembled to brainstorm new products. Oddly, it had nothing to do with bras or underwear of any kind; this was for an electronics company. *Of course I'm the one to call when ideas and inventions are needed for electronics – whaaaat?*

These gatherings took place in a downtown hotel conference room. There must have been eight to ten of us – none of us appeared, on the surface, to have any connection to each other. We were a mixed lot of nuts, from extremely shy to, dare I say, obnoxiously loud. Thankfully, there was only one of those. There was only one other woman. And nearly all came from the tech world, a couple from toy manufacturing. If there had been a photograph, it would have been easy to answer the question, "Which one of these things does not belong?" Me! I had no real job other than the one I made up every day – certainly no nine-to-five life. I came to understand that we were chosen because our brains were known for spewing ideas and because we were not constrained by rules. *Tell that to the long list of my frustrated teachers who constantly threw their hands up in the air for that very reason.* There was a leader from the advertising world who called what our idea-generating group was doing a process called *synectics*, which, in essence, meant opening up our creativity to seeing new ideas even in old ones. The fact that we came from different disciplines only added to the inspiration. We did all have to sign nondisclosures that any idea, product or system that came about from the games we played was never to leave the

Oops! I Forgot to Save Money

room. Plus, all ideas belonged to the company that hired us. We spent three days banded together in that room, never for a moment feeling bored or under house arrest. Food and drink magically arrived without ever interrupting our brainstorming, as we spun some gold out of that volcanic air. The energy in that room was exciting, sometimes electric and always rousing. We were paid handsomely and even better, I was brought back time and time again. It was and remains one of the most stimulating experiences I have ever had. Inventing and creating ideas from my imagination is the sandbox I am happiest playing in.

As my pregnancy progressed, so did my fear. It wasn't about my unborn child's health or wellbeing. It was about mine. Our professional lives were so filled with happenstance and unpredictability; it was not dissimilar to playing slot machines in a casino. *The irony is not lost on me that I have no appetite for throwing money into the fickleness of spellbinding machines.* I rarely knew where or when our next paychecks would appear. When they did, they sometimes could be quite substantial but then they would have to last us for an unknown period of time. Or they may have been tossed away on something providing instant gratification instead of smartly saving for those rainy days. But post-strike, our paychecks had diminished in comparison to the rising salaries of the actors who graced the covers of endless magazines. We were firmly embedded in the ninety-nine percent, versus those one per centers at the top - the rich were getting richer and the rest of us, no matter what our profession, were being edged out of the formerly comfortable middle class into a category yet to be clearly defined. Still, none of it scared me straight into finding a more secure job.

I thought often about what one of those might be like and what it could be. If I were even remotely Catholic, I would have made a very qualified Mother Superior. People always confessed their deepest, darkest secrets to me. Perhaps, I could be a teacher. I do like to be in charge…but I would always have favorites. That's never good but it's my nature. Could I be an architect? I love the grandiosity of creating beautiful buildings. But I don't have the patience for all the detail work that goes along with it. *To say nothing about the 6 years of post- graduate education it would have required.* I truly loved what I was doing and like most artists, that siren call was the only one I listened to. I believe it's imprinted into our DNA before we arrive on the scene, there to frustrate our families and friends who want to protect us and themselves from our unpredictable lives.

I was five months pregnant but given that I had more than my fair share of adipose tissue, I just looked like I had made a few too many trips to the all-you can-eat brunch at our neighborhood deli. I auditioned for yet another role as a therapist in a low budget film. 'Low budget film' means they can get away with paying actors at the lowest rate humanly possible and still be deemed legal by the union. *If they could have paid me in birdseed and gotten away with it, birdseed is what I would have received.* The common fallacy that actors make a lot of money is far from the truth. It used to be that working actors worked their way up the pay ladder just like in every other career but just like in every other vocation that has seen the middle class stagnating or worse, the same can be said of actors. Movie and TV stars make a lot of money but they are the exception. Shooting the movie was a piece of cake since for most of it I could be found sitting behind a desk, swathed in scarves and chunky jewelry. I was thrilled that no one would notice my 'condition' if I kept my ham-like swollen feet elevated. I was grateful for the paycheck, no matter the amount.

I knew, as the sky is blue, that I was having a boy. I knew from the moment I found out I was pregnant. And now I couldn't help but worry about how we would take care of his future. My due date was in the fall. It was now August and I felt I was in danger of exploding. The watermelon that temporarily housed my ever-growing baby was dropping lower and lower, putting pressure on all my lady parts. I desperately wanted a custom port-o-potty on wheels to accompany me wherever I went. As I was about to be a mother, I was haunting all the best baby shops to inventory the mountain of stuff that I kept being told I needed. I understood the need for a car seat and a crib and of course a stroller but a diaper changing table? *Couldn't I just use the bathroom counter?* The list of necessities was already going to be an astronomical amount of money. The suggested three breast-feeding bras alone were off the chart expensive. *I am and was a big-breasted bird.* I was breathing hard and too fast, well on my way to an anxiety attack. I bee-lined toward the nearest rocking chair and began a rhythmic and calming meditation. There have been babies since the beginning of time. Cave women had babies. There were even sharper objects around back then: flints, axes, and arrows. No way were they baby proofing their caves. They didn't have strollers that also separated into car seats, while making cappuccinos. *Because they didn't have cars.* The hunters hunted, the gatherers gathered. There were no baby monitors. Babies screamed and mommies dressed in flea-infested deerskins answered the calls. A very nice saleswoman approached me with a glass of water. She uttered two words I didn't understand. "Braxton Hicks". I shook my head and said, "No, Monica Parker." She laughed but then saw I was serious. I detected a small eye roll as she asked if the reason I was sitting down was because I was experiencing Braxton Hicks contractions. I stood up. "No, I don't know what those are. I'm just freaking out. Babies aren't cheap are they?" Again she laughed and stopped when she saw I was serious this time too, maybe even more so. I bolted from the store as best a pregnant woman with a front loaded U Haul can do.

I couldn't sleep well. There was no position that worked until I stuffed a pair of foam pillows between my legs and I was gone…

Rain is coming down in sheets. There's no one crazy enough to be out in this weather. Arlene careens into a parking spot across the street from a bank. With hoods pulled tight, we leap from the car. I grab my young son into my arms and run across the parking lot and into the bank. We are soaked and try to shake off as much water as possible but our hoods remain on. We make our way to the counter. The teller smiles and makes a comment about the awful weather and how it's only good for ducks and tadpoles. I am trying to dig through my purse to find a residual check I need to cash. Arlene grabs my son as I dump out the contents of my bag. Bits of broken goldfish crackers tumble out, various piles of used tissue, my sticky wallet and my boy's toy gun clatter onto the counter. I'm still digging around for that check. I find a crumpled bit of paper that I think must be it. I shove it towards her. The teller stops talking. I throw my hands up in frustration. My child begins to cry. The teller is getting edgy. Arlene looks aggravated. The teller reaches into her drawer and slides out a large wad of cash. I am tossing even more bits of purse scrapings onto the counter. I sweep all of the junk back into my bag. I thank the teller and grab my wailing boy out of Arlene's arms. The three of us exit the bank in irritation.

We are sitting in a café drying out. My son is now happy as he has a chocolate donut attached to his face. Arlene is happily scarfing a muffin. Mine is already finished and I'm picking at crumbs. A siren wails in the background. The TV is on. We are half-watching a story about a nearby bank robbery. A grainy black and white picture comes on the screen, showing two women in hoods, one carrying a young boy. They are being described as tough, no-nonsense bank robbers. "The large one had a gun," says the teller… OH MY GOD! THAT'S OUR TELLER! OH MY GOD! SHE'S TALKING ABOUT US! OMG! I'M THE LARGE ONE! WHAT A BITCH! Arlene grabs my purse and begins to dig into it. Her face says everything as she pulls out the toy gun and… a wad of bills. I feel panic begin to rise up in my throat. I barely whisper, "Did we just rob a bank?" We look at each other in horror. We simultaneously look around to check that no one in the café is on to us. We look back up at the screen. We are totally unrecognizable in our hoods except that I am large-ish. Arlene's first response, "We've got to ditch the kid!"

I sit bolt upright in bed, drenched in night terror sweat. I protectively touched my bulging belly and felt my unborn baby kicking. I was still shaking from the nightmare. Gilles, always the perfect husband, sat up and cradled me. "What's wrong?" I wailed, "I dreamt that I used our future son as a distraction to rob a bank!" Gilles laughed but then saw the distress on my face. He spoke softly, "It was just a dream." Fully awake, I whirled towards him. "I don't think it takes a dream analyst to explain this nightmare! We are having a baby who will become a person and people are expensive." With his usual soothing but magical thinking, Gilles said, "Everything will be as it should be." I fell back to sleep…but less than a minute later my eyes popped open. "What the hell does that mean?" *I know exactly what it meant. I wanted to park my grown up self on the side rail and have Gilles be the hero. I wanted him to ride in and rescue me.* Most of us

141

want to be rescued; it's a universal fantasy. But ultimately, we are all responsible for ourselves. Taking on responsibility can be exhausting but when we succeed, there is no greater reward.

My body was busy finishing baking my baby, who seemed to be ready to vacate the premises as he was very actively seeking a way out. He kept pushing, kicking and reaching to find an exit. Clearly he had a lousy sense of direction. I thought about eating alphabet soup with only letters that spelled out 'Down' and then 'Out this way'. With swollen feet and my massive swollen belly but no possibility of getting any real rest between the peeing, kicking and terror of actually giving birth, I decided to kick my entrepreneurial inclination into high gear as a way to make some extra money.

I had let the chocolate idea go. As good as I knew it was, I didn't have the patience to dig deeper into all the marketing and research that needed to be done to take it to the next level. *I am now more than a little aware that not doing the grunt work is the road to nowhere but back then, I don't believe self-awareness was on the table. I just moved on, leaving one more going-nowhere, coulda-shoulda idea in my wake.* I had been so inspired by my synectics product brainstorming experience, that I decided to put together my own brainstorming group. I chose a group of eight friends. A few were writers, artists and actors, along with an interior designer, a realtor and even a physicist. They were all longtime friends and creative thinkers. I sat like a gestating queen on a comfortable chair with my feet up on a matching ottoman, while everyone else lounged on cushions on the floor. Of course Gilles had done everything to provide a beautifully prepared buffet. Who can come up with a bazillion dollar invention of the magnitude of a Joy Mangano mop on an empty stomach? Once the eating, laughing and joking around were done, we began to focus. With no actual leader designated to run this group of funny, mouthy and easily distracted 'children', the process was akin to herding butterflies. But everyone finally settled into the task at hand - coming up with an idea that was fresh, innovative or quirky enough to capture the imagination of the entire world that would then translate into big bucks!

Ideas were percolating and then began popping out of everyone's mouths like an exploding bag of popcorn. "Margarita In a Bag" made a million dollars in its first roll out – we could do tequila Jello-shots that could be prepackaged. That idea got shot down in flames almost instantly, given that Jell-O would need to be made portable, and like nitroglycerin, not that simple as it needed refrigeration. That spun into how "nitroglycerin shots" was such a great name for Jell-O shots. We all agreed, but we were still stuck on the how. Our physicist friend was assigned the job of finding out the possibilities of making portable Jell-O. Someone, it might have been me, raised the issue that we would need to get Kraft on board as they are the company that holds the Jell-O brand. It didn't take long for the whole Jell-O shots idea to fade into oblivion as the prospect of negotiating with Kraft's bank of lawyers about putting alcohol into a reputable and much loved kiddie favorite was sure to be a no-go. We then got stuck on a merry-go-round of food related ideas. We unanimously liked the idea of cookies that had the added boost of caffeine. Coffee always went well with cookies. The names began flying, "Big Buzz Cookie." "Cookie Kick." "Cookie Jolt". I hated to be the voice of doom, but having learned a few things from my chocolate fiasco, I knew that food products were not that simple to get to market as they needed test kitchens and endless money or backing. No one was daunted. Ideas were pouring forth, from the great to the impossible. This was creative playtime on steroids.

We agreed that whatever venture we entered into needed to be simple to execute and flashy enough to grab attention. One that made the cut for further research - a sensor that could be added to a car's roof for all those who at one time or another forgot their coffee or purses on the roof of their car. Who hasn't done that? My friend Yves, a renowned jeweler, once left his briefcase filled with diamonds on the roof of his car. It wasn't until he was on the entrance ramp to the freeway that he remembered, almost causing a chain reaction accident as he came to a screeching halt, car horns blaring as he leapt from his car. His prayers answered, it was still there. Another big idea was so simple that we were sure it must already exist but we all agreed it was still a good idea - a sling holster that could carry any umbrella over the shoulder, leaving hands free. By the time the night ended, we all had assigned homework. Did an umbrella holster exist? How to patent our ideas? The cost? Could we use a commercially available sensor and package it to suit our needs? Everyone left feeling gung-ho and ready to blaze new trails to fame and fortune.

When we gathered the next week, only two people had done their assignments. The evening took longer to kick into gear as more time was spent eating and chattering but promises were made to do better. The third week, the same two were the only ones prepared and two of the others cancelled at the last minute with excuses that were transparently fraudulent. The commitment felt like it was losing air. By week four it was deemed to be a great and fun experiment but hearts and minds were not all in. After some serious thinking and researching about why this extraordinarily inventive and enthusiastic group flamed out, the conclusion I came to was that creative people love the birthing of ideas and even expanding on them. What they don't enjoy and therefore don't make the same commitment to, is the less fun work of research and implementation.

A lesson learned - not to put a group of people together who share the same kind of creative DNA. Next time I put a group together; I will make sure that at least one third of them have marketing and business skills. We all have our talents but we need to gain strength and abilities from each other.

Laura Robinson is an uncommonly good-looking woman of a certain age, blessed with charm and humor. She is a human idea factory and a wonderful singer and composer. Back in her twenties, she and a former boyfriend came up with the idea of packaging a much-loved parlor game that almost everyone has played at one time or another, commonly known as the dictionary game. They called it Balderdash. It's the hilarious classic bluffing game where players make up phony definitions to strange words and everyone has to guess which is the true definition. It became one of the most successful board games in history right up there with Trivial Pursuit, Pictionary and Taboo. More than twenty million were sold worldwide.

There were other games and endless ideas, some of which did well, while most just fizzled. Then Laura put together the very successful television show, 'Celebrity Name Game', featuring the appealing Craig Ferguson as the host. It succeeded beyond her wildest dreams, winning two Daytime Emmys and yet was unexpectedly cancelled after three seasons. For a couple of years, it seemed to Laura that her run might be over. She had never considered that as a possibility. She sunk into a "Laura-esque slump", meaning you would never have had a clue that she was suffering from self-doubt or a possible failure. She never stopped generating ideas, taking on suggestions from others, possibly overextending. Even though she was undergoing a crisis of faith in herself, she got up every morning and kept on both barnstorming and brainstorming. Into each life a little rain does fall but if you put on a raincoat and splash through the puddles, you might just be rewarded.

Laura just found out that she has sold a new television game show. Its title, which will be familiar, is under wraps until production is done. The dry spell is over. She also found out that she has sold a new board game for parents and kids.

∽

Note to Self: When life gets difficult, it's time to take action, not stick your head in the muck where it's hard to breathe and solves nothing. Follow-through is important. Having ideas is great, but often it takes not just will but capital to make them a reality. As artists we know that work is sporadic and you need accessible funds to carry you through the dry spells. But everyone should put money aside to be prepared for the unforeseen. Conventional wisdom *(of which I had none)* suggests having a 6-month cushion.

Recommended Medication: Dark chocolate or milk chocolate, with nuts, raisins or toffee chips; in squares, blocks or as chocolate torsos if the need is great enough.

CHAPTER 10

SMOKE AND MIRRORS

The Cost: The stress that goes hand in hand with accumulating debt.

Remarkably it was only a few weeks later that I did the most creative thing I have ever done, along with a team capable of making that happen. I gave birth to a ten pound, eleven ounce baby boy. I immediately had a fantasy of seeing him lying on a large serving platter surrounded by leafy, green garnish. But one look into those serious green eyes and I knew that he owned me forever.

The whirl from the all-consuming care and feeding of our baby boy, Remy, took over our lives as it does for every new parent. Every day was a dip into the magical mystery tour of baby-raising and the constant prayers that we were getting it mostly right. Cloth diapers were good for the environment, but the cost of the laundry service was astronomical. Everything that was part of our new normal came with sticker shock and it had only just begun. I was a stay at home working Mom, not to be confused with one that was on Mat leave. I was home AND working. I felt blessed that both Gilles and I could conduct our business from home even when sleep deprived, which was every day. We were the proud parents of a baby who never slept. I discovered a brilliant form of relief that worked for one hour twice a day. I would strap our ever-alert bundle of joy into his car seat and place it on top of the clothes dryer, and then set it to 60 minutes of sleep inducing vibration. *Defensively: We did whatever it took and I don't want to hear from the naysayers. It's not like I put our child 'in' the dryer! I hope it inspires a tired Mom or Dad to do the same.* It was precious time when I could shower, sit at my desk and hope my eyes would stay open long enough for me to write a few pages.

Like most parents, we wanted to give our child every opportunity to develop all his gifts. Living in Los Angeles, this was made even more daunting because as he grew, every activity was a magnet for the money that spewed like gilded confetti. It didn't take long for us to understand that the best 'free' schools' were in Beverly Hills. The private schools were so far out of our league we didn't even bother to find out in what well-to-do enclave they were located. It might have seemed like folly for us to be looking in Beverly Hills. We had thought through this choice long and hard. It wasn't just about the schools… We wanted our one and only child to have a quality education and access to opportunities. *Oh the apple didn't fall far from my mother's tree.*

We left our sweet cottage situated in the death-defying car-racing canyon where I was never insane enough to push my precious child in his stroller beyond our fenced yard. A charming and affordable duplex apartment in the 'flats' of Beverly Hills came on the market. We bee-lined to the address only to discover there was already a crowd desperate to nab this hot ticket of an apartment. When it was our turn to fill out the form, we discovered the old woman who owned the building was a crotchety émigré who had been raised in Algeria. Gilles immediately began chatting with her in French, while I followed the other hopefuls from room to room, immediately envisioning how our furniture would look in each room. This was not movie star central or the much-photographed streets of the rich and famous. There were still some high-end homes to be found but most streets were filled with lovely but more modest Spanish influenced houses that remained unfenced and clustered together in real neighborhoods, where trick or treating was as typical as Main Street Anywhere, USA. The same could not be said of the far glitzier side of Beverly Hills dotted with its gated mansions. Those were the houses where, on Halloween, children were given their candy by housekeepers, or possibly security guards. By the time I got back downstairs the always charming Gilles and our future landlady were sharing some mint tea and conspiratorial laughter.

Evan and his wife also moved into our new neighborhood. We continued to work together and even though our scripts were getting positive responses, this was a hungry town, overflowing with smart and talented writers, actors, producers and directors. Every one of them was hustling to become the next breakout success story. My mechanic was trying to sell a script, as was my dry cleaner. Many of these paper peddlers were ruthless and some were connected by blood; we were neither. We picked up jobs here and there but the going was tough. But that's when the tough get going. We continued to keep our heads down and work hard.

We settled into our new neighborhood and once more our home was open for fun, food and friends. The garage at the end of our driveway was soon turned into a studio space for Gilles, a refuge for him to design, sew, and see his clients. It was a great space that we soon made glamorous with the bounty from many a late night cruise of the wide alleyways to the north of us, canvassing the items our fancy neighbors cast aside, just waiting for the junkmen to pick up. Not a chance – we were faster. A somewhat tired chaise, reupholstered by Gilles in deep red velvet, became magnificent. A cast away chipped gold frame was soon repainted and repurposed as a mirror. Even a mostly stringless harp found a way of becoming a clothes hanger.

We both worked from home but all work still requires time and focus. Through friends of friends, we got very lucky finding wonderful and relatively inexpensive live-in child-care. I discovered the incredible salvation that resulted from hiring au pairs: young girls from far-away places who wanted a safe and free place to live, along with a nominal sum of money in exchange for helping with child-care. Our first au pair came from Brussels, Belgium; she was the sister of a good friend. Arianne was a fresh-faced beauty with a sense of humor and a generous spirit. She fit right into our lives like a daughter. Along with her caring for Remy, she also offered to type my scripts. I was elated. She was with us for a year. We remain friends today as we do with many of the other 'girls' who came into our lives. I learned soon enough these twenty-something young women had a built-in time clock. Their child-caring attentions ran out consistently at about the eleven-month period. Then they were done. Over the years we had a mini United Nations worth of girls living with us. They came from Belgium, Germany, France, Ireland, Israel, Sweden and Denmark. We only had one that was so wrong for the job. Our French au pair, a long-legged beauty, was the daughter of a single mother who was barely around as she was a high profile acting agent. She took better care of her famous French film star clientele than she did of her only child, so perhaps Genevieve didn't have any role modeling for mothering. She spent hours blow-drying her beautiful long hair and choosing her perfect outfits. We soon came to believe she had come to Los

Angeles to piss off her mother. It's also possible she thought that looking after Remy would lead to an acting job, and further infuriate her mother. She had zero interest in child-care, so much so that she often wore a very tightly fitted t-shirt that said, "This is not my child!" We quickly found her a secretarial job with a producer. Having young women come and live in one's home is not for everyone. It was a perfect fit for us. We loved the opportunity to learn about other countries and we were comfortable with the emotional upheavals that came from their youth as well as their being strangers in a strange land. Both Gilles and I genuinely loved the exchange and felt we all benefitted so much from it. Our son learned a smattering of many languages and became open to eating everything from schnitzel to falafel while in the company of a variety of pretty young women who weren't always tired. We were happy and feeling fulfilled.

How dare we? This was a magical fairyland of our own construction. But it wasn't grounded in reality. We couldn't afford this lifestyle. But we damned well kept pretending… until the bottom fell out. Talk about a fall from grace.

We were not the only ones struggling financially. These were rough times; many people were desperate to keep their heads above water. The protracted writers' and then actors' strikes had taken their toll on a large percentage of the industry. When there are no scripts or actors, the costumers, hairdressers, makeup artists, caterers, party planners, travel agents, drivers and on and on are out of work, too. Los Angeles is as much a company town as Nashville is for music and Pittsburgh is with steel. We were not alone. There were many stories of writers, actors and producers who had to let their housekeepers go and/or pull their kids out of private schools. Deluxe Hawaii vacations were put on hold. I felt bad letting my once every two weeks cleaning lady go.

She had already lost so much work. Some went back to their hometowns in far-flung corners of the country. All had been seduced by the endless affluence and few were ready for the reckoning.

∽

A neighbor, the wife of a producer friend, revealed to me that she reported her very large diamond ring as lost. She told her insurance company that she had absent mindedly left it on the edge of her sink and when she went to retrieve it a couple of hours later, it was gone. She searched everywhere and even asked her husband to check the plumbing to see if it had fallen down the drain and become stuck in the pipe. She told them he had taken the pipe apart but no ring was to be found. She added that the house next door was under construction and it was possible that their house had been broken into. She laughed when she told me that they cut her a check for thirty thousand dollars. I didn't know what to say. I felt a wave of revulsion.

Apparently there was a rash of insurance fraud in those challenging days as I heard another story from a close friend that had a similar theme. A pair of writers, who may have seen or written too many movies, had opted to fake a hit and run car accident at the top of the fabled Mulholland Drive late one night. One of the duo owned a very expensive Ferrari acquired during the good times. Now that he had been out of work for a few months and his debt load was strangling him, he convinced his pal that he would split the insurance payout with him if he helped. This was no simple scam. They paid cash for a junker of a car, bought in another municipality, and then used it to hit the Ferrari hard enough to send it over the edge of the cliff, with the driver's door open but no one in it. The owner then actually rolled himself

Oops! I Forgot to Save Money

down the embankment and then climbed back up to Mulholland all scratched up with torn clothes. His partner drove the junker car far away to another town and left it hidden in a car scrapyard.

It took a few months and an investigation but the Ferrari owner got his money and made good on the payout to his 'partner' in crime. This happened sometime in the eighties. I believe that with computers, car cameras and all the technology that is available now, it would be harder to pull off today. They would have been found out and prosecuted.

∞

We were invited to a friend's surprise fortieth birthday party at a very high-end restaurant. It was a beautiful and festive evening. Champagne glasses were refilled without asking. Toasts were made to the birthday 'boy'. His wife had seen to every detail. There was a fantastic band that never seemed to take a break. Normally, this would have been one of the best parties I had ever been to. We were surrounded by some of the best people we knew and loved. I threw myself into that evening with a performance worthy of an award. I looked like I didn't have a care in the world. Gilles also seemed to be pulling off a magic trick as he too looked like he was having a great time. I knew better. Not for a moment did the relentless gnawing at the back of my brain stop. I knew I appeared like a well-feathered duck floating along on the waves of that evening but if anyone could have seen below the surface, they would have seen my feet paddling fast and furiously in order to keep me from drowning.

∞

A year ago a woman called Marla befriended me. She was at first pass someone I liked instantly. Her warmth and humor were enticing. However, it didn't take long for me to realize she was a compulsive shopper, over-spender and a true wannabe. She worked for a high-end florist, doing setups for huge events and very lavish weddings. She talked relentlessly about the wealth of the clients she met. She loved being around those who could afford to buy whatever their whims dictated. Marla didn't hide her envy. Instead she tried to keep up. She spent money she didn't have on designer clothes, shoes, and purses: anything that she could flaunt on social media. She used to laugh off her expenditures by saying she was really good at reselling all those labels to those who suffered from FOMO (Fear of Missing Out). I was only at her tiny condo once; it looked like a small warehouse filled with packing supplies and racks of clothing. It didn't look like she could ever sell enough of her once-worn stock to make back the money spent.

There was something about all that consumption that went way past a red flag. I knew then it was Marla who suffered from FOMO. Her real life was not enough for her. She needed the posture of 'posing as rich' in an Instagram world to fill the void within. Her light and breezy persona was an act.

Marla frequented every high-end department store from Saks to Neiman Marcus, picking up the latest coveted brand name labels. She wore Gucci, Tom Ford, and Yves Saint Laurent gowns to the very over-the top weddings she was invited to. But she returned the dresses a few days after wearing them, with excuses that they didn't fit properly, or that her mythical husband didn't like them. It all worked until it was discovered through social media, where Marla was seen wearing all those labels, that she was a frequent abuser of the 'purchase and return after wearing' scams. It wasn't the tiny spots of makeup on the necklines or dirt on the hems but the sheer number of times she returned clothing. Her house of credit cards came tumbling down when those stores refused to refund the money she had charged. It was just another sad story about trying to feed the beast of needing to belong.

~

God help us, our child was growing bigger by the second. More new shoes. He was following in our misdirected footsteps; he was displaying eccentric and artistic leanings. Why couldn't he have been interested in teeth? Dentists make lots of money. Now, fencing and art classes and private flute lessons strained our already limited budget. Of course we wanted to foster his interests; he was going to be who he was intended to be. Living on the right side of the tracks had its pluses and minuses. Good free schools were worth almost all of it. High-end grocery stores were not. I didn't know that struggling to keep afloat in a sea of well-heeled Joneses would exact such a toll.

Pressure! It leached through my pores. I regularly found myself awake well before the sun came up. My chest was relentlessly tight from self-induced pressure.

The pair of insistent harpies that lived in my head were reinvigorated. I say re-invigorated because I believe they had always lived inside me but they pushed their way to the forefront because of my inability to face reality. They had two very distinctive personalities. One was rebellious and almost always bordering on anarchy. She pushed me to behave in a somewhat outrageous manner, meaning without a filter. *There's a unique defense if I ever heard one.* The other voice was afraid of chaos and instability. She was an order freak. She came through in the form of an obsessive-compulsive need to have all objects remain in their assigned places. An unmade bed made my heart palpitate. Any artwork or photographs that hung crookedly brought on flop sweat. *And I could easily have had a smack down with anyone who forgot to pick up after themselves.* Together they totally banned me from any freeway driving. They were characteristics that intensified when I hadn't slept well or was drowning in pressure - like now. I was unable to terminate their residency, so I named them. Harriet was the loud, pushy one and Pearl was the more sensitive fraidy cat. I wasn't going crazy.

I really was mirroring my mother's life.

SLAM! The hammer came down hard.

BANKRUPTCY.

For some, losing homes, furnishings and businesses would be very difficult to recoup. I knew people who handled their debt in ways I could barely comprehend. We knew of one friend who suffered so deeply from declaring bankruptcy that he spiraled into a deep depression. His failure to keep his home and family financially secure ultimately caused him to take his own life.

For me, bankruptcy was a strange savior, but the stench that came with it permeated so much of my being. I struggled with the guilt that came from not paying our bills in full but was grateful for the bankruptcy giving us a new start. I knew we were some of the lucky ones. Our credit had been decimated but I also knew it could be rebuilt. We had lost face but in a strange moment of clarity, I saw that licking my wounds would be short lived. We didn't lose our home. We didn't own one. We had no mortgages or real estate holdings to lose. We primarily worked for ourselves, or on a per contract basis and no one would ever know the humiliation we had gone through by having our credit cards cut up. Our businesses would survive; they were us.

For the first time our marriage took a hit. Apparently money troubles are notorious for doing that. When the going gets tough, Gilles slows right down, his paralysis protecting him from the freight train that is me. He could barely put one foot down in front of the other. I on the other hand flipped the switch - desperate to get into the nearest station - and he was in my way. I needed answers. I needed direction. I needed to find a way through this. We could no longer shove anything under the carpet of pretense. In order to clean the slate we had to take one hundred percent responsibility. No blaming and no complaining. We got into this mess together and we would have to find our way out: if not together, then I would have to do it for us. We had to make genuine changes to the way we had always lived and that would require getting some professional guidance along with a whole whack of discipline.

Note to Self: Debt is a heavy burden to carry around. It's like wearing a coat made of lead. It's always in the back your mind. It ruins sleep. It ruins relationships. It can make one sick. Don't sabotage a family or friend relationship over an unpaid promise or debt. Pick up the phone or knock on that door and tell them you are embarrassed and feel horrible but you will make it right and pay them back. Arrange to give them whatever you can every week, whether it's ten dollars or fifty. Do without until you have paid off what you owe. Not dealing with your debts will create a toxic situation and ruin your reputation.

Recommended Medication: Open the fridge, the pantry, and every secret chocolate stash and prepare to eat a larderful of humiliation and fear.

CHAPTER 11

TRUST YOUR GUT, NOT THE SCAMMER!

The Cost: Losing everything we'd worked so hard to regain.

I learned to do the hustle from my mother but I also learned more than a bit of paralysis from dear old Dad. Now, I needed to get over it and get on with it. Tighten my bra straps and take charge of my financial life, probably my husband's as well. So be it. It is said, "Into each life a little rain must fall." In this case it had come in a torrent big enough to create our economic sinkhole.

I needed a paying job. I ran down the list of my skills. I was tidy to a fault and hyper clean. I thought about cleaning houses. I felt a shiver run down my spine at the thought of a one-of-a-kind Burmese glass sculpture slipping from my soapy hands, and shattering into a million pieces. Scratch that. Oh hell, I have no traditional career skills. Writing and acting require third and fourth and fifth parties to make those jobs a reality. Acting in my living room or anyone else's wasn't going to fill my wallet at the speed I needed it to. My full time gig is making stuff up! So that's what I did. I wrote personalized birthday poems, Bar Mitzvah speeches and the occasional obituary.

I have always lived with an independent mindset and I don't want that to ever change. But that requires financial security – something I had never made a priority. I have made many money mistakes but I was finally seeing them as the teaching tools I needed to wake up. Richard Branson said, "At least when you fall on your face, you are still moving forward." Luckily I'm resilient and resourceful and determined to do just that. Much like my mother – *one foot in front of the other.*

We scrimped and saved and gradually got ourselves out of debt, although our credit rating would take time to right itself. We were still working on a better way to communicate with each other about the hard stuff that we (Gilles) would have preferred to remain unspoken. Gilles worked tirelessly, making and mending whatever he could out of his converted studio. It was a beautiful space unless it rained and then it was a flood zone. Carpets had to be rolled up. All the fabric bolts were kept in waterproof barrels while the sump pump released copious amounts of rushing water that pooled in through the door at the end of the sloping driveway. Gilles got a commission to design the newest soon-to-be Mrs. Michael Crichton's wedding dress. *You know, he of Jurassic Park and West World fame.* The sun was shining and all was well. We started a college fund for Remy, which made us both feel responsible and adult. *I would have to say, that was a first.* We began to feel that we could hold our heads up once again. We had tripped and fallen hard. We were in recovery from being bruised and battered but hopefully we were now a lot wiser. The brilliant partner and wife of Salvatore Ferragamo, the famous shoe designer, gave each of her twenty-three grandchildren a silver doll with a weight at the bottom, so when it fell over it stood up again. This was to remind them not to be scared of failing. I was trying to do just that. The anvil-like weight from the shame and mortification that had brought us to our knees had begun to fall away. In spite of the dire warnings that we were to be completely locked out of the credit market for

Oops! I Forgot to Save Money

seven years with scarlet B's for BANKRUPT splashed across every known record of our former spending habits, warning all with power to SHUT US DOWN should we try to storm the gates of any department store or loan department, credit cards were thrown at us. They came in the mail on a regular basis. We wanted no part of them and cut them up, except for one, just for emergencies. It was necessary to have one credit card if we needed to rent a car or buy a plane ticket. Not that we were planning on going anywhere anytime soon. I was working really hard on separating want versus need.

In one of life's surprises, Evan's and my agent introduced us to a famous animator. He had an idea for a movie he wanted written. We hit it off. After pitching him our ideas for the screenplay, we were offered the job. The animation studio was in Dublin, Ireland. We had set the story in New Orleans. We could not believe how lucky we were. Both locations were beautiful, exciting and we were paid to spend time in both. We loved every day of our working experience and we were paid reasonably well for our time. *I guarded those pay checks like a grizzly protecting its cubs.* The movie was called 'All Dogs Go to Heaven' and it became a classic.

I lived in my lovely neighborhood of regular folk while all the moneyed folk lived just on the other side of those gilded tracks. They were flush with the kind of money that they thought nothing of tossing around. I tried to quash the midnight bouts of lurking envy. This was made especially hard given that my rebuilt bank account was whispering loudly that I deserved a splurge. Nothing big. I found myself wandering the Beverly Hills' golden triangle filled with all the glossy goodies on display in some of the most famous and pricey shops in the world. *Old habits really do die hard.* I strapped on my best, entitled persona and hit Neiman

Marcus. I circled the store like a shark in search of a juicy surfer to bite down on. I inhaled the scent of Eau de Affluence that permeated the air. After fifteen minutes of ogling and touching fabrics made of gossamer and angel's wings with price tags to match, I accepted that if I wanted to buy anything, I'd best be seeking out chum. I came home feeling virtuous with some deeply discounted thank you notes and a lipstick. Cruising the store "as if" seemed to have satisfied my hungry inner beast. *Possibly for a day - maybe. My addiction to pretty things needed to remain in remission.*

    Gilles was nothing like me in this regard. He required little. He wasn't ambitious or complicated. *He had me for that.* I always thought nothing would make him happier than to step back in time and work the land. He loathed waste. Gilles believed everything could be repurposed. Amazingly, with his magic touch, he delivered. Our much-admired home and countless others were filled with his stunningly recovered, rebuilt and reinvented pieces of furniture and found objects. Gilles had an eagle's set of eyes when it came to catching his favorite prey - the detritus tossed on the sidewalks by people with a need to upend everything when they grew tired of a certain color, shape or possibly a spouse. They would have been surprised and possibly tempted to buy back their castaways after Gilles was done turning them into covetable objects of desire.

    Out of the blue, Gilles' sister, who knew nothing of our recent financial spiral, called to tell us about an opportunity she wanted to make sure we got in on. Her husband had the inside track on an investment. He was a man I couldn't quite take to or trust. But he was my brother-in-law. I did my best to move beyond my feelings and listen to what she had to say. *Oh, oh... A person should never ignore the twinge in one's gut, whether it's for medical or intuitive reasons or if a relative comes a knocking* with a *'sure thing'. That feeling is demanding you pay attention.* The aptly named Dick was an accountant who made a lot of money from investments of one kind or another. He had invested heavily in a mine in Northern Quebec that was fully stocked with a mother lode of untapped gold. He laid out perfectly rendered specs, diagrams and videos to support his pitch. Two major mining companies were sinking a fortune into building the infrastructure to get the gold out. He wanted the family to be among the first to get in and get out with huge profits. Everyone in Gilles' family put money into this venture. The pressure to join them came at us with genuine excitement and conviction. Gold was flying very high then. We talked about the pros and cons. *I hear you even now screaming; "Don't do it!"*

Not only did we do it. We convinced several members of my family and a few friends to jump in too. We had just put our financial house in order but the seduction of hitting it big gripped us hard. We had drunk the Kool-Aid and were now as zealous as my sister-in-law. We were believers. *In hindsight, I feel grateful that we weren't being offered that Kool-Aid by a messianic cult leader. I wouldn't be here to tell my story.*

Trepidation crept in as we waited and waited, our anxiety on code red. We blindly repeated the lies that were told to us to those who had 'bought in' because we had bought in to the promise. We desperately wanted to believe the projections were true. There was always a reason to keep us dangling. More positive projections were presented. And still we waited for our ship to come in. Every dinner with family or friends became more and more awkward. We felt we had sabotaged our son's future. One couple we had brought in got a divorce. It wasn't only about the investment the wife had made but it was a contributing factor. He left. She got the house and a new pair of boobs. Both were very valuable assets. They didn't blame us, but we blamed ourselves. Still we wanted to believe even though the strand of hope was becoming more of an ever-thinning vapor trail. A couple of months later, this foolhardy episode was dead in the water. Excuses were made. "The mine was so deep, that even though it was filled with all the gold that had been promised, it could not be extracted without additional investments and partners experienced in newer excavation techniques could be found. Blah, blah, blahhhhhhhhhh!!" The brother-in-law was suddenly a megaphone gone silent. "Aaaarrrrggghhh!!"

My twin demons resurfaced and both were competing for top dog position, dueling for the takeover of my body and brain. As Pearl took dominance, I scrubbed and cleaned like a madwoman. Attempting to scour away my sins. Harriet fought back by having me swear like a storm trooper, while making sure to toss all of Pearl's work into chaos. My only escape was sleep.

I tossed and turned. I felt Gilles' was equally disturbed. We curled up together in joined fetal positions and finally fell into uneasy sleep. We were jolted awake at 4:31 a.m. by what sounded like a freight train accompanied by violent shaking.

EARTHQUAKE! It was a resounding metaphor to wake up to. I leapt from the bed and charged toward our son's bedroom. Bookshelves, books and breaking glass were raining down all around me but I didn't notice. I grabbed Remy into my arms and followed Gilles as we made our way down into the safety of the stairwell. The thunderous vibration sounded like a freight train coming off its rails and taking everything down with it. The shaking and the shrill, screaming choir of car alarms that followed went on and on. Remy seemed to be only mildly disturbed. He was safe in my arms watching the chaos, taking it in with the same pleasure he got from watching the destruction

Oops! I Forgot to Save Money

of a Lego block castle he had just kicked. Then came the sound of walls pulling away from their struts. Crazy fast moving cracks zigzagged across the stucco of our Spanish duplex. We could hear bricks and mortar hitting the ground. The inside fireplace pulled away from the wall and tumbled to the floor. The chimney outside could be heard ripping from its moorings, then the crashing of more bricks. Dishes, glassware and bottles filled with everything oily and sticky flew out from the wildly swinging cupboard doors and smashed to the ground. The piano careened across the floor, only blocked in its trajectory by a fallen armoire. We were most startled by the ringing of our phone. It was my sister nearly three thousand miles away wanting to know if we were okay. How did she know? It was seven thirty in the morning in Toronto and she was watching CNN when the bulletin that a six-point something earthquake had done major damage to parts of Los Angeles. I assured her we were fine. Our house was still standing but had sustained damage. Then the doorbell rang. It was a couple of friends and neighbors. It was still well before five a.m. in Los Angeles, but they knew no one was sleeping, not after that jolt. Soon enough other neighbors began to stop by. Even in the middle of a crisis we were the place to rally. Gilles picked his way through the rubble in the kitchen and put on the coffee. We rescued some broken cookies. The upended chairs were put upright and it was breakfast, albeit not quite as usual. Suddenly there was another violent shake. More crashing as things fell. The car alarms wailed once again in tandem with loud barking from every dog in the neighborhood making their presence known. We all held our collective breath. Then it stopped. None of us moved. There was an eerie silence. We were too afraid to open the door.

After a long period of calm, we all went to the door and looked out. Our street was full of people assessing the damage. There was so much of it. Most everyone had chimneys that had come down. Pieces of sidewalk and road had cracked and opened revealing dark deep holes or had pushed upwards, creating mini hills. One house looked like Godzilla had stomped over it. We were the lucky ones. In other neighborhoods, whole buildings had crumpled. Bridges were gone, People died.

It took months, possibly years to make good on all those insurance claims. We learned in those few minutes that life was precious and deserved to valued.

Note to Self – Part 1: Never give up hope. The timeline may not be exactly as you want but keep on doing the thing you love and believe that it will pay off.

Note to Self – Part 2: Never invest in a 'sure thing' without doing some serious investigating. Don't get suckered by glossy graphs and renderings and reams of glowing statistics. Anyone with computer skills can make those. Always beware of friends and family who 'know' a sure thing. There is no such thing as a 'sure thing' in investing. And never gamble with money you can't afford to lose. Do your due diligence. Learn about the product and check out the person doing the pitch. Get references and check that those people are legitimate. Learn to listen to your gut. As the old adage goes… "If it sounds too good to be true…it probably is!" Trust that it often knows better than your ego-driven head. As awful as this may sound, do a background check on your brother-in-law, uncle or co-worker. It's your job to protect yourself and your money. I learned the hard way… or so I thought.

Recommended Medication: Wine. Lots of wine.

CHAPTER 12

HAVING THE COJONES TO FACE UP TO FEAR AND FAILURE

The Cost: My dignity and the courage of my convictions.

Our many blessings surrounded us every day in every way.
Gilles and I marveled at the gift of our rock-solid marriage that always got better on the other side of the challenges that could have broken many. We had much to celebrate. In spite of that ill-conceived investment almost plunging us back into a financial sinkhole, we persevered. We had too much in the plus column to crush us; that was my daily mantra. I was determined to give myself over to living in gratitude for all I truly had. *It was a bit harder to live with the snake in the family grass that had conned us into investing in what turned out to be a bogus gold mine. The fact that he was always going to be sitting at the big family gatherings would be a test of how much grace I would be able to muster in order not to put a pillow over his face and a hex on his head!* I shoved all my angst into a sealed vault, deeply tucked away in some distant part of my inaccessible medulla. I had just come back from Vancouver where I had had a great time being in the first episode of the X-Files. I invested heavily in the joy I got from raising our beautiful, interesting and headstrong son. *Where could he have gotten that trait?* I also got unlimited

pleasure from trying to tame our equally headstrong and independent new dog, Balto. This husky was an endless source of amusement, frustration and expense. There was no lock he could not pick and no leash he could not untether. His love for running any and all golf courses made us frequently deny ownership. As loving as he was, he was also a wild thing who occasionally escaped to do unspeakable acts. The odd guinea pig or suddenly silenced singing bird snatched from its locked cage did give us more than a little anxiety. *Luckily he was never nailed as the culprit.*

Most of the parents at my son's school were wealthy and almost all were hugely generous people. When they threw parties for their kids, they were as lavish as Bahraini weddings. A basket of Apple stock was often the kind of birthday present that ten year olds were being given. Okay, the Apple stock wasn't in a basket – it came in the mail in the form of stock certificates. A cool first tattoo was more my speed. Those birthday parties surpassed excessive. The entertainment was often by magicians one had seen on television or on stage in Las Vegas where occasionally the children and nannies were flown along with the parents. Or there would be live animals. I'm not talking about those found in a petting zoo; more like those found in the Serengeti. These were for ten and eleven year olds! When our boy turned ten, we knew better than to try and compete. *As if...* Our one goal was to provide a gaggle of mostly overindulged kids a memorable and fun time. After much thought, and taking into account budgetary constraints, we opted to throw a party at a closed summer camp. We had pizza. We had cake and a cool cheerleader of a camp counselor who came to teach the kids archery. With their skills honed, he staged a full on battle with Nerf bows and arrows. Soon every child was armed and dangerous and in heaven. *Score 100 points for this Mom!*

I worried that living so close to all that wealth would potentially make our son feel that he was less worthy or feel envious. We were

Oops! I Forgot to Save Money

always clear that being wealthy is not a guarantee to living a happy life. We went out of our way to never make comparisons. It wasn't that we pretended the other half didn't have so much more in acreage and disposable income. Instead, we opted to celebrate our lives just as they were. We had great lives filled with friends, family and unexpected adventures. Wanting to travel the world is in my genes. Everyone in our combined families was born in another country. It made for quite a list including Scotland, England, Ireland, Austria, Hungary, California, and Quebec. Given my career as an actress, there were, sometimes, travel opportunities. Films and television shows are often shot in far-flung locations and out of the blue, I got an offer to go to New Zealand to shoot an episode of a televised Ray Bradbury story. My co-star to be, the wonderfully talented and incredibly kind John Glover, gave me his other first class ticket. This meant that Gilles and Remy could join us. Travelling on a production company's dime is a perk that doesn't come along often enough. When accommodation, meals and transportation are taken care of along with a few days off during the film-shooting schedule, it's a good as winning the lottery. We crammed as much sightseeing as humanly possible into those precious days. Given that New Zealand is on the other side of the world, we knew this was a rare and special opportunity. The people we encountered were amongst the friendliest and most helpful we had ever met, inviting us into their homes and feeding us. The sights were like nothing we had ever seen before: from steaming geysers to volcanoes. And the experiences ranged from learning how to shear sheep to climbing down through a cathedral-like cave to an underground lake where we experienced an unforgettable boat ride, the only light coming from thousands of glow worms that flitted like stars all around us.

The glory of experiential wealth reminds me of an acquaintance of mine, who talked often about the conflict of her upbringing versus the life she was currently living. Leah grew up in a moneyed world where everything was done for her. She told me that she had no idea how her dirty clothes would disappear and then reappear, cleaned, pressed and folded. Her parents gave her everything except a fiscal education. Tragically, they died young. Leah was left to figure things out on her own. She was raised in the high life and lived it, with no thought to the future until the money was gone. Even as an adult she continued to live life with no thoughts for tomorrow. She worked as a management consultant, work that she loved but never took too seriously. She married an accountant who did well but not well enough to support her ongoing lifestyle of travel and deluxe experiences. He wanted Leah to worry more about money but she didn't ever take her changed circumstances seriously. He often told her she was a bad influence on their kids but Leah truly believed in living in the now. In spite of her big spender ways, they were happy. Neither of their two children was given any kind of understanding about money or responsibility - an oddity given their Dad was an accountant. This is a true cautionary tale as both of her kids, now grownups, have made bad financial decisions. Both have children of their own and no jobs or responsible partners. At various times they have both come to live with their parents. Leah admits to having enabled them and even rewarded them for their bad behavior. She justifies it by saying she only does it because she wants to make sure her grandchildren are being taken care of.

One of the many ironies in her life is that a few years ago her CPA husband had to declare bankruptcy. Yet Leah is adamant that she has no regrets about choosing lifestyle above savings.

Oops! I Forgot to Save Money

She added that back during the 2009 stock market crash, when so many of their wealthier friends lost so much of their money, she felt that they had scrimped and saved and then lost it all, while Leah and her family had invested in a lifetime of experiences instead. Now they were even. Leah actually believes she came out ahead; she would always have her memories.

I asked Leah what the future might look like for her. At sixty-six, she now has a good job where she at last works to make money, but it doesn't come with a pension. If any unforeseen circumstances come their way, they are in trouble.

Leah says there's no point in living with regrets. Their circumstances are what they are. She wishes she had had the foresight to do this financial thing better but she didn't. There is a momentary twinge when she says, "I guess it didn't have to be an either or when it comes to having carved out a rich life. I could have travelled a bit less and saved a bit more but ... it's too late for the 'shoulda, coulda, wouldas.' My circumstances are what they are and I choose to be happy. I can't live with a bleak-house mindset." She and her husband buy lottery tickets every week, calling those outings 'work.' If they win they will have 'worked' for that money. Admittedly, my jaw dropped when she told me this. She laughs a bit and says, "I can only hope for that lottery ticket to make up for the 401k we don't have." When I ask her where she thinks she will be living in her golden years, Leah takes in a breath and says, "Hopefully one of my rich friends will give me one of their guesthouses." I felt more than a twinge of anxiety for her. It seemed like she may be banking on smoke and mirrors.

There are some things that one can't change no matter how many lessons are drilled into one's head. Those are the things that are at the very core of one's being. It may not be free will. Not everything is a choice. It may be DNA. Some things are just what they are; those traits that make us unique just like a fingerprint or a snowflake. They belong to no one but oneself. Coloring only inside the lines is not my forte. Thinking outside the box is the only way I know how to think. I'm not sure I even believe there is a box to think outside of. There are so many things on life's menu that I want to taste and try. One thing I do know, I don't like being boxed in.

Los Angeles was a company town where the favored currency was power, followed by youth and beauty. Being funny was also a commodity. I had just finished a pretty decent role in a film called Switching Channels, starring Kathleen Turner and Burt Reynolds when I was unexpectedly summoned to the offices of one of the most powerful and legendary show business managers, Bernie Brillstein. He had seen my demo-tape. *There's a term that is showing its age.* I walked through a set of imposing doors and was greeted with enormous warmth by one of the many assistants. Did I want water, coffee, whatever soft drink I could dream up? I was doing all that I could to not appear overtly impressed. I was soon ushered into the great star-maker's office where I was greeted by a bearded bear with a huge hug. Bernie was warm and yet still imposing. I sat opposite him, attempting to feel at home. After telling me he really enjoyed what he'd seen of me so far, he cut to the chase, asking me what I was hoping for regarding my career. I felt very confident in answering. "You know those actors who appear in a ton of movies and no one ever remembers their name but people always say, I love that actor or actress. That's who I want to be". Bernie's eyes locked onto mine and he said, "Let me see if I have this right. You're an actress but you don't want anyone to know your name?" I felt my spine stiffen and my righteous indignation begin to swell. "That's right. I want to have a career where I work a lot but don't carry the weight or responsibility of stardom but yet make enough money to live well. I want to travel and write… invent things and…" I caught his wide-eyed appraisal. I plunged onward. "I'm more interested in a well-balanced life. I think fame kills that." Bernie stood up, offered me his hand so that I too would get on my feet and before I knew it he had walked me back to those same imposing doors. "I am pretty sure that given what you are looking for, you are in the wrong office. I felt the door whisper closed behind me. I was not sure what had just happened. I felt angry about being dismissed. But I was sure I was right.

It took me four years to understand what I had done wrong. I woke one morning drenched in flop sweat. "I'm an idiot! I was invited into a room with the biggest deal-making manager in Hollywood, not in Des Moines or Toronto. I was supposed to say, I want to be a huge star. I don't want to grab at just any brass ring, I want the platinum package!" I didn't want to be a star. I wanted to be a working actor, a writer, a producer and an entrepreneur and that's what I am. All I have ever wanted was the opportunity to create, both ideas and experiences. More than money or fame, it's the only thing that keeps my battery fully charged. But when friends asked how my meeting went, I tossed my hair and held my head up high and lied through my teeth. "It wasn't a good fit. If one hotshot manager is that interested, there will be others." The truth was, I still wasn't ready to risk.

An extremely well-known actress was a close friend of mine for many years - so much so that she was the Maid-of-Honor at my wedding and I held a similar position in one of hers. She had a quality that was innately part of her being that I admired and perhaps even envied: ambition, along with a laser focus. She sought out roles that suited her and then figured out how best to go after them. Whenever possible she was determined to take her destiny into her own hands, never leaving anything to chance. She heard about a film that was to star Jean-Paul Belmondo, who was a huge star in France. They were looking for an actress who was fluent in both English and French. She came to my husband, Gilles, for help. She wanted him to work with her on the audition, so that her French would be impeccable. She spoke very little French but she didn't want anyone to know that. The audition was to be videotaped and she planned on only speaking French from the second she walked into that audition room and opened her mouth. To that end she had written a scripted greeting to Mr. Belmondo. She asked Gilles to translate it into phonic French, which she then memorized. She got the role! I admired her tenacity, work ethic and determination. It wasn't that I didn't work hard. I did. But I didn't have that burn to be 'the one'! Being a star was not on my radar

A small postscript to that story: She may have gotten the role but her French was never really good enough, so after the film was wrapped, a true French speaking actress was brought in to dub all of my ambitious friend's lines. C'est la vie!

∽

At night, I again went over and over the humiliation of being tossed out of that fancy Hollywood office as if I were an old apple core. I wasn't sleeping much. Instead of counting sheep to lull me into dreamland, I spent the night counting how much money we needed to live a modest but good life. I added. I subtracted. Essentials versus modest luxuries. Some people count sheep, I counted the money in our separate accounts, the money I stashed in various pockets and other hiding places. I counted over and over again. It never added up. Mostly my dreams were haunted by thoughts of how possibly I could have been the next Rosanne with all the trimmings that went with being a huge star…If only I had said that. If only I had wanted that. I tossed and turned, still adding and subtracting, mostly the latter. *Yup, that 'never let them see you sweat' thing was a total smoke screen to fool people into thinking everything was always fine. Just fine… Liar!*

Times were tough. Some did well in our circle but more did not. None of us had that mystical superpower of being able to see into the future. If we did, it might have saved us from making mistakes but it also would have wrenched open the doors to unforeseen illnesses, accidents, broken hearts and funerals we couldn't have imagined attending. There's no pleasure in watching friends going through hard times. *I'm willing to bet no one knew about ours. Until now…*

∾

Frances Fisher, the wonderful actress best known for playing Kate Winslet's mother in 'Titanic', shared with me recently that, in spite of being a very recognizable actress, who is regularly seen on film and television, she is far from rich. This was a surprising and honest admission. Frances is bold and doesn't hold back. She went on to explain that back in the day, meaning up until about fifteen years ago, it was easier for the middle class actor to make a living, and have their agent negotiate salary increases based on an ever growing profile. An individual actor's *payout was known as his 'quote' and a well-known name was considered a valuable asset in giving a project cache, or attracting eyeballs or advertising dollars. One starring role on a television movie could make for a good year. One of those in conjunction with guest starring roles on well-known series could make up for lean years. If the actor was disciplined, those roles paid enough to allow them to create a safety net. Out of nowhere, those days came to an end. It seemed like all the producers, networks and movie and television studios collectively decided they didn't have to continue to pay actors their quotes. They banded together to fight the actors' unions resulting in a gradual shift to 'take it or leave it' offers. Our unions didn't protect us. This meant that middle-class actors, if they were lucky may have enjoyed the rare $100,000 year, and could then afford to own a home and have stability, including padding for when jobs were scarce. Today, for the same amount of work, their take home pay is likely to be under $50,000 and still needs to spread out over those lean years.*

Being a working actor is no longer a safe zone. Luckily for Frances, she is a saver but is well aware that the stash she has put away is not going to last, given the long lives we anticipate. Yet, wherever she goes, she is recognized, the perception being that she must be wildly wealthy. That status is reserved for what has become known as the twenty million dollar club. They are the stars that we all see on the covers of magazines, while standing at the checkout counter of our grocery stores, as we try to distract ourselves from the rising cost of everything.

∽

I wore a mask painted with a smile to every public function. If you were a really close friend, you could probably smell my fear

Oops! I Forgot to Save Money

but to the bigger world, it was all 'never let them see you sweat', a shake of my blonde hair and "Things are fabulous darling…" And then I scurried as far away as possible. Other friends were more honest, or their financial hits were just that much more obvious. I had several friends who could no longer hold onto their houses. The banks took them back or they sold them under market value just to get out while there was still a little to squeeze out beyond their overextended mortgages. I lamented about never being in the housing market. My friend Kerrie made it very clear that she thought we were the lucky ones. Her house had been decimated in the earthquake. Getting it put back together was as complex a job as putting Humpty Dumpty back together after his great fall but far more expensive and never ending. One of my dearest friends used her house as a piggy bank to pay off predatory creditors but it emptied out faster than she could have imagined and it was soon foreclosed on. It was harder to feel sorry for her. I had one friend who pinged from one financial disaster to another. She woke up every morning with the question, "What shit is life going to throw at me now?" That question upset me to my core. I felt and said that she was creating the outcome with the power of her thoughts. I worked very hard to remain positive and keep my fears at bay. *It wasn't always easy but I know as sure as I wear a size 9 1/2 shoe that our thoughts create our reality.* Whether you're trying to save money or get out of debt, the first step to realizing your financial goals begins in your mind.

It was around this time that the studios – those giants of the silver screen that had been legendary entertainment providers – like Disney, Warner Brothers, MGM, Universal, began to acquire television networks, magazines, and news corporations. Or was it the other way around? Either way, they became multi-national conglomerates with loyalties to shareholders and CEO's. Jobs were lost as companies streamlined to survive the mergers. It was hard to see friends losing their positions. Many highly paid executives found themselves reeling from unexpected dismissals. One good friend who lost his secure, high-paying gig was not only financially unprepared, his equilibrium was decimated as he went from having a daily phone sheet full of calls to having next to none. The shock of losing one's identity along with your status and self worth probably is a normal consequence of losing a power position that can supply work to others but there is no faster plummet to oblivion than the one that happens in Hollywood.

The truth be told, being out of work was not as scary for me. I was used to it and I knew how to navigate the feast and famine better than those who have always counted on a regular salary. But the essence of Hollywood had changed. It used to be a place where 'everyone knew your name'. Now, in this age of acquisition, with Internet companies taking over movie studios, everything was product and nobody was irreplaceable.

Note to Self: Know what you really want and who you really are. If it's a career choice, make sure you find out all the pitfalls and if you still want it, make sure you have the goods to become successful. Be kind; make yourself indispensable and always go the extra mile. Today's temp could one day become your boss. In my case, yesterday's assistant became my theatrical agent and he still is. Don't let money rule your emotions. Resentment, jealousy and envy are the trinity of the insecure. Above all, be prepared to withstand the ups and down's of the occasional sinkholes that threaten all our lives.

Recommended medication: Caviar for the ambitious, fish sticks for the rest of us.

CHAPTER 13

THE QUESTION OF NEED VERSUS WANT PUSHED ME TO WANT ALL OF IT

The Cost: $650 for blowing the opportunity to learn money management.

The beginning of the Millennium came loaded with panic scenarios. We were ending 1999 and the rumors of impending doom were spreading like a freeway-jumping firestorm. Something called Y2K was going to rain catastrophic hell down on all our computers if we didn't shut them down, burn them or send them to rehab. Scaremongering from the media and 'experts' was rampant. *Rolling my eyes in mock surprise.* Our response was to throw caution to the wind. *A recurring theme as a life choice, it appears.* We invited all our favorite people and everyone brought a candle. We placed them across our lawn to read a defiantly optimistic '2000'. We laughed, sang and enjoyed a wonderful dinner accompanied by lots of champagne as we spoke aloud our wishes for the next century. Even though I wanted to wish for a much thinner body, I let that one go for a more new-century selfless response. World peace was asking for too much. I went for kindness that would ripple out to all we knew and all that they knew and on and on – it was similar to a financial crowd funding campaign but one that would fund the heart on the seeding and growing of love. *In my head I was still wishing for a smaller body and a bigger bank account.*

Only when the clock turned to January 01, 2000 was it revealed to be much ado about nothing. As with all beginnings of a new year, resolutions were made but rarely kept. Mine was to stop all needless spending. It felt powerful to put that into the universe. I obviously forgot that I had made the same resolution last year. I made a list and I was astonished by it's length and truth.

Lattes – *The inflammatory cost of the addition of foamed milk was insane.*

Lipsticks – *I already had every pink and red ever made but there was always a new shade of peony that would call out my name and I needed to resist.*

Shoes – *Always pretty but guaranteed to pinch or topple me so what's the point?*

Hardcover books – *Libraries offer them for free.*

Magazines – *A glossy expense that can be found on the Internet.*

Restaurants – *Meals often not prepared as well as what we made in our kitchen for far less. But I'll give them marks for presentation.*

Baubles, bangles & beads – *One neck, two wrists, two ears. 'Nuff said.*

Lotions and potions – *Guaranteed to break their promises and my bank account.*

Bottled water – *The greatest scam ever perpetrated on humans and the worst thing to happen to the environment.*

Exercise equipment – *Wishful thinking. Definitely useful for hanging clothes on.*

Clothing – *The lure of pretty colors that often guaranteed instant humiliation in the 'as-if' part of my closet.*

Scarves – *I already owned a thousand of those, because they always fit!*

Things on Sale – *Seem like a good idea at the time but usually come under the heading of useless gluttony.*

Chocolate – *Not up for discussion. It stays!*

I was determined to keep my promise to ditch all things unnecessary and to cut back on the celebratory or therapeutic spending. *This was akin to promising to do one hundred one-armed push-ups every other day.*

I found out I was to do a guest spot on ER. I had auditioned for the show several times and finally I got cast. *Often acting can be a numbers game, and perseverance pays off.* I was so excited. My storyline interacted with Juliana Margulies and the divine Mr. George Clooney. I knew I was going to be playing someone with a rare disease. I hoped that it wouldn't require red blotches or some bizarre loss of hair. I wanted to look as good as possible for George. *Yes, I was well aware I was married and happily but we are talking George Clooney! This was long before Amal captured his heart. He was still in his serial dating phase. A girl can dream.* I went to my trailer to put on my wardrobe, only to discover that my costume was a shapeless hospital gown. That wasn't the bad part. Most of the guest stars on the show wore those. My disease was so rare that I couldn't be exposed to any potential pathogens so I had to wear a full-face gas mask... the entire time. It's not possible to flirt while wearing a gas mask! As if it would have produced a different result. Both Juliana and George were lovely and kind. *George was lovelier.* The scenes were done so fast, there was no time for the witty repartee that I had practiced over and over in order to have a chance of impressing either of them, but really for George. And just like that, it was over. Two weeks later, my check arrived. Of course, I celebrated by taking Gilles and Remy for an expensive dinner. *You can lead a horse to water but....*

Like a recovering addict, I was determined to climb back on the money-saving train. I asked Gilles if he wanted to take advantage of the inexpensive adult-education money-management classes at Beverly Hills high school. He had no interest. He was sure that he could manage better than he had before. I wasn't so sure. Uncharacteristically, I didn't gang up on him. I needed to find out how I could be smart about some things and so stupid about others. I asked my best guy-friend if he would go with me. I couldn't face it or myself alone. Trevor was a very successful television executive but ricocheted from being overly extravagant to being worried he'd end up in the poor house. He was looking for some financial balance and agreed to come with me. Without a second thought I whipped out that damn credit card and paid for both of us. *Breaking bad habits was proving harder than I thought.*

The misnomer was the phrase 'adult education'. Like the former bored students we had both been back in the day, we automatically sat at the back of the room so we could whisper, gossip and giggle at the insanity of us being in this classroom in the first place. A youngish, but anemic former bank manager was explaining the fundamentals of finance. Papers with what appeared to be hieroglyphics were passed around. Endless graphs appeared on a power-point presentation. Our much more committed classmates were scribbling notes in their new, shiny notebooks. I tried to focus but my head began to hurt as the bank manager who loved his new center-of-attention platform droned on and on. I strained to understand the numbers and flow charts in front of me. My eyelids were getting heavy. I forced myself to listen and try to make sense of the endless algorithms. BANG! It was like a heavy wooden door slammed shut, followed by a clanking drawbridge being pulled up. I heard the sound of heavy metal locks closing. Then my brain died. I felt an insane need to sleep. My whole being was rejecting this life-giving organism called money-management. I managed to look at Trevor who seemed to be exhibiting the same symptoms. Our eyes met. Simultaneously we rolled our eyes. Stress induced giggles began, erupting into unexplainable convulsions. We had the attention of the entire class and highly irritated teacher. Unable to stop snorting and laughing, we tried to shut up and avoid each other's determined efforts to break the other up. But with one sliver of eye contact, it was game over. We bolted from that room. My remedial fiscal education endeavor came to an end in a hail of audible class and instructor disapproval.

Money is like a magic trick that some people are able to figure out instantly and others, like me, take far longer to puzzle over to try to make sense of. *If ever.* And there's little help for those of us in the latter category. If politics and religion are dinner-table hot potatoes, then money is that 'never to be discussed in public' pebble in our shoe. No subject is more mystifying and secretive than money-talk. *Maybe baseball statistics...* I knew I had to crack the code to move forward but it wasn't going to happen if the teachers in charge of the code put their knowledge out there with all the personality of peeling paint.

When I was young I had one of those china piggy banks that couldn't be dipped into unless you smashed it. Whenever my mother or her blue-haired friends played bridge, they'd put their winnings (small change) into that pig as long as I remembered to empty their overflowing ashtrays, fill their sherry glasses and replenish the large plate of vanilla Knipfel and other strangely named Viennese cookies. As soon as their mink and Persian lamb coats were on, the flowered scarves tied carefully around their heavily lacquered hairdos, I picked up piggy and shook it, desperately wanted to know how much money was in there. I was often tempted to smash it into smithereens but I liked its sweet face. I couldn't do it. After a few months, that piggy bank was getting seriously heavy. My mother couldn't believe I hadn't hurled it to the ground. I couldn't either. I think I liked having some money tucked away in a safe place. Too bad I forgot that feeling as an adult. But no longer. I had a whole new resolve. Having participated in my own follies along with watching how so many others had struggled with debt and misguided spending, I was determined to find out what was at the root of my cavalier attitude to money. If I couldn't get the lessons I needed from a boring and bad teacher, I needed to act as if. I had to become the person I wanted to be. It was time to take charge of my life and become conscious of where and what I was spending my money on. We were debt free. I was determined; no matter whether it was a full-flush month or a junk-hand month of earnings, I would put money into a savings account every month.

Isobel and Raymond were a couple that Gilles and I had come to know pretty well. I always found it interesting that when we went out for dinner, Ray and I inevitably squared off in a variety of jousts over everything from politics to religion. We both enjoyed our sparring. During these battles, Gilles seemed to spend his time counseling Isobel on the rifts she often experienced with various family members or friends. Isobel was a very attractive woman but back in the day, she had been a great beauty. She had an ethereal quality that made men weak in the knees. She was courted and supported and never had to want for anything. But as she aged, there were fewer admirers and patrons. She hadn't planned for the future. She had always counted on others to take care of her. She never learned any marketable skills. She became bitter and resentful that her life had not turned out the way she had expected. Ray was her second husband and had never quite lived up to her expectations. She had settled. Nothing was ever quite good enough. She adopted a defeated attitude, always expecting the worst to happen and did what she could, perhaps unconsciously, to help push it to the brink.

Ray was a modestly successful engineer and no angel but he did love Isobel. He had known for some time that he had had enough and when he finally couldn't take her complaining any longer he left. To his credit, he left her well fixed. She got a beautiful house that included a rental property as part of their settlement. Isobel was shocked at her new state of affairs. Sadly, she never outgrew her resentment or attachment to Ray. She pulled a variety of victim-like behaviors to try to get his attention She took several sleeping pills, almost overdosing. She continually cried poor (which she wasn't), eventually taking a hefty mortgage on her house because she was too distraught to hold down a job to keep on top of the upkeep. She decided, in one of a series of grass-grows-greener moves, that she would move to San Francisco where her sister lived

In order to make herself feel better - but really to impress the sister she didn't really like - Isobel rented a penthouse apartment in a prestigious part of the city. She then spent a large amount of the money she had made by selling her house on renovating her rented apartment. Isobel still had no job. She was always jealous of her sister's big career and happy marriage and this was her way of proving that she too was successful. The question that came to nearly everyone's mind was, "Who renovates a rental? That's just throwing money away!"

Isobel, now fifteen years since her divorce, is a sad and lonely woman who has no money and is filled with bitterness that others seem to have better lives. And, sadly, Isobel's story is not unique.

∞

Note to Self – *Part One:* Most mistakes are fixable. The way forward in life is to have a hard look at those mistakes and see if there's a pattern that keeps showing up. Using your house as a piggy bank will inevitably drain most people's biggest asset. If that money is not reinvested, your cash cow is gone. Beware the 'Line of Credit' and reverse mortgage!

∞

Carole was raised in a very traditional upper-middle class way. Her parents had extremely high expectations for her success and she didn't disappoint. She worked hard and became a doctor. Her mother was a stay-at-home mom. Her father was a lawyer. What Carole didn't know was that her father, who had come from very little, always felt the pressure to keep up with the far better off family of his wife. What neither mother nor daughter knew, was that he was a gambler. He gambled hard to augment his salary so that he could be 'the big man' in the eyes of his family and friends. When he lost, he borrowed more and his debts grew, but he always bragged that his daughter was going to be a rich woman when he was gone. He showed Carole an eighty thousand dollar check made out in her name that he was putting into an investment account. It did make money, but when Carole got married and went to find out how much she now had to contribute to buying her first house, she discovered it was all gone. Her father had dipped into it on a regular basis. He could have been disbarred, but he begged forgiveness and promised he would give it all back. Unbeknownst to her mother, he took out a second mortgage on their house. At a family dinner, he magnanimously handed his daughter and new son-in-law a check for twenty thousand dollars to use to furnish their new home. That was the only money Carole got. When her mother discovered the true extent of his fraud, she left him, knowing that if she were to survive, she would need to protect whatever was left.

***Note to Self** – Part Two:* When there is a gambler in the family, it affects everyone, especially when it is a hidden problem. There is confusion and lies about the family's finances, which can result in serious psychological, emotional, social and often legal problems. That web of deceit can ultimately unravel a family.

Recommended medication: Vanilla Knipful. Don't knock it till you have tried a couple of dozen of these white sugarcoated, melt in your mouth cookies. Whatever ails you is soon lost in a sugar coma.

CHAPTER 14

MONEY VS. ENVY, NOT ENOUGH OF ONE AND TOO MUCH OF THE OTHER

The Cost: Saying no does not always come easily to those who like to say yes.

We moved to another beautiful Spanish duplex a short block away from our first Beverly Hills home. It had a gated courtyard dominated by an enormous weeping willow tree. It took my breath away. The previous tenants were good friends who were moving back to New York. They had given us glowing references to the landlord who, magically and mysteriously didn't raise the rent when we moved in. It was in a real neighborhood where people knew and liked each other. But it still wasn't quite like other places. On my right lived an actual Playboy centerfold - at that time a witness in the very high-profile O.J. Simpson murder trial. On my left, a blindingly beautiful single mom with a pair of gorgeous multinational kids who looked like they had fallen out of a J Crew catalogue. Right upstairs from us lived the triple threat: three beauties who scampered about in the smallest of everything, much to my teenage son's delight. *If I had looked like they did, I would have been dressed or undressed much as they were. And I would happily have gone grocery shopping dressed that way too.* It soon became apparent that not all of their gifts were entirely genetic. In more than one conversation, I was instructed about how much it cost to look the way they did, leaving me slack-jawed. As it turned out, these women were all on the darkest side of thirty. *That was probably a lie.* It still didn't console me. Their monthly maintenance costs were staggering. I'd need scaffolding and a gold bar or two to afford the team of artisans they employed. At the end of it all, my ribs would still be buried under a layer of fat, camouflaging the much-coveted convex stomach I would never have.

The other side effect of living in Beverly Hills was the constant cover up of envy. I admit to having more than a touch of green about others being able to afford what I can't. I may not be jealous about those who can drop an enormous amount of money on some designer purse - I don't even carry a purse. I like pockets. These conflicted feelings harken back to growing up with a mother who created a faux-wealthy façade. When the scrim fell away, I was left with a sense of betrayal. And I wondered who I would be if I did have that kind of wealth. *Definitely a traveler!* The wealthy people I admire the most are those that are not seduced or beguiled by their money. They are sensible and sane in the ways they take care of their financial wellbeing. They also enjoy their money. They don't worship it. It doesn't make them all that they are.

I recently read a money advice book about how to maximize your potential for super saving, guaranteeing a very healthy and wealthy retirement plan. It was filled with advice about buying cheaper cuts of meat and day old bakery items, making one's own coffee or meatless lasagna, getting a roommate to split the rent, staying in to watch movies on a streaming site. Sometimes – yes! Always – no! That's not the life I'd want to lead. I think balance is more my goal. I'm not saving just for my retirement. I also want to enjoy the ride getting there. I feel moderation is a good

Oops! I Forgot to Save Money

idea but occasional splurges don't fall under the heading of failure. And I do understand that if one is in debt, then far stricter measures are required.

Christmas was approaching when a friend said she had found an affordable four-day jaunt to Cabo San Lucas that was also suitable for kids. We jumped up and down at the opportunity. It was only a two-hour flight. I was pretty sure it would do the trick to stick a cork in my travel jealousy.

We were but one of many happy and boisterous families thrilled to be on a getaway to sun, sand and fun. We were barely off the plane when we, along with every other passenger, were swarmed by rabid hustlers closing in on our personal space, waving endless promotions, promising everything from free drinks to expensive dinners and free nights if we were willing to sit through a short film showcasing a variety of the 'best' new condos and time shares. We girded ourselves against all the noise, determined not to get suckered by these relentless predators. We leapt into a taxi that would take us to paradise. We almost made it out of there but my single-mother girlfriend Sasha had been seduced by a particularly good-looking huckster. We waited and waited. My perpetually patient and good-natured husband was ready to murder her when Sasha, flushed with the possibility that she had found the love of her life - well, at least for the next few days - jumped into the cab, smugly waving a four hundred dollar voucher for our New Year's Eve dinner at a well-known Cabo restaurant.

It wasn't until we were lounging on our sunbeds, jumbo margaritas in hand, watching our boys having the best time along with an international scrum of other teens, that Sasha casually mentioned that our dinner voucher would only become activated after we had listened to a teeny presentation in a nearby hotel.

The added bonus... it was happening early the next morning, the day of New Year's Eve. Gilles was having none of it. But I fell right into line, suckered by the free dinner vouchers. *What the hell is wrong with me? I know there's no such thing as a free lunch...or dinner.*

A dull-tequila throbbing pain pounded in my head, as I stood grudgingly in a queue of likewise tired, hung-over fools. Sasha was fully made up and wearing her best sexy-morning wear, almost giddy in anticipation of seeing Luis, the Hispanic hunk she was intending to marry, or at the very least spend the next three nights with. The doors opened and we were shuttled into a utilitarian presentation room, masked with colorful piñatas. Thankfully, coffee was poured and overflowing baskets of fresh Danish pastries were placed on every table. A fairly innocuous presenter laid out the rules. We couldn't leave the room until the presentation video was over! We were to hold our questions until our consultant came to sit with us, when he or she would helpfully share his or her knowledge. Warning flares pierced through my headache. Sasha was oblivious as she scanned the room looking for her Luis. The video droned on and on. The video zoomed in on rooms with beds that looked like every other resort room with beds. *They all have the same amount of wicker and tropical colors and those weird towel-swans on them; they're all surrounded by infinity pools, Jacuzzis, several acres of hyper-pigmented green golf courses, dining rooms a go-go, and on and on.* And in every shot there seemed to be a stunning bathing suit wearing, much-in-love couple, frolicking hand-in-hand. I was done and dying a slow death. But I knew that the suffering would continue, so I ate ten more Danishes – *killing all chance of wear a bathing suit.* I drifted into my sugar-induced coma, only snapping back when an aggressively smiling Scotsman in an ill-

Oops! I Forgot to Save Money

fitting seersucker suit sat down with his clipboard in hand. He introduced himself as Jock. *A suit in Vacationland*! He was here to sell. He was talking nonstop about the amenities, the climate, and the instant camaraderie we'd have with others just like us. *Yes, they who got snookered into buying.* He had a practiced smarmy charm. I tried interrupting. He was immune. I tried a bout of easy-to-access hostility. He was still talking and talking. I closed my eyes and thought of the huge plate of nachos I was going to eat when I was released from this prison. I opened my eyes. Jock was leaning in to close the deal, pointing at where our signatures should go. Battle-worn and exhausted, I couldn't take one more second of the pummeling. I whipped out my credit card, as did a broken-hearted Sasha that her Luis was a no show. And just like that – SHAZAM! We owned a bloody time-share. The Scot was smiling and quiet… At last!

Houston, I think I have a problem. *What the hell was wrong with me?* I settled on having suffered a severe case of backsliding due to the non-stop pressure from a relentless salesperson. No one should be cudgeled into buying anything. Sober and furious, my war with the Mexican authorities was on, as was both Sasha's and my relentless mind-numbing battle with our credit card companies. I knew that in North America there was a three-day 'buyer's remorse' clause that would allow one to back out of an impetuous purchase. The vacation timeshare company put me on hold, while an extended torturous version of the Mexican Hat Dance played over and over. I was then transferred and transferred to anyone who could pass the buck until my ears couldn't take another second of the pain, which was their desired result. I fell into a rabbit hole of bureaucracy as I tried to find the person who would get Sasha and me out of this coerced purchase. I hit one brick wall after another until a kindly official told me I was wasting my time. Mexico didn't have such a thing as a cooling off period in which to change my mind. He added that there would be no timeshare business if they had that!

Both Sasha and I were exhausted from the runaround and frustrated that we had succumbed to being bulldozed. We were determined to not let it ruin the rest of our time in Cabo. The misadventure of buying a timeshare was temporarily put on hold. Let the surfing begin! We packed in everything that a great beach vacation had to offer.

Everyone came home tanned, guacamole fulfilled and happy – other than that gnawing voice inside my head that was still angry from being seduced. I was up before the crack of dawn with my credit card company explaining what had happened. I wanted them to cancel my fifteen hundred dollar deposit. They explained why they couldn't, but I wasn't having it. I asked to speak to a supervisor. After getting nowhere with the next person, I kept on moving up the food chain asking for the person who could cancel the deposit. I finally was put through to some department that I had never heard of. I remained calm as I retold my story for what seemed like the hundredth time. The part I left out was how easy it was for that wily coyote to bring this lamb to slaughter. To my shock and awe – It was handled instantly. POOF! The charge was reversed and it was now in the credit card company's hands. The woman I spoke to said it was her pleasure to right this wrong. They would deal with the timeshare company. It wasn't the first or sadly the last time they would hear this story. I wanted to hug her. Instead, I asked her to spell her name and followed up by writing a glowing note to the head office about her professionalism and compassion. Determination and persistence are necessary but sometimes it also requires the appearance of angels.

Sadly, Sasha could not get her credit card company to do the same. And I couldn't do it for her, as they would only deal with the actual cardholder. I'm not sure she was as insistent as I was.

It was back to life as usual. Gilles was off with Remy on a hunt for something he desperately needed for a school project. No one loved the thrill of the hunt for something obscure and inexpensive that could then be repurposed to make something amazing as both my husband and son did. I didn't have the patience to scour for the hours and hours they did.

I returned home from an awkward TV studio meeting with my writing partner. Evan had the pretentious habit of reflecting similar experiences back to whichever producer we were meeting with. It made me uncomfortable. I always felt it was a transparent form of sucking up. If the producer said he was heading to Florida for the holidays, Evan would say, "What part of Florida?" No matter where the producer said, Evan would immediately nod knowingly and then say, "Oh, that's where my parents winter." I could feel my eyes roll… Evan's parents were long gone. It was the same scenario, different suck-up at any and all meetings where there was a possibility of future work. I often felt embarrassed, but I did learn a great deal from our working together. We had had our share of successes but we shared disappointments too. That's simply the nature of living and working in Hollywood. We were a really good writing team if the only thing that we were to be measured by was our writing. But I came to see that our personal styles were in constant conflict. I had been feeling that way from the beginning although I kept making excuses, as I didn't want to rock our boat. But the things that bothered me were too important. Evan's integrity was often on a slippery slope. He always exaggerated the state of our careers making us sound as if we had many films on the go. He lied so easily, I found myself feeling queasy. Gilles often remarked that he never saw me as stressed as when I would see

Evan walking up the pathway to our front door. That can only happen if one knows something is wrong but continues to go along regardless. But it was when I found out he had been working with another writer and didn't tell me about it, that I knew that I was done. Ours wasn't a marriage, but we were a team. Given that he had kept it such a secret, it was the same as if he had cheated on me. I figured this betrayal was a cosmic exit visa. It's never easy to break up any kind of partnership, particularly when you have ongoing and shared product; it's almost impossible to lay claim to who did what. It's agonizing to have to start over. It would require creating a new body of work as well as constantly answering the questions about why we broke up. I simply chose to say that I wanted to find my own voice. That was true but really I could no longer partner with someone who was so ethically on such a different page. It was also terrifying to commit to going it alone.

I showed up at my desk every morning as usual. I sat there gazing out the window not sure what I was supposed to do. Ideas were not my problem. I had too many of them and they were all competing with one another for my sole attention. It felt like a massive freeway pile-up resulting in a gridlock of ideas. This went on for a few weeks. I would start one outline and then another idea would leap to the front of the queue. I prayed for writer's block just to stop my brain from exploding. I missed the back and forth as we spewed ideas. In those moments I worried that I had made a mistake leaving Evan.

I was temporarily saved when a good friend of mine, Barnet, also a writer, said that he wanted me to meet a woman who he thought would be a perfect writing partner for me. I wasn't sure that I wanted to get attached again but my friend was insistent that I meet her. Her name was Nancey and we arranged to meet at a nearby restaurant. It was almost love at first sight when this extremely pregnant woman with a wide-open smile and an even more open heart, sat down across from me. Nancey was funny, self-effacing and was blessed with a pragmatic wisdom that totally appealed to me. We immediately agreed to work together.

We met several times and tossed around ideas. We wrote one script together and it was a good and joyful experience. But it dawned on both of us, almost at the same time, that we wanted to work alone. We wanted to be free to express our own voices. I no longer remember which one of us found a writers' boot camp where we would meet once a week to create our own screenplay. It was the best thing for both of us. I needed that swift kick to move forward on my own. The discipline and camaraderie from having to show up and show our work to a whole room of writers was exciting and terrifying and it ultimately proved to be the foundation for both of our future careers. The added bonus was that Nancey and I remain the closest of friends to this day. I was never afraid to write alone after that all-consuming boot camp. In fact, it is the air that I breathe. I love the discipline of looking at a blank page and then spinning words into stories. Risk really is its own reward.

Note to Self: It was good to see that at least some of my new found financial direction had begun to take hold, but so bad to know I could still be tempted. The struggle of saying no doesn't come easily to those who prefer to say yes. Learn the difference between wanting and needing. We needed a new car desperately. Ours was twelve years old and falling apart. We bought one… but only when we could afford it. And then we paid for it in full! Yay. Being rich may look great and it may well be happiness for some, but never envy anyone's life. You have no idea what troubles they may have that are more serious than your own.

Recommended Medication: Tequila on the rocks or in your mouth straight from the bottle. The perfect relaxant after having a rotten day.

CHAPTER 15

SECURITY AT LAST, BUT NOT WITHOUT READING THE FINE PRINT

The Cost: Sleepless nights and fingernails nibbled down to the quick.

The need for freedom to follow my creative muse wherever it takes me does feed my soul, if not always my bank account. Some people have no choice regarding the jobs they do; they simply have to have a reliable paycheck in order to survive. At the rate most women are underpaid, they sometimes need to work two jobs to put food on the table and pay for childcare. I am well aware that not everybody gets to do what makes him or her happy. I feel blessed in that department in spite of the risks that come with it. I know that no matter who you are or what your job is, we all go through hard times of one kind or another, often making us feel anxious, scared, and depressed that we will never come through these difficult times. Having faced the shock and humiliation of bankruptcy, I know that it's possible to climb out of a black hole and reclaim the future. I had made many changes and was feeling whole once again. I put money into a savings account with the same regularity as I now paid all bills. I was still in shock that it had taken me so long to get this elemental bit of practicality through my thick skull.

Growing up, most of my generation were told if we fussed or didn't finish our dinners that there were starving people in a variety of countries who would be grateful if they were given even half of what we had on our plates, even if it was only every other day. And much as we rolled our eyes and hated to hear it, it was true. Even more so today. But in this era of concierge parenting, every home in the affluent west may as well have menus on the tables. Each child is overly catered to. "Brooklyn, what would you like for dinner tonight? What about you Presley?" Am I being judge-y? I come from another time. We kids didn't get a vote. We got what was served to us. I ate what was on my plate. *And what anyone left on theirs.* Choice wasn't on the menu.

I understand times change. But we are supposed be living in the age of enlightenment. It feels more like the age of conspicuous consumption and waste.

I am shocked about what we so cavalierly throw away: from food, plastic everything to disposable cheap clothing. Having everything gets us nothing but bigger problems. The cost to the environment will cost all of us.

Alexandra and Lindsay Lorusso, twins in their early thirties, grew up in the waste management industry. Their father owned a thriving company dedicated to the disposal of waste. It seems serendipitous that they took this knowledge and parlayed it into Nudnik, a company they built from the ground up to combat fashion waste. Companies like Burberry, along with other fashion giants, burn everything unsold. The global fashion industry is the second largest polluter next to big oil. So much of the cheap, fast fashion is made of a mix of synthetics and natural fibers, creating the same problem as the simple to-go coffee cup. The lid is made of plastic; the cup itself is made of paper but with a plastic liner making it nearly impossible to recycle. Tossed into landfill, the sheer volume is catastrophic to the environment.

Lindsay and Alexandra are uniquely qualified to understand how the disposal of fast, cheap fashion is just as hazardous as throwing plastic into the ocean. They are committed to changing the status quo. Self-funded, along with a small bank loan and hard work, they went directly to the source of where most of the fashion waste is found - Bangladesh and China. They made deals with the factories for their waste material, saving the producers' disposal costs. Nudnik then turns it into sustainable, repurposed fashion for children. Their innovative approach has won them grant money, allowing them to expand their operation. Theirs is truly a story of turning trash into treasure.

∽

Happily, 66% of Millennials are more motivated to buy quality garments from ethical brands. The emergence of clothing swaps and DIY wardrobe hacks indicates an increased consciousness. Just like when shopping for food, we are becoming educated to read labels and see what things are made of. But the lure of cheap fashion seems to have superseded common sense for many. A thousand designs a week are offered online for next to no money. They are on trend but are not made to last, ultimately costing us huge money. Cheap is not the answer. Buying too much is an epidemic. Throwing things away hurts us all. And it does nothing to grow our bank accounts.

I have always felt I lived a charmed life, money or no money. I have been lucky in so many ways, *my short stumpy legs notwithstanding*. I have a great family when they are not driving me to eat. *Oh... that's not their fault.* I am always gobsmacked when the well is in danger of drying up and out of the blue, the phone will ring, or there will be a knock from above and a new opportunity arises. I am always ready to step through that door and step up to the challenge. Or at least, I fake it until I get it.

    I finished my first solo screenplay, Big Mouth. *Not an autobiography even though it would be a perfect title.* I had just given it to my literary agent when I was given a book to read by a friend. She thought I'd enjoy it. It was a first novel from a wonderful writer. The book was called Hunger Point. It told the story of two sisters, one of whom triumphs over her own self-destructive tendencies (anorexia). It offered a powerful and most human exploration of the complex relationships that bind together a contemporary American family. I knew immediately it would make a terrific television movie. Evan and I had sold a couple of our original television movies, but on my own now, I had not. I wrote up a very extensive outline and packaged it with the exceptional reviews the book had received. I gave it to the head of movies at Lifetime Television and waited. *That's what one does in Hollywood. Wait. It's not the rejections that can kill you; it's that the clock may run out on your life while waiting and waiting...*

    It was months later, when that life-changing call came. The executive I had given it to called and said he wanted to have the book adapted into a screenplay. I was over the moon with excitement. I immediately shared my ideas for how it should be adapted. He responded that he didn't want me to write it. It was as if a huge boulder dropped from the sky and crushed my very being into oblivion. I was speechless. I felt a pool of stinging hot tears filling my eyes. My throat was constricted. I couldn't speak. I tried to find the ability to protest that he was making a terrible mistake. He was speaking but I was too upset to really listen until he asked if I had heard him. I hadn't. He repeated that he wanted me to come on board as an executive producer, given how

Oops! I Forgot to Save Money

passionate I was about the project. He added that he wanted to introduce me to a very experienced woman, Ellyn Williams, who he thought would make an excellent executive producing partner to bring this movie to the screen. Somewhere I also heard that I would be making far more money than if I was the writer.

At first, I was scared that I knew nothing about producing. I had been an associate producer on a couple of TV movies but that title was easily given to writers who wanted more money. It was a way of appeasement without raising the writer's fee. Being an associate producer meant sitting on a set all day but never having any real input. But it soon became apparent that producing was something I had been doing most of my life, starting when I was that child that put on plays in my back garden in Scotland and charged kids to come see them. Ellyn and I met and within minutes we knew we would be great together. Producing this movie turned out to be everything that I was good at. I'm naturally decisive. *Think bossy.* Being a producer basically means being captain of a large ship that provides employment to roughly two hundred people, from the director, the writer, the cast, the cinematographer, costume department, hair and makeup people to even the transport and the person who does payroll. It also means that you must present every choice that's made to the network for approval. They are the people who hold the purse strings and therefore have the final say. This means a heavy dose of people skills are required. Both Ellyn and I had those in spades. Making a movie is about managing everyone and making sure that it all happens in a timely fashion. So much money is on the line. What it really meant was, WE WERE RESPONSIBLE FOR IT ALL! – The good, the bad and the "Oh shit! How will we fix that?" No one ever talks about the sixteen-hour days; much of it spent putting out fires and problem solving. I flourished in that

203

Monica Parker

high stakes enterprise. I loved the responsibility and relished the hard work. The film turned out to be great and we were responsible for giving the relatively unknown, beautiful redheaded Christina Hendricks the lead role. She later went on to be one of the breakout stars of Mad Men.

    I took a large chunk of that paycheck and banked it. I also invested a bit, but cautiously. Baby steps! Ellyn and I soon put many movies into development. None were as easy green lights as Hunger Point. Finding inspiring true stories or dramatically interesting, socially relevant tales was often harder than the gory and dark tales of the depraved and demented. They may grab the headlines but not my heart. Given that we would be spending a great deal of time researching the full backgrounds of the heroes or heroines of our stories - from finding them to getting them written and often rewritten, then if we were lucky, we would get to spend even more time getting the films ready for the screen - I knew I didn't want to invest that much time with the Jeffrey Dahmers of the world.

I found this story many years ago in the Los Angeles Times. An attractive, creative and dedicated homemaker was seemingly happily living in the modestly affluent neighborhood of Westwood, California with her successful husband and teenage daughter. Her world was rocked when she discovered her husband had been cheating on her for two years and unbeknownst to her, had been making plans to exit the marriage. He went out of his way to hide their assets and put the house in his name only, leaving her with next to nothing except her Volvo station wagon and his barely realistic child support payments.

Oops! I Forgot to Save Money

 After starting and then failing in her own startup catering business, she had to move to a small apartment near their former home, surviving with a minimum paying job working for another caterer. Her daughter hated the new apartment and their scaled down life. She convinced her father and his new girlfriend to let her come back to the house where she had been happier. Without child support, the woman was forced to move to an even lesser apartment, this time in a not-so-great neighborhood. She somehow managed to keep her head above water but eventually things hit rock bottom when she lost her low paying job.

 Not knowing what to do, she moved back into the familiarity of her old neighborhood even though it was now in her car. Through ingenuity and the friendship of a very resourceful streetwise woman, she took her homeless status to new heights. Dressed in her one good and always pressed suit, she hit the 'Happy Hours' and real estate open houses looking for free food, and visited hotel lobbies to keep up her newspaper reading, taking showers, and stealing naps in good beds in vacated hotel rooms by hanging the "Do Not Disturb" sign on the door.

A real estate saleswoman took notice of the enterprising Mom and offered her a job. All she had to do was be at her open houses early enough to set up the food and brochures. But she took it to the next level and began making her own floral arrangements as well as baking cookies to create a welcoming feeling. Soon enough, she got a full-time job and began making a new life for herself.

 This true story became the basis for a successful Lifetime movie that I produced called Home for Christmas. But I love the lesson one can learn from it about resilience…

~

More than twenty years ago, television movie producers owned the movies that they made in conjunction with a network or studio. That meant when they played in other countries over many years, producers got to share the profits. But for at least the last fifteen years, most networks now owned the product, meaning that making television movies is one of the worst business models currently in play. Producers don't get paid while their films are being written and developed. This can take up to two years and then it's possible those tales will have fallen out of favor and the networks will decide not to make them, meaning we worked for two years and didn't make a cent. So, we needed to have several of these movies in development to protect us; that way if one fell away, we'd have another possibility to fall back on. I had just found a job that I was really good at and enjoyed and that I thought would be a steady and profitable business. Not so.

Note to Self: No matter what your business is, don't spend any of the profits until the money is in the bank. Being an entrepreneur is a high stakes gamble where all the pieces need to come together to bring any venture to life. When an idea comes together you are a God and when it doesn't, you are nothing. It's always necessary to have more than one fully formed and solidly prepared idea waiting in the wings. No matter what entrepreneurial venture you are on, think of it as similar to those old plate-spinners who run from one end of a table filled with plates on sticks to the other, trying to keep as many as possible spinning.

Recommended Medication: Truffles: sweet and chocolaty, and those found in the forest. Because a hike is always a good stress buster.

CHAPTER 16

THE UNPARDONABLE SIN OF GETTING OLDER IN HOLLYWOOD

The Cost: Ouch! How did I not get it until that brick hit me in my head?

3:10 A.M. The LED on my clock was flashing... and flashing! I had been tossing and turning for hours, begging the sheep to stop bleating and just let me count them quietly until I could shut out the noise.

At 5:17 A.M. even the sheep couldn't take my restlessness. I was making mental lists of my assets, primarily those I could attribute to my character rather than the brick and mortar kind that could end up in actuarial tables - I didn't have any of those. But I'm smart. *Sometimes*. Or at least, I have a bright-ish mind. I'm decisive. I'm creative. *How's that working for you?* Shut up. Shut up. Shut up. I needed to sleep. Once again I was hit hard. I just found out that two movies that we had been told were likely 'go projects' were now 'no goes'. They were not going forward and not because the network didn't like them but because the person in charge of our movies had been fired and a new president had come in and wanted to put her stamp on things. Therefore she was, in effect, tossing the previous executive's 'babies' out with the bathwater. The security I thought I finally had attained had just fizzled like a dying party balloon. I was in shock. These movies were supposed to be sure things – well, as sure as anything in Hollywood can be. I had been around long enough to know there are no sure things. There is always the unforeseen, no matter how solid the ground appears. Much like Los Angeles, where the earth can fall away in a microsecond - a true metaphor from the National Geographic Files. It's the same in every freelance business. Until the check is deposited and made real by the bank, it's not real! *Crash! Burn! Survive! Rinse and repeat!*

    The slab is icy cold. It's deathly quiet, which makes sense given that I'm lying on it naked. *Oh God Noooonoooo!* There is an almost translucent, zero thread count, single bed sheet draped across most of my body. A far too good-looking pathologist is sharpening the tools of his trade. I'm being autopsied. Oh great, my fat cells get to spill out along with all the acids of my self-inflicted stress-busting, binge eating ways. There will be traces of French fries and triple crème Brie as evidence. I'm more concerned that he will dig into the long-locked vault of my brain. That's where the real damage will be exposed. My slippy-slidey, not always real, optimism will reveal itself to him in the total lack of serotonin held within. All my darkest fears and phobias will leap to the surface as soon as the light is focused on the recesses where my secrets have been safely kept away from exposure. I am right. *Small satisfaction.* He writes a scathing report stating, "The large cadaver revealed a life lived of fakery and pretense that all was sunny when clearly this was far from the truth. This woman was not as she pretended. She was all sizzle and no steak. She had some savings, but not enough to protect her from life's tsunamis. And now it's too late."

    I jolted awake from the terrible nightmare! I shook off the terror and tried to rock myself into a state of calm. Thank goodness, it wasn't real.

Oops! I Forgot to Save Money

6.02 A.M. I had given up trying to sleep. I was sitting wide-awake, bleary eyed and really off my game. *So get it together.* It's time to take inventory. Okay, let's start with what's working. My greatest resource is my tenacity. I don't give up. I'm not letting a little insomnia change that. What else do I consider an asset? I have unlimited positive energy. *Not at this minute.* I inspire others to do their best. I have a large network of talented, smart and deeply loyal friends. *That's just a distraction to keep from getting on with it.* That being said, it didn't take a clairvoyant to know the opportunities lessen, as one gets older. Our networks shrink, as does our stamina. Shut up! It's too early to be doing battle with my own lippy little Tinkerbell. I'm not stuck for ideas; I know how to zig when everyone else is thinking zag. Never having had any yoke, I roam the fields of my imagination and I'm really good at creating work where there isn't any. *Basically you exist on dreams.* Shut up! That's not it. I make dreams and bring them to life. And that is what I'm going to do with the insomnia that has given me this time to think. See, a silver lining. And I always bounce back from adversity. *Then get up and out of that bed of your own making and get on with it."*

So what WAS my problem? I knew answering this question meant having to take a hard look at my liabilities. First off, having a freelancer life would be considered a problem by any normal, business minded person, although other artists and entrepreneurs would disagree. Creating is oxygen! *You are supposed to be having a hard look – remember!* I sipped my tea wishing for something stronger, like a pillow over my head. I knew I had to change my way of being and doing. How? I didn't have the answer, yet. My brain chatter was rapidly sequencing the "not good enough" versus the "I can do it all" narrative colliding in my head. I knew I needed to look deeper. I began to think I must have either a fear of failure or a fear of success. But I wasn't quite sure which. Couldn't I have both? I do like an extra helping of most things. I am sure they both produce the same result, that is, more fear and feet of clay. The devil isn't in the details. It's in ignoring them.

But not today! No more ruminating, agonizing, procrastinating or fantasizing. Do the grunt work, and pray for miracles on the side. I spent the morning reading a pile of old scripts that I had written, a few done for hire but many written because I am a storyteller and I have tales I am driven to tell. There's a peculiar phenomenon when reading a script or story that you have written some time ago. It is almost like reading something for the first time. It appears, page after page, as if it had been written by someone else or by a part of the brain that was suspended in an altered state during the process. I picked out two of them that I thought had stood the test of time and technology and sent them off to a select few agents that had come highly recommended. I took a real leap of faith, a few deep breaths and called my current agent. It was time to cut her loose. We had run our course. I needed someone hungry enough to sell me! We had the usual 'appetizer' banter about the heat and the awful smog that somehow also provides Los Angeles with some really spectacular sunsets, or 'smogsets' as many Angelinos call them. I kept trying to cut to the chase. I had called to fire her. Not because she was a bad agent but she wasn't a good enough one either. She wasn't getting me enough work. Most of my conversations with her were spent, *as in wasted,* in a kind of verbal foreplay that took far too much time. We always talked about the weather first and then her hair. I wish I were kidding.

HER: "What do you think, are my streaks too stripey?"

Oops! I Forgot to Save Money

ME: "I wish I could offer up a better opinion but given that we are on the phone, I can't really tell. They looked great last time I saw you. I want to talk to you about…"

HER: "Yeah, I should have stayed with Lorenzo. He got me. This guy, not a clue… Do you know anyone who does good blondes?"

ME: "Well, I'm still with the same hairdresser and you weren't happy with what he did. Anyway, I need to …"

HER: "This town is crawling with blondes and they're all great looking fakes." How hard should it be to find someone who can make my hair look that fake good?"

ME: "You're right. Uhm, okay so… I'm sorry to interrupt… but I am leaving you… Uh, you're a lovely person but I think I need someone… uhm… who… uhm…"

HER: "Okay then. Best of luck."

ME: "Thank…"

A dial tone replaced her nasal voice. For a moment I thought she was still droning on about the terrible tragedy of her very stripey streaks. Oh my God, I did it. I finally was able to breathe. I didn't need to worry about her. She'd find another writer/therapist with whom to discuss her hair.

I knew that waiting for any of the agents to respond to my work was going to make me hungry. All stress makes me hungry. But then again so does sitting at my desk, writing. I seem to be unable to clear the weeds in my brain without grazing. I keep a never-ending supply of trail mix by my computer to feed the beast of creativity. I'm like a buzzard in a cage of parakeets who finishes every ounce of birdseed in my feeder and then flaps and squawks in on all the other petrified bird's bowls, scarfing up all that I can until I can't open my beak to shovel in another bite. But this was a new day and I wanted to let go of habits that did

211

nothing to free me from anxiety. No more negative babble. No more self sabotage. I began the job of actually de-cluttering my office. I'm not really big on living in a mess. I need order to function. All surfaces are a lie of apparent neatness. Just don't open a drawer. My filing system consists of fifty plus years of birthday cards all tossed in one drawer, with stacks of scripts flung into another. Bar Mitzvah invitations! Why did I have these? There are endless news clippings that at one time or another I thought might make great fodder for potential movie scripts, except that, once they were tucked deep into that file cabinet from hell, I never, ever looked at them again. But I struggled with throwing them out. New day. New resolve. They were tossed.

The Bar Mitzvah invitations, however, stayed. I felt they were so excessive and in such bad taste that some future anthropologist might want to expose them to the world. *Right… because an anthropologist will immediately be summoned to your house upon the globe-shattering news of your demise.*

A select overview: A lumpy thirteen-year-old boy dressed in a tuxedo, posed as James Bond holding a passport and a martini glass with the time, date and location of where his secret spy mission/celebration was to be held. There was a second, even more preposterous, spy-themed invite in the form of a small, realistic looking cardboard briefcase which, when opened, blasted the theme from Mission Impossible as a beanpole in a designer suit appeared in a photo, along with his thirteen year-old, pitch-breaking voice, inviting you to accept your mission and open the red box revealing the address and date of the big, and I'm sure costly, event. One more showed a pimply pubescent standing next to a private plane with a bevy of scantily dressed, real-life showgirls. *Not kidding.* The Las Vegas location of this party was emblazoned on the side of the plane. There was an invitation written on rolled parchment to resemble the Dead Sea scrolls but with glitter. Another was a Bat Mitzvah invite for a far too high-heeled and extremely unfortunate looking girl, clearly seen as a great beauty by her doting parents as they had her dressed in what I think a forty-year old divorcee on the prowl might wear - a strapless shiny bejeweled mini-dress and those shoes. She was held aloft on a flowered throne by beaming parents. These were real invitations that came to my son from some of the less sane Beverly Hills parents at his school.

Oops! It's so easy to cruise right into a distraction. An hour wasted I'll never get back…fun though.

I turned to a mountain of stuffed bags and file folders to look through at least ten years of tax papers and receipts. As I began to sort through all this paperwork to see what I had to keep and what I could dump, I was horrified at the many reminders of extravagance and wastefulness, but also warmed by great memories of dinners, celebrations, theatre and the many beautiful and exotic places to which we had travelled. I was happy to still find those absolutely worth 'the spend'. Most of my follies showed up in the black and white receipts for unused gym equipment, diet supplements and far too many impulse buys. *Otherwise known as lapse-of-judgment stress-busters.*

Unnecessary kitchen equipment that didn't do as advertised: A strawberry huller that didn't, an immersion blender that needed to go to remedial immersion classes, along with dresses I would never fit into unless I was slammed with a horrific, extended bout of wasting-away consumption. Shoes that pinched but I had to have, convinced that they would loosen with time. As all the evidence was bagged to give to an overweight women's shelter or fed into the trash or the voracious shredder, I was struck with an epiphany. This is exactly what I did whenever I was on one of my endless diets. When I cheated, candy wrappers were instantly tossed with another, less 'telltale' item, covering any verification of my transgression. If you can't see it, it never happened.

I had a second burst of clarity. It was about my sweet Gilles. I had been far too hard on him. Now that I had checked my assets and weighed them against my liabilities, I needed to do the same regarding his. I took a long moment to think about whom exactly this man is. He did not come up short in the husband/partner category. No one could be more supportive, loving and nonjudgmental. I had more than a twinge as I realized the same could not be said of me. I had judged him and tried to make him be something that he couldn't be - a captain of industry. I had pushed, pulled and squeezed him as if he were putty, trying to reshape him into my idea of who he should be. When he pushed back, I accused him of being stubborn. He had desperately tried to hold on to himself as opposed to my version of who he could be. I got it. *It took you long enough*. Gilles is an artist, the real deal. He makes beauty out of other people's trash. He turns the mundane into the magical. He elevates the normal to the sublime. He lives to make everything more accessible, more available and to help others. I felt remorse for every petty criticism and conviction I had thrown in his direction. He would never do that to me. Yes, I frustrate him at times but he doesn't lob stones at my flaws and I have myriad. With my blinders off, I saw that the alchemy that made us be us didn't deserve so much harsh judgment. I also saw that I had projected all my wants and needs onto him like some tattered Cinderella expecting him to show up with my glass slipper. What we really needed was a long overdue, mature conversation about our financial inertia, not his culpability versus mine. I asked myself again, how was it possible we had never had that conversation, which should have been mandatory before we even considered marrying? Unbelievably, it had never even been on our radar.

I live in my brain more than in my body. I am by nature an imagination hunter - a juggler of ideas - and Gilles is a doer who figures out what and how things need to get done with an engineer's problem-solving acumen. He doesn't care about practical things like money, and I do. Admittedly, I am late to that party. But we have both lived on the edge of financial devastation because we had put our monetary health into the smoke and mirrors of careers that have no guarantees. *Rereading that sentence has just made me feel ill. How could we have been so cavalier?*

Yet, we both love what we do. We love our independence and the freedom of being creators. We have been on this unstable but mostly gypsy-like, glorious voyage for more than thirty years, filled with more good times than bad, but when the bad hits… it hits hard.

The third epiphany of the day came crashing through. I have specialized in wearing the façade of positivity. Looking like a person who has it all together has been the armor I wear as protection. Everyone wants to be associated with success. The 'never let them see you sweat' adage is a great business strategy but when that mask begins to suffocate you, it's time to take ownership of the truth. If we love our independence so much, how will we be able to afford it when we are old if we don't have savings! Most of us will outlive our savings, living far longer than the actuarial tables have predicted. That's when the unexpected is to be expected. Long ago, when I intuitively decided to follow my passion, that choice came with a price. I didn't know then how steep it would be for the long game. Now that I do, I still wouldn't change my career choice or my husband for one second. I would however have committed to a savings

215

plan... even a small but consistent one. I only wish I had had the insight and knowledge to put some money aside. I now had to accept that it was going to require a whole new set of dance steps to catch up. The last thing either of us wanted was to put the financial burden of caring for either of us onto our son. What kind of parenting would that be? Shifting from mismanagement to management was the only road to salvation. That, and taking the heat off my husband... I have always been the bigger earner. What if money didn't ever become his priority?

My friend Sandi is a beautiful, smart woman who had a hugely successful career that she chose to leave behind. Sandi is the former Vice-President in charge of sales at Bugle Boy, a company that, back in the 1980's, had sales of close to one billion dollars before going belly up when trends changed. She followed up that position by starting her own licensing company.

She and her brother and sister grew up in Toronto, Canada as the children of an affluent suburban family. Her father was the boss. In Sandi's own words, he was the one who earned the money; therefore he had all the power. Those who didn't earn, including her mother, did not. At a young age, Sandi knew she wanted to be the one with the power. She wanted to be the one with the voice. So did her sister, who became a realtor. Watching their father do all and be all that he wanted to be and seeing their mother never complaining was the story they grew up with, until their mother, at age fifty-two, got her real estate license and began to make a whole lot of money and more importantly, discovered that she liked it. Having financial independence helped her find her voice and soon she began to assert her likes and dislikes for the first time in her relationship.

Interestingly, and to his credit, her husband, Sandi's father, found it difficult at first but it actually made their marriage stronger. It's harder for him now that they are in their mid-eighties and he is no longer working but she still is and she's reveling in it.

Back to Sandi: Along with having a stellar career and the money that went with it, back in the day Sandi was a hot ticket in LA's dating scene. She went out with loads of big-name actors, powerful agents and successful lawyers, but they did nothing for her. It wasn't until she fell in love with a starving artist, a writer, that she was surprisingly hooked. She much later came to understand that his far lesser financial picture made her feel secure. She truly believed that he wouldn't leave her. In her mind, it wasn't her that he loved but what she could offer him. Much like in her father's story, where he had all the power, so did Sandi. It's amazing how often we allow the false narrative we have invested in for so long to become the truth that rules.

Sandi and her new husband created a happy home life but gradually Sandi began to get frustrated with his inability to make consistent money. That changed when he landed his first gig as a film producer. It was far away on location and it was all consuming. Now, Sandi was scared. The power shift she had thought she wanted, terrified her. She couldn't sleep. She could barely breathe from the anxiety she felt. Now he had power. 'Now he will leave me' was the constant thought that ran through her head. He didn't but there was a seismic shift in their relationship.

In spite of his newfound success, his earnings were still sporadic. Welcome to show business. Sandi was still the consistent moneymaker, who, in Sandi's mind, meant that she still had the right to call the shots, and she wasn't always nice about it, admitting to even being a little bitchy. She had modeled her behavior after her father. Eventually he confronted her. He told her he loved her but he couldn't continue living with the way she treated him. "You either respect me and accept me as I am or I have to leave." For Sandi, this ultimatum was terrifying. She had always been the one with the control. She really had to ask herself, if this man were to never make another penny, could she love him and fully accept that this was their relationship? "Can I love my partner wholeheartedly and drop my hostility and need for control?" She knew she really wanted to, but it wouldn't be easy. And it didn't happen overnight. She had to work on it over and over again, to nip her old habits in the bud whenever they surfaced. The more she worked on her relationship, the more she found out about her patterns. In order to save her soul and her marriage, she made a radical shift, but not before almost losing the love of her life. She studied somatic psychotherapy and learned more about her own patterns, taking the focus off her husband's career. Not unsurprisingly, the more she let go, developing her own self-confidence, the more successful her husband became.

As she took more responsibility for her part and patterns, Sandi came to understand that what he gave her was exactly what she needed – a kinder, healthier, more well-rounded sense of self along with the ability to get out of her head and feel more, to love more, not just him, but to also love herself. She also began to see just how strong and self-confident her husband really was. How much strength and self-awareness it took for him to support, and truly partner with her. Her heart knew he was the one, long before her head caught up. And now they were in the dance of supporting each other and their individual dreams and projects.

It's not easy to cast aside these old stereotypes. There are many traditional tangos that couples do to conform to society's views. Sandi and I have shared the learning curve of having chosen men that are comfortable with their gentle side, men who operate intuitively and are in touch with their feelings. Some would say they are more feminine, and that she and I are more comfortable with our occasionally more competitive, masculine behavior. *I think the word you're looking for is dictatorial.*

A lot of us have grown up with the old stone age idea that men should be the ones bringing home the meat, while we attend to hearth and home. It's the picture that many women have grown up with, including Sandi, but not me. My single, working mother was absolutely the breadwinner and the boss, *although not so much a homemaker*; and my father was a ghost that occasionally made an appearance, as far as possible from my mother's irritation. Our more powerful parent's DNA infused both Sandi and me. It's difficult to break away from our early shaping and raising to create a newer, more comfortable dynamic. Sometimes, in our search for elasticity, both Sandi and I temporarily wanted to abdicate the power we were used to having. We tentatively handed off the reins to our mates. But when they took them, we didn't always like it. Giving up control can be a struggle. I know I never would have grown nearly as much with someone competitive and controlling. It would have always felt like a door slamming hard on all that I am. Most men have a far greater attachment to how money impacts their sense of self-worth. I have come to realize I am grateful that I have a prince of a man rather than a rich prince who would have likely inflicted his whims and ways on me. That glass slipper would never have fit either of my big feet, nor would the muzzle on my big mouth. I understand there's no one-size anything to fit all of our

219

accumulated baggage. Having partners who earn the big money can really affect one's identity. *I mean mine.* Finding balance takes time and willingness.

I consider both Sandi and I to be blessed to have found men who are secure enough to have made room for our strong-headedness without feeling threatened. They are our partners in the truest sense of the word, who lead with their souls and have taught us to do the same. It would have been so easy at times for either party to walk away, but we didn't and we grew closer and softer.

The Cinderella myth I thought I wanted was simply an excuse to pass the buck and make my dreams and desires someone else's responsibility. I decided to not put any more pressure on Gilles. I made peace with the fact that I was on my own in wanting to solve this money thing. But I had no idea how to course-correct our lifelong non-plans. I could no longer afford to not take our future into my hands. I decided to start by purging all excess along with the unnecessary. I needed a clean slate to begin my fresh start. I made a list of what I could get rid of, where to sell the things we no longer used, wore or needed. The few sterling silver bridge trophies that I still had, along with a pile of old European filigreed silver candy and nut bowls were the first things to go. I was thrilled at the possibility of never polishing any of them again. I swooped them up into an old pillowcase when the phone rang. It was an agent from a very well known, boutique literary agency who had read the scripts I sent out… and she loved them. *Oh-Oh. This is a test. Just as you try to get out from under those dangled fish, you are being reeled back in.* I couldn't discount the possibility that our crisis was over. It had paid off as many times as it had not. I was overjoyed that she had responded so favorably to my screenplays. She and I began to talk about which movie studio she thought she could get at least one of my movies set up at. Once the business portion of our conversation was done, we just started to chat. Laurel was sharp, funny and irreverent. We sparked each other. By the time I hung up, I knew we were both feeling the effects of a girl crush.

    Despite feeling high on all the appreciation and flattery, I was still pursuing my other moneymaking options and I was brought plummeting back down to earth with a call to a pawnbroker to see what my silver cache was worth. Without missing a beat, he barked at me, "Silver-shit don't sell. You gotta melt and smelt the whole shebang." Crushed, I went online to see where else I could unload the unwanted, tarnished silver and fussy, old-fashioned bric-a-brac I had inherited from various aunts I never knew. Amid the interweb noise, I discovered that 'gold parties' were all the rage, as the price for that precious metal was through the roof. I made a few calls and soon I was hosting a gold party for a bunch of eager girlfriends with the promise of cash for gold.

    The loot that poured out of purses, pockets and plastic see-through bags was astonishing. In front of each woman lay a pile of outdated baubles, broken bangles, single earrings, even some miniature gold bricks and some long ago discarded wedding rings. I had cobbled together, with help from my sister and my niece, the rose gold legacy of my European roots. My mother had sold most of her adornments right after the war in order to put a roof over her head and food on the table but she had recouped a fair amount over time from relatives and generous patrons. Fueled by bottomless bottles of wine and chemistry, outrageous and very juicy personal stories were shared as each piece was weighed and tallied by our savvy gold-party impresario, Marni, who, much like the Tupperware sales force of an earlier era, had several parties on the go at the same time, run by her newly trained staff.

My impetuous friend Michelle had brought the aforementioned gold bricks and tipsily told us they actually belonged to her mother's ex-husband. She giggled that he didn't realize she had them. She stumbled upon them in a worn leather box with a pile of things that her mother had given her. When our gold expert weighed them and told her that the melted value would be well over nine thousand dollars, Michelle almost fainted. There was no love lost between her so-called stepfather, as was made graphically clear. She handed them over and a check was given immediately. Michelle was unable to stop whooping. I was shocked that my gold-garbage brought in the tidy sum of two thousand dollars. Everyone left happy and richer and a fair bit drunker.

    I had just finished cleaning up when the doorbell rang. Through the intercom, all I could decipher was a high-pitched voice hyperventilating. After a few moments of crackly non sequiturs, I realized it was Michelle and I opened the door to an open coated, pajama clad, full-on hysterical woman filled with guilt and panic at having sold her mother's legacy gold bricks. With another glass of wine in hand, she told me she had shown her Mom the unexpected windfall, offering to give her the money. Her mother had been appalled and accusatory, saying that what she had done was no better than stealing. She said that her ex-husband may have been a bastard and possibly had forgotten about the gold bricks but he'd remember one day and know they were somewhere. He had told her they were worth about fifty thousand dollars! With this revelation, I thought Michelle might pass out. She shakily stood and stuttered that she had to get those bricks back! I was about to respond when we both shared a sharp intake of breath… remembering the moment when our buyer had mentioned she always took the gold directly to the smelter so that she wouldn't have to be nervous about it being stolen. For a moment there was no sound. I'm not sure we were even breathing. We both snapped to and began scrambling to track down the whereabouts of the gold. Marni's cell phone was off. We had no information on her other than what was on her shocking-pink website. I sent her an email. Michelle sent her eight more emails. Now it was my turn to panic. Was my check a dud? Had I brought a scam artist into my home? Had I caused some of my closest friends to be ripped off? Michelle was practically keening from the visions she was having of the white-hot smelter oozing a lava-like stream of gold onto a stone slab. I was feverishly scrolling through Google to find smelters within a twenty-mile radius. There was one just a few miles away. It had to be the right one.

We were in the car and screaming out of the driveway when my cell phone rang. Oh my God! It was our golden girl, Marni! It turned out she had thought about the stamped gold bricks a lot and worried that they were really worth a lot more than the simple gold weight value, so she had made the decision to wait until morning when she had intended to call me to get Michelle's number. But after having a shower, she had seen that her inbox and phone messages were lit up like the Eiffel Tower on Bastille Day. Michelle begged Marni to let us come over right now to make the exchange. It wasn't easy for Michelle to hand back that hefty sized check but she knew she wouldn't be able to exhale until she did. *Easy come, easy go.*

With that near catastrophic episode behind me, I headed to a high-end jeweler tucked in a corner of a very discreet Beverly Hills courtyard, weighted down by a pillowcase filled with the Sterling silver bridge trophies and other silvery bric-a-brac. I must have looked like a cross between Santa Claus and Black Beard the Pirate, yet I was greeted graciously by a tall, bespectacled man named

Norbert, who led me to a tasteful corner of the store and offered me jasmine tea while he looked through my overstuffed pillowcase. As each piece was weighed and calculated, Norbert asked its provenance. He was very impressed by my mother's obvious bridge-playing skills, wanting to know if I, too, had the same talents. Perhaps a bit too hastily, I shut that conversation down. Much like the laments of golf widows, I still felt the sting of being a never-home bridge-player's daughter. But once all those trophies and nut bowls were fully tallied, I walked away with a neatly folded pillowcase and more than sixteen hundred dollars in cash. It had been a great week for de-cluttering. With both the check from the gold and the cash in hand, I headed to my bank, which happened to be right next door to a very seductive looking travel agency, its windows filled with the eye-candy of sexy beach scenes and glorious old European cobbled streets. It was like crack cocaine to a twitching user. I had a huge wad of cash burning a hole in my pocket along with my ever-present travel lust. I felt a shiver of desire pulling at me. My hand reached for the door handle. I took a moment, let out a whimper and practically ran into the bank, plunking that money right into my first tax-exempt retirement account. This was followed by a medicinal stopover at a nearby French fry stand. It was a small compensation prize for having beaten back the devil of impulse spending. I hoped that, in time, having a growing stockpile of money in the bank, along with peace of mind, would permanently replace the temporary fix of impulse spending.

∽

I recently got together with the wonderful and extremely talented Jean Smart of 'Designing Women' and 'Fargo' to name just two in the brilliant string of television series she has helped to elevate

Oops! I Forgot to Save Money

to cult status. We talked about her views on money and life. Jean comes from a typical middle class family, one of four children born to a stay-at-home mom and schoolteacher dad. Both her parents survived the depression and it left its mark. Her father's family was dirt poor even before the depression, which meant that even though he now earned a decent living, he never took anything for granted. During the summer school holidays, he would paint houses and in the winter, he taught night school. Her Mom was a frequent bargain shopper who also loved a good tag sale. Jean said, even though her parents were frugal and didn't lavish their kids with gifts, she never felt she wanted for a thing. As a child, Jean loved saving money. Leading up to Christmas, she would begin checking her little bank book to see how much she could spend on presents for everyone in her family, and then would scour the junk stores for the best prices to maximize her buying power. I can attest that her generosity continues to this day.

In spite of having a very successful career, even remarking that she's shocked that at her age it is doing the opposite of slowing down, this is the most prolific and highest paid period of her life. Jean laughs that she is just like her mother; even when she can afford full retail, she can't pass up a good garage sale. She loves the thrill of a bargain along with the feel of it being a treasure hunt.

She then remarked on the behaviors of young couples that don't want to start off their married lives in a small, comfortable house, waiting a few years to trade up. They don't seem to have the patience or desire for anything other than a fully renovated house replete with the requisite granite kitchen and giant-sized bathrooms. "If you believe you can buy everything you want immediately, how does one develop patience? There is a genuine feeling of satisfaction and joy brought about from hoping and wishing and that can't happen if it all appears instantly."

I asked Jean what advice she would give to young people. Without missing a beat, she said: "Don't assume anyone else will pay your bills. Make sure you can take care of yourself. It's not that hard to learn a few necessary basics about saving and spending wisely. Educate yourself. It's not that complicated. There are endless books and videos and professionals who can offer help."

∞

Laurel and I continued our weekly love fest along with status reports as to what was going on with my script. I was thrilled but wary. I was old enough and wise enough to never get too excited; I had been around this block many times before. It's filled with excitement and big plans and lunches with producers full of flattery and blindingly white-toothed smiles. All those on the way up and on the way down want to attach to the potential of the next big thing. Yes, it could be mine… but those in power have short memories and tomorrow they might be presented with another potentially big thing. That one could come with a big name star attached, or blackmail from a brother-in-law, or it could be that another competitor wants it, making it far more desirable as it comes with the bloodlust of the chase, potentially relegating my offering to the heap of forgotten former prizewinners. In an even worse scenario, my script could actually get into development, which comes with the lure of big money down the road. *Never to be seen, just promised*. Development-hell as it is unaffectionately known, is the hard labor camp run by an ever-changing stream of low-level executives who all want to have their input, meaning raising their legs to pee on my script because everyone wants to take credit. I knew that Laurel was young because she was so arrogantly confident that she could make this happen. I was more skeptical. She was probably thirty-something, if that, and I knew she thought I was about the same age, which was why she was so enthusiastically hitching her wagon to my star. I wasn't going to ruin our agent/client love affair with anything close to reality; I kept on just being me, which would work as long as we never actually met. And I knew I could never meet anyone she was pitching my script to. In movie buying years, I was stale, burned toast.

Waiting for my items to be scanned at the checkout counter of my local grocery store, I caught a bold headline over the image of a beautiful wavy haired cover girl. It said, "Thirty five and still looking good!" Thirty-five! I should hope so. An army of goose bumps popped up out of nowhere. Only a few years ago, I was just a smidge over fifty. *Smidge? Seriously!* Whatever. I had no idea my age was about to become an impediment. I was a fat actress who played character parts, not leading ladies. Even though in my real life I am a wife, lover and mother, none of that could ever happen on film. In my early career it meant playing best friends and waitresses. As I got older, I was endlessly cast as hookers, landladies and more than a few mental patients. I had since graduated to madams, psychics and therapists and that would continue until I moved into "old ladies brandishing canes", "homeless trolls", and "landladies who didn't speak a word of English, walked with a limp and were crusty and mean", and… probably more mental patients.

Incomprehensibly, it gets even worse in a writer's life. I knew the perils of going into studio meetings to pitch film ideas to twelve-year-old producers wearing the type of tight, shiny nerd-suits that we laughed at on Pee Wee Herman but were now in fashion. I could walk into any of these sleek mid-century decked out offices and instantly read their minds: "Fuck, who set this meeting up. I'm going to get them fired! This woman could be my mother! Maybe my grandmother!" But then I'd sit down and somehow make them relax and laugh. Soon they'd be enjoying my company but I knew that there was no way in hell they would try to sell my movie. Their asses were on the line and they didn't want to get that call. "Did you set this meeting up? That woman could be my mother! What the hell are you thinking?" I was thinking that Laurel would make the perfect front man to pitch my movies: Christian to my Cyrano.

My reverie was interrupted, by my cell phone announcing a call from Laurel. We shared another laugh-filled conversation as I loaded my groceries into my car and continued as I sat with the car idling in the parking lot for another fifteen minutes. Before hanging up, Laurel casually tossed out that she had made a reservation at a popular Beverly Hills restaurant for early next week. She said, "We have so much in common and already can finish each other's sentences, it's time we had a face to face and take this friendship to the next level." I joked that soon we would be borrowing each other's clothes. She said she wore a size two. I laughed and said my dress size had a two in it. Damn! She loved my humor. I felt a shiver run down my spine. It was at that moment I knew what it felt like to be some geezer with a comb-over and bad knees, posing online in a jock photo and flirting with a pretty twenty-year old blonde, pretending to be as cool as she is. I knew this day would come and I knew I had run out of excuses.

I lay awake for most of the night, trying to figure a way out of this and still keep my hot young agent. Finding some younger, thinner, cooler version to pose as me was proving to be a dead-end. I finally got out of bed and washed and fluffed my hair, even going so far as to cut long bangs in order to cover as much of the truth as possible. I slathered Preparation-H under my eyes to diminish puffiness and lines. *The tube said it shrank soft tissue.* I kept a skin-plumping masque on my face for well past the recommended 20 minutes. I went for a youthful dewy pink lip-gloss. My outfit was, of course, black. Everyone in Hollywood, the land of bright and incessant sunshine, wears black. Always be prepared for a funeral. I certainly was… mine. I sat at the bar of the trendy uber-cool restaurant Laurel had chosen and waited. I was on my second double espresso. I needed to be truly alert. I smiled at no one, not wanting to have any frown lines crack my perfect, lighter than air makeup. A tall reed in black with shiny, shiny extensions cascading past her shoulders and carrying an expensive purse half the size of a cow stood at the door and through her oversized black sunglasses did a sweep of the room, passing right over me. I could see a little frown trying to sneak through the Botox barrier when she couldn't locate her new BFF. I breathed in slowly, knowing I still had time to get out. I could walk right past her – even give her a little bump as I exited and she would never know it was me. I shook my bangs further into my face. It was time to end this thing. I raised my arm and put her out of her misery, or right into it, as I waved. Laurel's Botox and her frown were now at war. I thought I saw a little crack break through that plastified face. I could read her thoughts as if they were in neon. "What?! This can't be real! That is not the person who I gave some serious intimate cred to – No way!" She looked around in the vain hope that there was someone behind her waving at the middle-aged woman who was smirking right at her.

    Laurel barely sat down when out of her perfectly pouty mouth sputtered, "Oh My God, I thought you were younger. Like a lot younger!"

    I couldn't hold back. "And I thought you'd be a lot less rude!"

And then and there began the most uncomfortable thirty-five minutes of either of our lives as we tried to recover our equilibrium. Our blind date was officially a disaster, as was my future as Laurel's client, in spite of the fact that she had loved my voice as a writer, had loved me... But that was gone, baby gone. She had no idea how to sell this 'me' to her peers. My talent hadn't changed but her perception had.

If we are lucky, we get older. We just must never look it. The cut off for being saleable in Los Angeles is apparently thirty-five…maybe forty if one is really connected. Ageism happens everywhere and in every profession, at least by fifty. *Not true. Embalmers can be any age as long as they don't have the shakes.*

We wrapped up the lunch. I let her pay just to help her through the awkwardness of the silence. As Laurel gathered up her iPad, iPhone, iPurse, iSunglasses, she actually said, "We'll talk soon." I replied, "Absolutely. You can reach me at Sunny Acres, the retirement home. I'll be checking in this afternoon."

Note to Self: If you want to be rescued, be your own knight in shining armor. Start small. Put a few dollars into a savings account every week. Watching it grow brings on the glow of accomplishment, which leads to growing your self-worth emotionally as well as financially. And for God's sake – DON'T GET OLD!

Recommended Medication: Bread Pudding, cheap to make in its basic form. Perhaps with an added salted caramel drizzle over the whipped cream, butter cream and ice cream.

CHAPTER 17

CHANGING THE PAST REQUIRES CHANGING

The Cost: Down coats, warm mittens and an aching heart.

The day after my 'bestie' literary agent and I parted company, Gilles and I were stuck in the sub-human snarl of traffic as we drove to San Diego for a long planned, Labor Day beach house weekend. The stop and go traffic was making me nauseous. I hadn't slept well and I was in a dangerously black mood. My very sweet husband tried to joke me out of my misery but I was not having it; I was locked in deep. The sound of silence reverberated through the car as we crawled along for several more agonizing miles. We passed the remains of a horrific accident. The wail of an ambulance could still be heard. The incinerated remains of what had once been a red and shiny but now unrecognizable model of car was being cranked onto a tow truck. A fed up child in the lane next to us was screaming. The mother snapped and began screaming back. I felt a sudden tightening in my chest. I wanted to scream too. The collective rubbernecking had reached critical mass. Everyone was stuck in this mess. The pent up frustration was as enveloping as a severe case of heartburn as we lurched forward. With a snap of the traffic god's fingers, the lanes ahead of us opened up. It was as if a race flag was waved and we were off! We were back in the competitive sport of lane changing at warp speed. My legs turned leaden. My breathing was becoming strange and static. There was a lurching in my stomach. I was in the throes of a major anxiety attack. It was coming at me like a pair of hollow-point bullets from a double-barreled shotgun. Gilles took one hand momentarily off the steering wheel and reached across, taking my hand. He could see something was wrong. But now I couldn't speak, even if I wanted to. He re-took the wheel with both hands and like a possessed madman careened across all eight lanes of traffic and pulled onto the shoulder. Honking was unleashed in strident fury.

We sat in the car on the side of the highway, Gilles gently rubbing my back until my breathing became normal. He asked me if I needed to go to the hospital. Did my chest hurt? I shook my head, no. He asked me if I could explain what had just happened? I nodded and said, "I'm day old pastry… dry and no longer desirable." *This metaphor was totally lost on Gilles. He loves day old pastry.* He looked at me not comprehending. "I'm done. I'm too old. My sell-by-date has passed." I told him about my ill-fated lunch. When I got to the part about me telling Laurel that I was checking into Sunny Acres, he started to laugh. Our eyes made contact and I began to laugh too, loud and hard, so much that we didn't see or hear the police motorcycle pulling up behind us. A fully kitted-out patrolman – a ringer from the CHiPS movie - tapped on our window. I pulled myself together. My full acting chops were on display as I slumped down into sickly non-English speaking mode, convincing him in broken English that I had eaten something that was off and I had had to throw up. I didn't want to do it in the car. He sternly suggested that next time something like this happened I would be better off soiling the car than endangering ourselves and everyone else on the freeway. *He had a point.*

Oops! I Forgot to Save Money

When we arrived in San Diego, our happy housemates greeted us loudly. Our glasses were filled with something sweet and potent and we were led out onto the deck. The view from our rented beach house patio was just as advertised: "A magical expanse where the sandy shore, shimmering water and blue sky instantly transport you to a feeling of bliss and calm." We were sitting on the long bench overlooking the water in complete silence along with our normally loud and funny group of longtime friends. The only sounds were an occasional seagull, the lapping of waves and intermittent sighs of pleasure. I was quietly still churning over the ramifications of my anxiety attack. Had I been put out to pasture? I wasn't old… maybe in dog years. In wolf-whistle years, I was totally invisible which made me nonexistent by Hollywood standards. I had been voided, erased, reduced to rubble like a Hollywood tourist attraction. "Come one, come all…See the ruins of an aging, un-Botoxed former working writer and actress. But on the bright side, I would never have to work out or diet again, given that no one gave a damn. I headed straight for the kitchen and pulled out everything needed to make a panful of sinfully delicious brownies. *I know… I know… Sugar is the enemy of all mankind.* Neither assault rifles, nitro-glycerin bombs, Sarin-gas, tripe nor jellied-aspic, are as reviled and feared in Los Angeles as much as sugar. Too damn bad. For me it is the ultimate pain reliever and numbing agent and it works. While stuffing my face, it occurred to me that the North American obesity epidemic is especially hard on women. And it hits us hardest the moment we hit the age where we become ghosts. Shoving food in our faces is calming but makes us bigger… *Maybe that way we'll get noticed!*

Soon enough, I was back to being able to fake my sunny disposition… so much so that, just like those occasionally elusive orgasms, it became real. Guitars were produced along with some makeshift percussion instruments. A little tequila and a whole lot of Bar-B-Q later (or was it a whole lot of tequila and a little bit of Bar-B-Q later), everyone was singing and dancing barefoot around a fire pit in the sand. I took a step back and took in the unbridled fun of this Gidget-Goes-Wild flashback. A pair of bikinied young women walked along the sand. They stopped to look. I think what they saw was a Gidget-Goes-Grey bunch of oldies desperate to hang on. They laughed and moved along.

We laughed louder!

By seven in the morning, everyone else was sleeping or passed out. I'm a morning person no matter how much fun I've had or how little sleep. It's just the way I'm wired. I was already on my second cup of coffee, having walked the beach while scooping up some beautiful shells and been mesmerized by the mysterious life forms in the tide pools. I was sitting on the deck in front of my laptop. I had read The New York Times from cover to cover. The day's obits were not as fulfilling in their tales of lives lived as they sometimes were.

I squirmed a little uncomfortably at the one where the son wrote in the most poetically descriptive manner how horrible his mother was. I said a protective prayer that would not be my fate. But I did love the one where the recently deceased woman had taken the time to write her own in advance, "I finally have the smoking hot body I have always wanted, having been cremated. Please come say goodbye and celebrate my wonderful life with my husband and his special friend Dorothy who is now lovingly taking care of the horse's ass".

I moved on. I read and 'liked' several Facebook postings and banished those who posted sentimental odes to cats. With the morning stillness still shrouding me, I casually Googled 'houses for rent' in Toronto, Canada. I had gone on for years about missing Toronto but had always been told by countless friends that I was suffering from grass-grows-greener syndrome. I looked out at the hazy sun breaking through clouds, making the water sparkle like diamonds. It was breathtaking and even though it was early in September, I knew it would still look like this in January when everyone in Toronto would be shivering and shoveling.

I didn't think it was a case of the grass being snowier. I had been going back and forth between Canada and California for twenty plus years. I missed my family. Not many people I know have family in Los Angeles. They are all from somewhere else, having come west to seek their fame and fortune like the gold prospectors at the turn of the century. Some found it, but most didn't. I think my need for Toronto runs deeper. It's a very stable city, filled with endless red brick houses that have stood the test of time and weather. It can be a little stuffy but with that comes a consistency that I was craving. It's unflappable. By comparison, Los Angeles is where the ground is unstable and I, too, was no longer sure where I stood. I kept searching the rentals. I landed on a pleasant looking house on a street that I knew and loved. I impulsively picked up the phone and called my girlfriend Wendy, also an actress, who had moved back from California and asked her if she'd mind having an up close and personal look. She was so excited at the thought of having us back that she said she'd go to look right away.

It felt like barely any time had passed when she messaged me that yes, the street was lovely but the house was dark and foreboding, giving off a vibe of some unspeakable crime that had gone on there. She was one hundred percent sure we'd hate it. *Can't imagine why she'd think that?* I thanked her for checking it out and apologized for her having to deal with such an unsettling experience. I was surprised at how disappointed I was. Still, no one was awake yet and I was left to my own devices. I'm not sure why but I obsessively went back to my house hunt. I didn't really know the neighborhood I landed on next, but I found a charming red brick Victorian house on a street that brought up visions of drug deals and muggings in some part of my brain that had connected to some idea of its unsavory history. But it was a really pretty house fronted by a white picket fence. I called Wendy again and asked her if she minded looking at just one more house. I mentioned that I thought it was in a sketchy part of town. She laughed and told me that there were no 'sketchy parts' of Toronto anymore. It had all become gentrified. She dutifully stepped back out to have a look. Less than thirty minutes later, my phone rang. It was Wendy, breathless with excitement. "This is your house! It's light and airy and even has a basement apartment where you can stick your twenty-year old son and his child bride for the duration of their dumbass marriage." *And that's a story for another lifetime. A mother doesn't rat out her child, not if she doesn't want a scathing obit.* I asked when it was available. After a short moment, Wendy came back and said, "Now!"

I was on the deck, drinking my third cup of coffee and eating my second muffin as people stumbled out of the house. Gilles was the last to appear. He loves sleeping in. He leaned over to kiss me. I was fighting nerve endings that were twitching and shimmying. I smiled and asked him how he had slept but before he could answer I told him we were moving. He didn't miss a beat. "Tell me which direction and I'll order the moving truck."

The writing was on the wall as well as pretty much rubber-stamped on my forehead. My sell-by date was looming as far as Los Angelinos in positions of power were concerned. I have never been one to overstay my welcome. I prefer the 'leave 'em wanting more' philosophy. I think this time I may have miscalculated. As a writer, it shouldn't matter what age one is, as long as our memories are clear and we still have an appetite for telling stories. But in LA it does. As a character actress it shouldn't have mattered one whit except that in the film and television business youth remains supreme. Young beautiful actresses have shorter shelf lives than pole dancers and older character actresses are so plentiful and desperate that many will work for peanuts. My category when I was younger had far fewer chubbies to choose from, giving me the edge, but nature's joke on movie stars is that no matter how much you spin in circles to keep aging at bay, you get older. That and a few failed relationships, result in binge eating and drinking, in partnership with weight gaining menopause. A lot of former famous beauties were now much heftier and muscling in on my territory. After a lifetime of starvation dieting to keep up their appearances, I can't say I blame them for throwing in the towel. I hope to one day thank them all for giving me the shove I needed. But at that moment I was still pissed, a bit bitter and a lot scared.

 I knew I needed to get out of Glitter Gulch and go to a city that didn't want all females to have thigh gap; a place where not all women looked like Vanna White, never aging, held together with Gorilla glue and Botox, strutting in heels as she flips those letters for the three hundred thousandth time; a place where my man could look in the mirror and see his true reflection without having the pressure to remain permanently boyish. *Like most TV weathermen - looking as if blown backwards by a tornado.* At the very core of this proposed move was the idea that I needed to relocate while I was still young enough to lay down a new foundation before it was too late.

 But before we could leave, I had to confront the hardest part of this new chapter. I was about to leave a community so loyal and precious that I felt they were irreplaceable. I knew telling my friends would be difficult but I had no idea how hard it would be for some to hear our news. Every friendship plays a role in our lives. My girlfriend Nancey was my beautiful wise sage. We took her to dinner to tell her our news. No one could have prepared me for her reaction. Her face went from pink to a putty-grey just before she pushed away from the table. She stood ready to walk out of the restaurant but not before saying, "Now what am I supposed to do?" She was inconsolable. And soon I was, too. It was as if we were both hanging on to a tree branch in the middle of a windstorm that was determined to shake us off but in different directions. Arlene's response was a touch less dramatic. In spite of being heartbroken, she decided to handle the news in a completely different way. She threw us a party and invited everyone she knew I would miss. She went all out decorating her garden with fake snow, saying, "If this is what you want – we can give you that." She made the most beautiful album and got everyone to share something, a poem, a story, or a memory to remind us of what and whom we would miss. *She certainly wasn't making our move any easier.* The topper was that everyone was instructed to bring us scarves, mittens, anything that our soon-to-be harsh winters would require. When the Consul General of Canada and his wife gave us a farewell party with all those same friends in attendance, it was humbling to be surrounded by so much love and out of control laughter and it made our decision even more daunting. Our biological relatives may have been in Canada, but these friends were our chosen family. I thought I was overdue for a visit to a psychiatrist. What had I done? It should come as no surprise that I have too much of everything except friends. Despite their number, they are all irreplaceable.

As we prepared for our exodus, Gilles gave me a rare ultimatum. We were renting a seventeen-foot truck and whatever we couldn't fit in it was not coming on the cross-country journey. Now, I have been a collector of eye candy for most of my life. I have bought, found, or been given a fantastic collection of many things eccentric, beautiful and unusual. Having been blessed with these extraordinary and generous friends, parting with the things they had given us was not as severe as abandoning one's children but it was painful nonetheless. I didn't care if my clothes or most of our furniture didn't make the cut. *Liar, liar, pants on fire. You wanted nothing left behind. You will want it all to be with you in your arty-farty mausoleum when you are dead.* I fought back my tears as I cherry-picked my way through my treasures to first give away to friends and then ruthlessly sell everything we could to finance our move. Somewhere in this process, I discovered what all those de-cluttering gurus have been trying to teach us borderline hoarders - there is something incredibly freeing about letting things go. I only hoped that feeling would carry over into our new life.

I had so many loose ends to tie down in LA that I didn't arrive in Toronto until early November, a month after Gilles and our son did. I had no idea what this new chapter would hold as I was now a stranger in what was once a very familiar landscape. I felt a twinge of something uncomfortable in my gut. I shook it off as I pulled up in front of our beautiful rented Victorian house. The sun-dappled trees on both sides of my new street, still resplendent with their golden orange leaves immediately calmed my nerves. But when I awoke the next morning, on the first day of my new life, a powerful wind had blown through overnight and brought every single leaf down to the ground. Enough snow had fallen that the cars parked on our street looked like giant puffed marshmallows. It overflowed my new mid-calf winter boots as I shoveled the path while planning my escape. I felt a tear freeze on my cheek. What had I done?

Note to Self: Starting over can be paralyzing or filled with renewal if you can overcome the fear of stepping into the unknown. A new beginning is an opportunity to course-correct mistakes made in the past. It also offers a chance to reinvent, reinvigorate and reignite your life.

Recommended Medication: A double scoop of burnt marshmallow ice cream with chocolate and caramel and strawberry sauce plus a little whipped cream on the side to anaesthetize against all rash decisions.

CHAPTER 18

BIG RISK, BIGGER REWARDS

The Cost: Stepping out of my comfort zone onto an untested limb.

I woke up feeling disoriented. Where was I? I took in the windows that looked as if they were etched with a silver pen. It was nature showing off. Intricate and delicate patterns made of hoar frost covered every inch of glass. I shivered, not quite sure how I had landed on this frozen, alien space ship. I looked at Gilles sleeping soundly next to me. He was deeply shrouded under our duvet, breathing softly as if he had not a care in the world. I felt an irrational fury at his serenity. My feet touched the floor and I shivered. I wrapped myself in not one but two shawls and I was still cold. I pulled on some furry Ugg boots over my pajamas. I caught my reflection in the bathroom mirror. I couldn't help but laugh. I looked like a Latvian peasant woman. I just needed a babushka.

I stood at the kitchen sink and looked out over the icy wasteland I had chosen to call home. I caught a glimpse of something small and furry dart into a hole and disappear under a mountain of snow. I imagined it had no intention of coming back out until spring. I wished I could do the same. Unpacked boxes were still piled in corners. Our furniture had found its place; it was clear I hadn't. I was aware that finding my place would take time. I knew better than to think I could just waltz back into Toronto and everyone would be waiting for me. I was not the same girl that had left and my friends here had changed too. I knew well enough that the vacuum we left when we originally moved to California had been filled. I looked out the window at the picturesque row of snow topped Victorian houses. It took a few minutes before I flashed back to about ten years earlier when I was here visiting family and friends.

I was driving up this very street with my girlfriend, Deborah, when she had pointed to a "for sale" sign in front of one of the houses. "You should buy that house". I asked why on earth she would think I would ever live in this somewhat derelict neighborhood. She responded, "because they are really great houses and they are undervalued right now but the neighborhood is changing. You can afford to buy one." It was true; I had just finished a big movie and could have taken that money and put it down on a house. But at that time I had no thought of moving back to Toronto. Her idea made no sense to me. Damn! How right she was! These houses were in Toronto's version of the very recently gentrified Brooklyn and are now being snapped up as soon as they hit the market for well over a million dollars. As the song goes, "Regrets, I have a few…" In my case, more than a few.

I changed out of my peasant garb and instead piled on so much mismatched, wildly colored polar fleece over my puffy down coat that I now looked like a Christmas parade float. I waddled out onto the snow packed walkway and headed to what I thought might be my car. Half an hour later, the polar fleece was tossed onto the fence. I was hot from scraping and brooming the windshield and windows that had never seen snow before. Perhaps that's why it shuddered before I skidded off to the grocery store. Only I had no idea where the grocery store was in this neighborhood. There were few recognizable landmarks. I was lost. *There's an understatement if there ever was one.*

I developed a kind of brain fog. It would envelop me the minute I woke up. It was disorienting to be in a city that I once knew so well and now was continually trying to find my way in. I was a stranger in what used to be such familiar terrain. My friend Wendy assured me that I would find my way in every way but it would take time. She said it took her a couple of years to really land. I didn't feel I had that kind of time. I was all business. I had banked on moving back to a kinder, gentler town than Los Angeles; a town where I was still young enough to lay down the pipe I needed to carve out a career that I hoped would ultimately allow me to sock some money away. I could do that on more than a couple of fronts, as a writer, an actress and as a producer. But not so fast!

Ageism is everywhere, although it certainly wasn't as blatant as it was in LA. And maybe I did have a leg up. New and shiny is always appealing and now I was a new kid in town. I was no longer as connected here as I had been before I left. Many of my old contacts had moved on and become realtors, decorators, or had built house-staging businesses to take advantage of the booming market. They too, knew the writing was on the wall. Show business was too unreliable. They were padding their nests for the future by having taken on safer careers. I let the brain fog envelop me in a strange but protective shroud. I unpacked boxes. I found the organizing of things to be soothing. I had no real direction. I was rudderless. I kept getting lost in the city I needed to rediscover. *Oh… yet another metaphor.*

A long ago friend bumped into me on the street. We made small talk as we reacquainted ourselves. After about ten minutes, we hugged our good-byes. I began to walk in the opposite direction when she breathlessly ran back to me. She told me she was having an afternoon gathering of writers and actors and she would love it if I came and read something. I didn't know what else to say, so I said if I could, I would. We hugged once more and walked away. I really doubted I would show up at all. There was something about the time warp of going to an event where there would be a room full of women I hadn't seen in more than twenty years that made me uncomfortable.

I was truly happy to be in such close proximity to my family. It grounded me unlike anything else I was feeling. But the three thousand miles between my California life and my Toronto one was as gaping as the Grand Canyon. I was well aware no one had made me do this. I was so far out of my comfort zone. Twixt and tween. I was feeling untethered. I didn't know where I belonged.

∽

Being anointed with the label of most likely to succeed is a form of pressure that can disable the best of us. When I was in my twenties, I was smack in the middle of a group of thusly anointed. Weirdly, many of us found ourselves living on the same street. No doubt this happened because, as soon as there was a vacancy, we made sure one of our peers grabbed it. It was a charming boulevard filled with large, airy and affordable duplexes. Casseroles, baguettes and bottles of wine were carried from one house to the other. These were our Big Chill days. We celebrated each other's successes and commiserated over the failures, which were few.

To be a freelancer or an entrepreneur requires the patience, skill and courage of a high-wire-walker. But the biggest requirement is balance. Not everyone gets that. One of the most talented amongst our group, Barbara, was a strikingly attractive and savvy young woman. She was a marketer's dream who could sell anything to anyone, especially if it was in person. Her looks and forceful demeanor were her gold-plated assets. She started out selling a line of her own cosmetics to various high-end department stores. It wasn't always easy as the money it took to produce her line was staggering. She jumped at the chance when she was sought out by one of the most successful cosmetic companies to become the face of their brand.

Barbara had always been one of those people who needed the trappings that came with money and success. Now she had it all, maybe because she so desperately wanted it all. She had always lived above her means but now her need to impress was stratospheric. Bottles of Dom Perignon were ordered along with lavish meals in the most expensive restaurants. Travel was always first class. As her position grew larger so did her spending. She married a moderately successful man but she was sure she could make him over into the power broker she felt she deserved. They soon had a daughter, Peony, and she too was indoctrinated into their grandiose life. If she and her family could have travelled everywhere on the Orient Express, she would have. She sent their daughter to the most expensive boarding school in Switzerland with the children of royalty and rock stars. She was raised to believe the well would never run dry. But it did. Barbara had no understanding that even though she was the face of the company she worked for, everyone is replaceable, and she wasn't getting any younger. That and her demanding ways were a fast pass to the end of the gravy train. She had had a good run at making big money but she spent it all. She hid the fact the she was having money problems, in order to keep up her image. She saved nothing. The big jobs got fewer. The big money got smaller. It would have been a humbling experience for most but for

Barbara, it produced arrogance, denial and ultimately, bitterness. Her husband left her. He was exhausted from not being able to live up to her expectations. She went back to the city where she grew up and where she was still considered a big deal. It was the only place left that allowed for her outsized ego, which I learned much later was really a mask for her insecurity.

As Barbara grew older, sadly, she couldn't get any work even there. With no savings and her still hugely expensive lifestyle, she had to withdraw her daughter from her expensive boarding school. Like a deer in the headlights, Peony found herself wandering the halls of a public school in a fairly down market neighborhood, wearing far too expensive clothes. She was lost and isolated. It didn't take her long to take comfort in alcohol.

When I last encountered them, it was tragic: each one of them struggling and damaged by their fall from grace. Barbara was living with the now adult daughter and her young son, surviving on bad but cheap food. Peony was in and out of rehab but Barbara remained in denial, believing that the circumstances that had befallen her were because of other people's mismanagement. Denial is the armor we wear to protect ourselves from confronting the hard facts! Barbara's was a tragic and tattered tale. Most of our group went on to have far more balanced and successful lives. But it's important to learn from the cautionary tales.

∽

When the day of the salon came, I made the decision that I needed to go. It felt cowardly not to. I took a piece I had written with me but I thought it was unlikely that I would read it. I was surprised at how happy I felt in the company of so many old friends and acquaintances. There was a lot of laughter, great food and plenty of wine. The concept of time slipped away and it was as if none had ever passed. Some of the stories the women read were funny, a couple of them sad. And from the woman who had invited me came the shocking revelation that she and her husband were full-blown swingers. She didn't just read her story. She acted it out. It went far beyond colorful. It was lurid. There was utter silence from the previously raucous crowd. Mouths were open. Making eye contact was dangerous. In that moment, whatever fear I was hauling around evaporated.

It was my turn. I took the papers with the story I had written out of the recesses of my purse. I walked up to the improvised stage and I read. It was the story of a shame I had carried with me since I was twenty-one. "The handsome, somewhat older, but far more experienced, boy next door had asked me out. I was over the moon. He took me on a moonlight drive through the park, then to a fancy restaurant where I feigned an aura of sophistication I truly did not have. The evening was better than I could have imagined until my date picked up the water pitcher and emptied it on my head. I was frozen in shock. My false eyelashes crawled down my face like soggy caterpillars. The whole restaurant took in a collective shocked breath. A spark from the Steak Diane flambé had caught the nylon cord that wound through my carefully coifed updo, and then my hair. Harold, my date, had acted instinctively to put out the flame before a real disaster took place. I was at first horrified, then mortified. Harold led me from the restaurant, our meal unfinished. He took me to his sister's house to dry me off, promising me that he would take me for the best Sicilian ice cream to make up for the ruined dinner. There was no one at his sister's house. I stood forlornly at the bottom of the stairs while Harold went up to get a towel. He dried my hair and leaned in for a kiss. One was not enough. He wanted more, much more. I fought as hard as I could but soon he pushed me down onto the floor… and he raped me. There was no ice cream".

I had stuffed that pain deep away, praying I would never be found out. I didn't hold back in my telling of the innocence lost - about the emotional devastation that somehow was made funny. That's my way of sharing pain. This public airing of my embarrassment and humiliation came well before the "Me Too" movement. It was shocking when I shared it, but as we now know I was far from alone! We grow up. We no longer need to bury our heads. The response to my story was amazing. I felt something click into place. I didn't yet know what that click was. But I did know I had to keep writing.

My energy had rekindled and I was open to everything that appeared to want my attention. The brain fog had lifted and the snow had melted. I finally felt I had landed in my new home. A question kept floating around in my head. "How old would you be if you didn't know how old you really were?" I decided it really would depend on one's state of mind and whether or not both knees and hips were being cooperative. Or how much one had to drink. I was feeling open, ageless and excited. Since that afternoon soiree, I had been writing without knowing what form my musings and self-reflection would take, until it began to coalesce. I knew. I was writing about my lifelong struggles with my body. My joke has always been that when I was born I weighed six and a half pounds but one hour later I weighed sixty-two pounds and it went up and down from there depending on what diet I was on. My first enforced diet happened when I was twelve years old, mandated by my mother who was worried that I would never find a husband if I was fat. It's hard not to wince at that very notion. These often insane and punishing diets continued well into my forties. I spent a crazy amount of money on them. *That could have been a tidy little nest egg.* It was only when I came to the clarity that I was interfering with my biology and more significantly my mental and emotional health that I stopped. I was finally free of that tyranny. I knew this was a story I was intended to share. But the most important part of the story was about love.

I was cracked open and words flowed out of me with an ease and purpose I had never felt before. It was as if I was possessed. Before I even understood what I had written, it was done. It was too long, a bit unwieldy but something deep inside me told me I was on to something real and maybe even important. What is destiny but the sum total of the choices we make that gets us to where we are supposed to be.

Without wanting to seem as if garden fairies had kidnapped me, I found myself opening up to whatever the universe had in mind. *Finally you stopped believing you could control everything.* In no short order a friend invited me to join her at a political theater workshop being led by a very prominent director I had worked with twenty years earlier. I thought I'd rather have hot pokers shoved into my eyeballs but I said "yes". After the workshop, the director, Pam Brighton, approached me, saying, "I hear you have written a one-woman show and I'd like to read it." I at once said yes and sent it to her. Two days later, she called to say she'd like to direct it. And so it went... A close friend offered me the money that would be required to bring my show to the stage. The director, Pam, who lived in the UK, delayed her return and moved into the guest room in our house. We read my play over and over and whittled it down to a manageable size. We found a church to rehearse in and a lovely young girl who was excited to be our assistant for next to no money. And I kept saying yes. The hours were long, and living and working with Pam, whom I loved even when we were at loggerheads, was exhausting. I am a neat freak, especially when I'm working. I can't have clutter around me. It makes me feel anxious and weedy and there's enough of that going on in my head. Everything must be organized and in its place. Gilles and my son have always made fun of me for that. Remy was forever moving things ever so subtly to see if I would notice. Notice! I could walk into any room and in less than three seconds catch on if a throw pillow was out of place. Pam was more like... *I want to be kind, but it's not showing up.* Pam was like Pigpen, covered in flakes of ash and dandruff and smelling like an ashtray. Dirt seemed to catch in her wake and nothing was ever returned to its place. I had visions of hitting her on the head with the greasy frying pan she left out on my kitchen counter every day, along with the crumb trail that had Hansel and Gretel followed, would easily have led them home. My saving grace was I had to spend hours on my own every night in the sanctuary of my bedroom in order to memorize my ninety-page script. That amounts to an hour and half of just me on stage, alone.

Titles were bandied about. "The Weight is Over," "The F Word" (meaning 'fat'). But the title came at me at three a.m. with the velocity of an asteroid, "Sex, Pies & A Few White Lies"

Posters promoting my one-woman show appeared everywhere. There was even a full-page story in one of Toronto's most read newspapers. Opening night came and we had a packed house in the upstairs clubroom of a well-known restaurant. I stood backstage amid the pickles and canned tomatoes in what was laughingly called my dressing room, my lungs filling with anxiety as I heard sounds of glasses clinking amid the chatter and laughter. Our sweet assistant Megan came backstage to give my five minutes warning till show time. Pam marched in and in her loving but brusque way nailed me with her eyes and said. "Be good. They're all waiting." I felt my knees buckle. I hadn't been on stage in more than twenty years. I took in a few deep breaths to try to calm myself. *That was a waste of time.* I put my hands on my heart and had a few sharp words with myself. "No one made you do this! This is your dream. Now go out there and enjoy it."

I remember nothing of the performance. I heard laughter and lots of applause. It whizzed by like lightning. When it was done I may have been exhausted, but the euphoric adrenalin rush was palpable and worth bottling.

I woke up the day after with legs that were in agony. It took a few minutes to understand that I had been so tense when I first hit that stage, that I had planted myself so firmly, that I may as well have been nailed to the boards. Nevertheless, word spread and we had packed houses every night. The reviews were unanimously great. I was asked to come to talk about my show on a national radio show. One of the next calls was from The National Eating Disorder Association who had heard my radio interview and invited me to be their keynote speaker at a conference event to be attended by two hundred doctors and shrinks. *The irony abounds.* I invited them all to bring their couches and said I would happily volunteer to lie on every one of them. *I had enough nuttiness for everyone to have a go.*

Stepping into the unknown and taking a chance on something I had talked and talked about doing for years but never had the courage to pull off brought me the knowledge that putting it all on the line had just changed my life. I was now officially fearless. I knew this was just a preview of what was to come.

Note to Self: Whenever doubt creeps in, I remind myself that the words in my head dictate the outcome of everything. I cancel the negative and switch to the positive and say yes. The universe will hear me. My biggest take-away? To always take a chance on yourself even when you are terrified! Life is full of surprises. Always be on the lookout for inspiration and opportunity. When you do, it usually shows up.

Recommended Medication: A celebratory cocktail for everyone.

CHAPTER 19

EVEN SQUIRRELS KNOW IT'S IMPORTANT TO STORE THEIR NUTS

The Cost: The shock of discovering how dumb it is to not have a plan.

People talk to me. They open their hearts and their mouths and tell me the most amazing and revealing things. I'm always interested in how others navigate their lives. I have learned so much from them.

∽

While visiting friends, I sat down to share lunch with Tonya and Kimmie who spend seven days a week together sharing housekeeping duties for very wealthy families in a beautiful beach community in Connecticut. They were open, generous and absolutely open as they answered my questions about their lives.

Together they clean six houses a day, every day and need every penny they make. They are single mothers, one a former drug addict and the other a former alcoholic. They have both been clean and sober since they had kids. They are a formidable team with open hearts and indefatigable spirits. They work for a cleaning company that pays them fourteen dollars an hour for backbreaking work but they never complain, even though they know that the company charges thirty dollars for their services.

They laugh a lot, mostly at themselves. Tonya is the stronger of the pair, always moving at the speed of light. Kimmie has a fused disk in her back and can't stand for too long, so she spends most of her time on all fours as she cleans the floors and baseboards wearing thigh-high rubber boots. I met them while staying with friends at one of those gorgeous homes they keep ship shape. I asked them why they don't go out on their own. All the people they work for treasure them and would happily recommend them to their friends and neighbors. They were quick to school me on the facts of owning a cleaning service. From Kimmie I learned that a good vacuum cleaner costs about three hundred dollars and they would need two in case one breaks down. Tonya chimed in that that cost was just for the first pair but they'd need a second pair of vacuums for pet free houses. "Can't have dog hair falling all over someone's Persian carpets if they don't own dogs or cats." Tonya then added in the cost of cleaning products, brooms, brushes and hoses, and ladders to reach the gutters. A van would be required, insurance, gas and then the liability insurance in case, God forbid, they broke some expensive antique vase. Kimmie threw in that so far that has never happened. And above all, they don't want or need the responsibility. They have enough of those already.

During their very short lunch break, these two women made me laugh with their stories about changing their own tires, plowing snow and cleaning their gutters after they have finished a grueling twelve hour day cleaning houses. They have mastered the art of living within their means. They shop for the cheapest cuts of meat; they take their clients' leftovers instead of allowing them to be tossed. They throw nothing away, choosing to repurpose everything. They both believe that no one takes better care of you than yourself. They snorted that waiting for some 'boring' Prince Charming to come along would cut into their precious sleep time.

Every day is Groundhog Day for them. They are up before the sun comes up in order to get their housecleaning done before the sun goes down. And so it goes, yet they are grateful for the work and only pray that they remain healthy enough to provide a better life for their kids. They have no envy in their hearts as they clean the already highly polished floors in one over-the-top beach house to the next and so on. They both wished that they had received a better education but they didn't and they don't have much time between working and taking care of their families to get one. Tonya is making plans to return to school by putting away whatever tips she receives and bartering for babysitting. They are grateful for the lives they do have. They know all too well that happiness doesn't always come from having a well-stuffed bank account. They are a reminder of how blessed I am to live the life that I do.

∽

Sitting on a small ferry zipping across the Bahia de Mujeres, the sea constantly changing colors from deep blue to various shades of turquoise like a light show, it was hard to fathom it wasn't a special effect. I marveled not just at the water but how my life had changed since I took a chance on me by writing and performing my one-woman show. Here I was, a true example of risk reaping rewards, on my way to beautiful Isla Mujeres to be the keynote speaker at an International Women's Day conference. A Jack Canfield quote flashed through my head. "Everything you want is on the other side of fear." *Words I now strive to live by.* I came to understand that opening up about my lifelong diet struggles in a very public forum was incredibly liberating. I wasn't playing to a camera with anonymous viewers somewhere out there. I was speaking directly to roomfuls of women. I could see them nodding appreciatively. I saw tears flow in recognition and best of all I heard the healing sound of laughter as they recognized themselves in my many stumbles. When I shared that, more often than not, I landed on my head but I always surfaced stronger and bolder, I could feel their longing to open up come to the surface. I was in my element. I loved sharing every flaw and folly that I thought belonged to me alone. It was in these talks with women the world over that I discovered how much we shared. The darkest secrets usually centered around our perceived failures from our body image, to never living up to expectations as wives, daughters, and parents and on and on right up to our bank accounts.

    Someone, somewhere, suggested I write a book based on my one-woman show. Without a clue as to how I would go about taking on such a monumental task, I said yes… because that's who I have become! I asked everyone I knew who could give me advice on what to do to make it happen. Several writers and agents warned me that it was a daunting proposition these days, with more and more people writing and fewer actual bookstores – the business model for written product was like the shifting sands of the desert. I was warned that as a first time author, up against celebrity names and best-selling authors, it would be difficult to even find an agent. I listened and then I thought, if we listen to everyone telling us all the reasons not to waste our time doing something we have never done before, then we have no chance at succeeding. We are sunk. My inclination to fight back against the naysayers was in full force. If I were a bull in the ring, "No" was the red flag I needed to make me go for it. The challenge was on! I did more research into what I would need to

Oops! I Forgot to Save Money

do to be given that chance. I wrote a lengthy and detailed book proposal. It took me almost a year. Three most generous writers allowed me to use their names to send a cover letter to their agents along with my book proposal. In little more than a week, I heard from two of them. They loved my title - "Getting Waisted: (A Survival Guide to Being Fat in a Society That Loves Thin)". After talking to both of them, I was thrilled to hear they were interested in representing me. I chose the agent with whom I felt I had the most rapport. I wrote and wrote. And then rewrote. The pride I felt when I finished that manuscript was like nothing I had ever felt before. I felt I had grown wings. Although, that high may have been exceeded when I was invited to read from my book in front of packed audiences in major bookstores in both Los Angeles and Toronto.

"Getting Waisted" came out it 2014. It was a hit. It garnered almost one hundred percent positive reviews. I floated on air for months. And I learned it's really difficult to make money even if a book is covered in five-star reviews, unless one is lucky enough to get on one of the big American morning shows or is kissed by Oprah's sun. To have that kind of PR agent costs really big money… money I didn't have. I was still thrilled as my book sold thousands of copies. *And not just to my family and friends.*

I knew in some way that moving away from the warmth of Los Angeles to the freezing winters of Toronto had helped to make a dream I didn't even know I had into a reality. I could now add author to my string of self-propelled careers. A second book followed a year later. "OMG! How Children See God" also got amazing reviews and an enormous amount of free publicity. I had been curious in this day and age of ever-growing secularism and extreme fundamentalism, how children were thinking about God. Their answers and drawings were illuminating, funny and sometimes

257

extremely touching, so I put them together in a book. It, too, did really well.

I knew that I loved the challenge of sitting at my desk, allowing the characters in my head an opportunity to come out and play. If the old adage was to be believed, that one should write about what we know, then I knew exactly what I wanted to write about next. Money! And how little I knew about it! This would be the book I needed to write to help me understand myself and hopefully for others to come to understand themselves in their recognition that much of me is also them. For a moment, the old insecurities flared. Who am I to write a book about money? I am definitely no specialist in the high-flying world of global economics. I took a deep breath. I do have way more than the ten thousand hours required to make me an expert in struggling, fearing and hiding from everything to do with money. I have earned more, saved less and not cared enough. I had PTSD in what not to do in order to create financial stability. But I am fearless about telling the truth; I have an excellent track record in that department. Who better than me? I hoped it would change my outcome and help others to do the same.

I recently asked my son what was his take-away from having us as parents. Barely taking time to blink, he responded, "I'm risk averse." He is, at thirty-four, a successful software engineer with a retirement plan already in place. I looked him in the eye and said, with a hint of irony, "Say thank you." I'm not sure if he smiled or winced.

I have always been a glass almost full kind of person with the occasional financial tsunami showing me that life can be unpredictable. Before I could make sense of the choices I had made, I needed to understand why I had made them. Money was not what I had chosen to focus on. I pretended I didn't care about it. But I cared. It was an out of sight but never out of mind quirk in my persona. *Let's call it what it was - a colossal failing.* My 'ah ha' moment crystalized. I needed to understand the why. Why had I not cared enough about money? Why had I unwisely chosen ignorance instead of education? There were so many questions that were coming to the surface. Questions I didn't even know I had. I couldn't contemplate writing this book without digging deeper. To that end, I sought out a qualified therapist to help me plumb the depths of my financial neuroses.

Lori welcomed me into her comfortable office. I told her I was interested in writing a book about women and money. After spending about five minutes with this remarkably open and insightful woman, I amended my reason for being there. I told her the truth. I needed to understand my obscure and conflicted relationship with this most necessary commodity. Over the next couple of sessions, the foggy vista began to come clear. It became obvious that in my most formative years, my role model was a single mother who lived far above her means, yet operated like a bumper car, hitting on something and when it failed, backing up and then hitting something else. She never had a strategy, just a lot of dogged determination to keep repeating the same pattern. She was always trying to push through to a better result, surprised when it didn't work. Added into the mix was my mild mannered, passive father who asked for nothing and so got little. Neither of them knew the first thing about parenting. In spite of the non-parenting I received, I somehow developed some of my better qualities like optimism, resilience and curiosity, laying the groundwork for my contradictory personality - my determination to do things on my own and my shadow-self that wants to be rescued. I felt a stab of recognition. The true epiphany landed when we began discussing my need for abundance to make up for the scarcity I feared most. I too had been a bumper car pinging from action to distraction and back to action with no conscious strategy. Behavior is developed young. Consciousness comes later. A rippling anger that had lain buried deep within surged to the surface. I wasn't angry with either of my parents. I was angry with me. How could I have been so stupid? So wantonly clueless, so reckless with our future? After the shame of that acknowledgment came relief. I had been hope without a plan. I had subconsciously known that. Perhaps that's what propelled our move to Toronto. I knew I needed to do something drastic to shake things up. I had made a decision to stop throwing everything against the wall in the hope that something would stick. I now believed that in order to succeed one has to commit in full to exploring no more than three ideas, choosing to focus in on only one at a time, then committing to doing all the homework that is required to bring it to life. My old habit of trying to do ten things at once was scattershot. And it had only lead to abandonment or failure. When my sessions with Lori ended, I felt I had been woken from a far too long sleep. I was no longer unconscious. I was damn sure that I wasn't going to let the past govern my future.

    I decided to write this book to help myself break this cycle and hopefully help others who are terrified that they are too late to join the party. According to AARP, statistics show that a healthy, middle class couple that are in their early- to mid-sixties today have a 43 percent chance that one or both partners will live to see 95. Savings need to be adjusted accordingly. There is no way of knowing what will happen to interest rates and inflation in future years. But for a retiree to generate $40,000 a year after stopping work, he or she will need savings of about 1.18 million dollars to support a 30-year retirement. This was calculated using average returns of 6 percent and inflation at 2.5 percent, according to Morningstar, a Chicago-based investment-research firm. *And good luck finding 6% interest on anything these days.*

"**Hello… HELP ME! I have fallen to the floor and I can't get up!**" I'm having a panic attack from having read Morningstar's statistics on what I will need to have saved in order to live in the manner to which I'm accustomed, which is certainly nice but not over the top in opulence. I'm not going to live in Panama or Croatia just because it's cheap. We want to grow old where our families are and not be dependent on them. But for those who had simply hoped for a reasonable retirement age, the recessions and economic trends in recent years have also worsened the finances of millions of seniors. Some bought homes during the housing boom and then found they owed more on their homes than they were worth and had to walk away. Others invested in the stock market and saw their investments shrink dramatically. Today, about 12.4 percent of the population aged 65 or older is still in the workforce, up from 3 percent in 2000,

My half-sister from my mother's first marriage is a great deal older than I am. She always told me growing up that she was old enough to be my mother. That used to infuriate me but now I am so grateful to have her. She will be turning ninety-three this year and has decided to give up skiing because, she says, at her age it would be stupid to fall and break something. I asked her how come she didn't feel that way at eighty-eight! She is blessed with remarkable health and fitness. She can walk rings around most people half her age. She was married to a doctor, which means she was left relatively comfortably off. But recently she told me that she really could only afford to live in the manner she is accustomed to for another five years. I jokingly told her that she'd be fine given she could get a job as a fitness instructor. But her situation is really no joking matter, as we are collectively living longer and there is that terrible fear that after having lived a fairly good life, one might have to face the end of it in poverty.

∾

I recently sat down with Bonnie Bruckheimer, the former producing partner of Bette Midler's film company; All Girl Productions. At the age of seventy-four, Bonnie is a vibrant and inspirational role model for forward movement. She absolutely embodies agelessness. When that part of her professional life came to an end - it was because of the studios increasing preference for making blockbuster action movies over more intimate female-oriented stories - she wasn't quite sure what the next act would look like. Several of her many female friends were in the same boat. Either they had aged out of their careers, or the companies they worked for were closing and they were cut adrift. They all wanted or needed to continue working, for their mental and emotional wellbeing and, for some, to pay their rent or mortgage. They couldn't afford, nor did they want, to just be 'ladies who lunch'. They decided to form a women's group to explore their possibilities and their dreams. They began meeting every other week to help each other answer the question, "What do I do next?" For one, it was being given the courage to write a book about her early years spent working with the Rolling Stones. Bonnie had the dream of teaching film to young people. With this group's support, she was elated when she landed a job teaching women's studies at the prestigious University of Southern California School of Cinematic Arts. But that wasn't enough for Bonnie's boundless creative streak. At a friend's suggestion, she transferred her sales and organizational skills to the home staging business. After a steep learning curve along with her incredible sense of color and taste, once again Bonnie is a star! As a positive reenforcing side-note, Bonnie says she got more support from her circle of friends to follow her heart and passion than she did from her parents.

~

I, too, treasure my girlfriends. We truly have each other's backs. When any of us has an idea, a performance or even what may sound like a hair-brained idea, we always show up to offer whatever we can do to support each other. *I love my man, but it's the women in my life that continue pushing me towards my dreams and enriching every part of my being.*

I will never retire! It's actually something I can't imagine doing or afford to do. But I'm not alone. There are countless people in their sixties, seventies and possibly beyond who will never be able to retire. They can't afford the luxury of even thinking about it. I think artists and writers just keep on keeping on because for us 'work' is an expression of life. The trick is to keep being paid for our efforts. I have often thought that my mother's talent and Gilles' artistic vision in concert with their gift for taking an idea and then turning it into something so beautiful that it can take one's breath away was worthy of an exhibition. The entrepreneur in me sees that there is a marketplace for the unique, one-of-a-kind things that my artist friends create from the filaments of their imagination. No one needs to fall into the starving artist category. Etsy is just one of the global curators of all things unique. They and others offer an online marketplace to showcase their offerings. Artists, entrepreneurs and rebels will always exist but now with a little effort, they can thrive. But it's not just artists; it's anyone with an idea and the will to push it forward. I can't emphasize this enough - a business plan is required to bring it to reality.

We are now living in the time of the Gig economy. Disruptors, as they are now known, crave independence, freedom and customized life/work balance. *I can relate...* We didn't think to name it when that's what we did. It was much the same but without the pervasive marketing and branding that comes with this new, ever accessible public millennium. They have brilliantly upended the world, as we know it. It's not easy for the cabbies that have been replaced by Uber and Lyft. Hotels struggle to compete with the Airbnb business model that has provided income to so many willing to rent out their basements or homes to those who want to find a less restrictive and less expensive way to travel. The entrepreneurial gifts from this new generation are often a mash-up of brilliance meeting necessity. "Why didn't I think of that?" comes as the highest form of praise. Task Rabbit is a global company that matches up the needs of pretty much anyone with someone in their roster. If you need pictures hung, they have that someone. Shelves built, homework help, groceries shopped for and put away and on and on. The ideas are endless, from companies that supply chefs and butlers, to those that will send you all the food to make your own gourmet meals. A few of the original giggers that come to mind are babysitters, lawn mowers and dog walkers. Today, they have an entrepreneur at the helm of almost every category that markets and brands their services. And there's room for more. If you can't find a job to pay the bills, then create a service or fill a need that will bring you the income you require. Do it alone or with friends. It doesn't have to be complicated. It can be something you already do. Bake from home, paint a porch, rent out a room, offer to care-take the elderly.

Wait! Bulletin! I just read more from AARP – "The worst thing you can do is thrown up your hands if the number feels out of reach. Save, save, save. Savers can double, on average, their nest eggs in the last decade or so of their <u>working</u> lives, thanks to the magic of compound interest." Says Michael Kitces, director of planning at Pinnacle Advisory Group. "Think about going from two cars to one, or cutting back on travel to keep spending low. If the market delivers a historically typical seven percent annually, your money doubles every decade." *Whew! That's good news.* Laurie Campbell, CEO of Credit Canada Debt Solutions confirms, "With perseverance and commitment anyone can undoubtedly increase their nest egg. I know the road to change requires taking baby-steps. Owning a life jacket is a necessity. In my case that means a savings plan big enough to weather all kinds of unexpected storms.

One thing I know for sure… From here on in I am the CEO of me!

Note to Self: To quote Bradley Whitford – "Infuse your life with action. Don't wait for it to happen. Make it happen. Make your own future. Make your own hope." I would now add to that, 'be sure you also make a plan in order to have a roadmap to follow.' One foot in front of the other… The steps all add up.

Recommended Medication: A Red Bull Ice Cream Float to keep the engine running.

CHAPTER 20

PEOPLE CHEAT FOR IT, STEAL FOR IT AND EVEN KILL FOR IT

The Cost: If we want money, we should save it, to protect it and ourselves.

I was feeling on top of the world. I had kicked my own ass and in the process I kicked some bad habits. I have come to realize that growing up with parents always living on the edge of economic collapse did leave its mark. Presenting as if we were well off played even greater havoc with my own financial identity. It was like living on a movie set. The big house looked opulent from the outside but when you walked through those front doors, there was no there, there.

When there was money in my bank account, I often displayed the anxiety of a person coming from scarcity. It didn't feel real. When there wasn't enough, I spent like a drunken sailor to make myself feel as if there was. *Paging Doctor Freud!*

I have wondered who my parents might have been if their lives had not been so brutally savaged by war. Their potential as emerging adults was severed on so many fronts. Emotionally, physically and geographically they suffered losses too horrific to imagine. My mother's family was torn apart. She continued to fight, to rally again and again, in spite of being a single mother

267

who knew no one in her newly adopted country. Her resilience was admirable. My smart but socially repressed father got swept up in other people's needs and wants, mostly my mother's. His go-to was to shut down, yet remain dutiful. Neither of them ever in my memory had constructive solution-based conversations about anything. Money-talk was always fraught. Those fights were the lullabies I went to sleep listening to. They both struggled and worked their whole lives. They were not around long enough. I, too, am resilient but also buoyant. I am a survivor's daughter. And I am a survivor. I am a fighter. I got all of that from them. I'm a human self-cleaning oven because I had to learn to care for myself. I am deeply grateful for the gifts I inherited from them.

If I have learned anything by telling my story, it's to be grateful that all I had clung to was no longer necessary. I have survived my mistakes and discovered that failure is often a necessary teaching tool. I have put it all out there. I have nothing to hide. And I now realize that living life filled with hope but no plan made me skitter and slide as if I was constantly on thin ice. Learning from failure has filled me with rewards. We now have zero debt. I have money in a savings account. I am a woman still filled with hope but now I also have a plan.

I have spoken to investment counselors, bankers, and financial gurus and the consensus is the same: We must face what's possible and what's not possible. For us to play catch up will require discipline and a far more conservative plan than someone much younger could take. We don't have time to risk the ups and downs of the stock market. Our plan is not a glamorous one. It's safe and turtle-like – slow and steady but moving onward and upward. Perhaps we will get to a place where we feel comfortable putting some amount of money into something slightly riskier with the possibility of a bigger return. But until that day we are not foolish enough to squander our hard-fought-for savings on anything too risky. By protecting our financial future from any unexpected nightmare scenarios, we can insure that there will always be a net to land in.

Discussions about money no longer require pulling the blanket over my head when things become uncomfortable. It's a loaded topic because so many of us have created complicated 'stories' that define our behavior and negatively impact our ability to manage money effectively. Money issues need to be healed to be able to move forward. But before you can do that, you have to identify the story you have been telling yourself. There is no shortage of scenarios, often stemming from our childhoods. Some cry poor in order to be rescued. Unrequited love can bring on overspending, trying to buy friendship with expensive gifts to get approval, or to soothe ourselves. Our lives are like the chapters of a really epic novel, filled with all the highs and lows the imagination can conjure, soaring success and crushing defeats, heart stopping romance to really powerful sex… Oh, *that's another book.* There could be broken hearts, spectacular blessings and painful, soul crushing episodes. It's life. But for women especially, money is overburdened with emotional meaning. We think we are not worthy, therefore we don't deserve success. And these stories can apply equally to gazillionaires as well as those living below the poverty line. But financial misbehaviors can be modified, although it doesn't happen overnight. First comes the recognition and admission that these behaviors exist and then the work to erase and replace them with healthier ones. The hole in our soul can be healed.

Money can mean opportunity, security, status, acceptance and power. I interviewed Elizabeth Bradley, a content executive who writes a blog called 'Chatting Money'. She says, "It's time for us to feel comfortable gathering wealth and therefore financial control of our lives. For that to happen, women need to be confident in their money knowledge." What I like about Elizabeth is her decidedly un-stuffy approach to money talk.

∽

"I've heard women utter a phrase "I'm just really bad at math" often enough that I want to chat about it. Sorry, what's that you say? I think it's honestly like going on a date and opening with, "I'd love a glass of chardonnay, and hey, I'm bad in bed." Says who? Who is this universal math judge that has determined your global standing? And is there a universal judge for skills in the bedroom? Is it a 10-point scale? 1 for mediocre at French kissing, and 10 for fireworks?" (I never want to know my ranking there.) Elizabeth continued, "Do you honestly think that some people are just innately better in bed, that they were just given a special gift? Or would we say that experience and knowledge, and a healthy dose of curiosity can improve your bedroom skill set? My personal view is that a desire to be good in bed helps you make sure you have some knowledge to improve your performance. Doesn't it? There is absolutely no reason we can't approach math in the same way – a bit of knowledge and experience levels the field. We're simply talking about the math you need to be financially savvy in life, daily skills, with no calculus required. It's definitely as do-able as sex is. Math is essentially just logic. I've seen some super-women figure out how to go to work, get the kids after school, prepare dinner (plus breakfast and strategize lunch), contribute to an online chat room, fit in a Pilates class, lead nonprofit organizations, send 3 work emails while transporting home, ensure everyone in the house is clean (ish), read to the kids at bedtime, AND occasionally have sexy

times with their partner – all on the same day. How on earth do women pull that off?"

We knocked back some more wine and Elizabeth gave me this last nugget. *"It's a logical (and phenomenal) juggling act, where you minimize wasted moments and maximize key details for efficiency. You know that's true because when your spouse takes the kids for 6 hours, you notice the details that YOU would have covered, somehow get dropped – and that's how you realize you simply do it more efficiently, right? I guarantee your partner or spouse doesn't say, "Shucks, I'm bad at parenting" after stepping in for an outing you normally do. It's just about getting familiar with the details. You simply make shortcuts and efficiencies for the details to be smoother. That is the core of financial math – not kidding!"*

∽

It's fascinating to me that we women know the calorie count of almost everything we put in our mouths and we can tally them with total ease but we are resistant to talking about, or handling our finances. Clearly, we do know how to do the math.

In the process of writing this book I video/interviewed almost one hundred women about their relationship to money. Many of them have never before had a conversation about money with anyone. It's as if they were being asked to unlock their secret diary and share their most private of thoughts. But as I have said before, people talk to me; they tell me things they wouldn't normally share with others. And yes, they know they are being recorded. I tell them how important this conversation is. It needs to be shared. I don't judge and I am the first to throw open the door to my failures and follies. Their honesty and openness has educated, humbled and inspired me. I know that cracking open these powerful, sometimes secretive, shame-filled and ultimately stirring conversations will help others just as they have me. I believe Gloria Steinem when she says, *"Women's progress has been a collective effort."*

∽

I had a surprise lunch date with a girlfriend who found out I was back in Toronto. When I had last seen Diana, she was a successful creative director at a stellar advertising agency. The minute we saw each other, it was as if no time had passed, even though it had been at least a dozen years since we had seen each other. Over a lunch of salad and some high-end twigs, we reminisced. I shared all the exciting things that had happened for me. Now it was Diana's turn. She started by sharing all the good things happening for her college-attending son; the only downside being how expensive everything associated with the experience was. In spite of this, she proudly added that this was AFTER a full scholarship. "It's the extras," she admitted, "the travel back and forth from university to home, the books, the food and insurance, and on and on." I asked about her lovely husband. Sadly, he had died of a heart attack three years earlier. My heart went out to her. I saw she was on the verge of tears. So I listened. It was the best gift I could give her. She simply needed a safe place to let go. After a few minutes I reached across to comfort her, and that was when she could no longer hold back her tears. She was simply worn out. She gradually pulled herself together and, in one of those insane conversations that I think belong to women, we laughed and cried over the litany of unraveling life events she had been dealing with.

To hell with any pretense that we could stick to our clean eating plans; wine and chocolate mousse were ordered. It was the perfect accompaniment to the revelation of her mother's encroaching Alzheimer's, and the realization that every qualified facility that could give her mom the care she needed cost a small fortune. Her mother's pension only covered some of the costs; therefore it was on Diana to make up the rest. It was also exhausting to pick up whenever her mother called. She called a lot, not always knowing why she called or even to whom.

In spite of always having been proactive about savings and investments, Diana had not been prepared for her mother's dependence or the mess her husband had left behind. He had no will and his finances were a disaster. It had taken her a year to locate his passwords so that she could find some of the vital information she needed. Diana had left her job after he died (she had been just too overwhelmed) and now that she was ready to get back in the game, in spite of a shelf full of awards, she couldn't. The truth was she had been 'aged out'. I inhaled my dessert and listened.

We have to remind ourselves we can ask for help. Before we parted, I hooked Diana up with one of my cousins, a wonderful woman who is also an Alzheimer's specialist. I also remembered I had been given several gift certificates by my friends before we left Los Angeles. I dug into my purse and happily gave Diana one for a relaxation spa day. I hoped that somewhere in my network there was someone in a position to offer professional advice to Diana, maybe even a job.

∽

I know this much, friendship needs to be a team sport; we need to keep sharing, and keep talking. In the grand girlfriend community, we are each other's best resource. I have learned so much on this journey about bringing money conversations into the light, but the one lesson I have come to appreciate the most, besides the value of compound interest, is that as women, we are the gold.

This is my third book and I know that even with a truckload of great reviews, some magic is involved. That being said, magic is not something I can bank on. *I can't pretend I'm not wishing for pixie dust to land all over this book.* What I know for sure is that my story is universal and not often spoken aloud! I'm happy to say I already have several invitations to talk on how I turned my financial failure into possibility. I no longer grab at filaments of something that may or may not become real. To think you can manifest abundance without action is simply wishful thinking. My plans are more grounded now. I will always be a risk taker in the creative arts gamble; I still have the courage required to be a freelance writer, actor and producer. But I have also made changes that offer stability. I am a recognized speaker, willing to share my stories about being a fat woman in thin-land and about aging disgracefully in a world that values youth. And now on a broader stage, I can share my tale of having survived bankruptcy and taken my financial destiny into my far more conscious hands. I am making more than fifty recorded hours of "Women Talking About Money" available to view on my website.

Money is not a dirty word. I want people to know we need to talk about it. We need to demystify its power over us and become the power over it. That's why I wrote this book; It's not a How-To, more like a Don't Ever. But I have learned from my many mistakes. Money is a basic necessity and a wonderful tool that allows us to achieve a kind of freedom that provides us with the ability to follow our bliss. There are no do-overs but there are change-ups. Here's to waking up and stepping up!

Always remember, the power to change is in your hands. Go for it!

I choose now to live by this principle and I hope you will too: If it doesn't bring you income, inspiration or orgasms, it doesn't belong in your life!

Note to Self: From Carrie Battle: Start by defining your personal goals, and balancing your risk comfort level with the true purpose for your money. Holding a diversified portfolio of financial products such as stock and bonds, and revising it occasionally has proven to yield better results for investors. Just ask Warren Buffet. The road to responsibility is about baby steps. Educate yourself and manage expectations. Don't bother listening to or reading about how much you need to live out your life in comfort. That'll just sabotage doing what's possible for you.

Recommended Medication: Whatever the hell you feel like. You've got this.

EPILOGUE

THE DAY THE WORLD STOPPED

The Cost: Almost everything we hold dear.

The Economist - March 17, 2020:

OF THE SUPPOSED five stages of grief, humanity's response to the covid-19 pandemic has seemed stuck in the first three: denial (it will not happen to us), anger (it's another country's fault, or our government's) and bargaining (if we make modest changes to our ways of life, it will leave us alone). Monday March 16th may have been the day when the last vestiges of these coping strategies evaporated. Much of the world moved on to the next stage, depression—the heart-sinking realization that billions of lives will be seriously disrupted for weeks and probably months; that, before it is over, many people will die; and that the economic implications are beyond dire.

∼

The ominous sound of an iceberg shedding an enormous island-sized chunk of ice is both eerie and deafening. It starts with a hissing sound, nothing to panic about, but it's followed by a ripping, groaning sound, ghostly at first, followed by a thundering explosion as it smashes into the ocean; then, the silence. The feeling that sound provokes reminds me of the collective ripping-away of our lives being decimated, followed by the ever-expanding silence that began to push in, closer and closer, the day the world stopped. "Now what?"

Back in the old, normal, sun-dappled city of Los Angeles, I was in a department store filled with shoppers. I was half-heartedly perusing the plus size section for a bathing suit that would cover me from neck to toe. Unfortunately this was February 01, 2020 not 1920. I gave up, realizing I had no intention of going swimming on the cruise on which I was about to embark.

This cruise was to be a celebration of thirty years of friendship between fifteen women, spearheaded by our cheerleader-in-charge, the party-loving Linda Hart. Her last name spawned what had become an annual all-girl Valentine's Day party. As it was the thirtieth anniversary of this loud, funny, diverse group, at Linda's suggestion we had agreed to take the party to Cabo San Lucas, Mexico, on a one-week cruise. *We also managed to get a screaming deal.*

There were rumblings of some terrible virus happening in far off Wuhan, China. It was nothing for us to concern our 'pretty little heads' over. We continued checking in with each other as to what we should bring on the trip. I knew this group, famous for lavish gestures, would be bringing gifts for all in our party, ranging from the sublime to the weird and wacky. But as with every group venture, I also knew there would be cancellations. The drumbeats were getting louder. This virus was no laughing matter and unlike in the days of yore - when planes were packed and landing all over the globe every few minutes - the rumors and low-grade fear had begun to set in. Our rooms were fully paid for and allowed for two people. We lost a few to fear of the encroaching virus, as well as to the predictable 'unforeseen', but we gained three husbands, mine included. I promised Gilles he could roam the ship at will and not be corralled into any of the all-girl activities. I asked him only to join us at our evening dinners. He agreed.

Wednesday, February 05, our sailing date, was around the corner. News was now emerging about the multitudes becoming sick and dying in Wuhan. I could feel the bubbling apprehension beginning to spread. Calls were made to the cruise line. Assurances were given that everything remained a go, and that there was nothing for us to be concerned about.

Linda, not one to take things at face value, made the trek to San Pedro, our port of departure. She somehow managed to convince the cruise director to give her a personal tour and show her the efforts that were being made to keep everyone safe. *It wasn't until we returned from our trip that we found out she had packed a pair of Hazmat suits for her and her husband, and thirty face masks just in case...*

On Monday, February 10, with only some minor trepidation, we climbed the gangway to the enormous Royal Princess. I had more anxiety about being on a ship with so many potentially raucous, hard-core partiers than any ship-borne virus. I was pleasantly surprised from the moment we came on board. Our room with a balcony was lovely. And everyone, from the passengers to the staff we encountered appeared warm and friendly. This was a Valentine's cruise and much like Noah's Ark, most people arrived in pairs. Many were wearing matching outfits.

Gilles and I had one medium sized suitcase and a backpack between us. I knew that Linda had planned many events that required dressing up, but I'm a really good packer and planner. I had mix and match clothes rolled into one another that would serve for any occasion. *When I saw a few of the other 'girls' dragging what seemed to be enough luggage for a three-week F. Scott Fitzgerald inspired, French Riviera cruise back in the Roaring Twenties, I thought perhaps I had underestimated the wardrobe demands.*

    The ship was a microcosm unto itself with little to no news from the outside world. There was one shared moment when several of us stepped into a crowded elevator and an older man emitted a massive sneeze. Everyone held his or her collective breaths in a moment of horror. But we soon forgot about it as the partying continued. Our celebration was full tilt fun. There was costume night and white dress night, many margaritas in Cabo San Lucas, and finally Valentine's evening, our last, with all of us dressed in red. It was loud and filled with expected gift excess from lavish hand-made cards, giant fans with our faces on them, to colorful bathing-suit toppers and hand-blown glass hearts. Bursts of laughter and tears flowed at how wonderful this special time had been.

    On Saturday, February 15, after a long and crowded, snake-line disembarkation, we were on the freeway back to Los Angeles. The conversation between Gilles and me was all about how much fun we had had and how we had all worried about nothing. That was when my throat began to hurt. I blew it off as coming from the salty sea air to the dry-as-dust, California weather. But by the time we were back at the house we were staying in, I was wracked with body pain like nothing I had ever felt. I had a slight fever and immediately fell into bed. I ate next to nothing and just wanted to be left alone in misery. The night sweats were jungle worthy. Four days later, the pain morphed into severe facial neuralgia. And the day after that I was completely fine. I knew it wasn't the flu. It didn't feel like anything I'd ever experienced before. All I knew was whatever it had been, it came on with a fury and was now thankfully gone. Gilles returned to Toronto a couple of days later and then he came down with something, but his symptoms were worse. After a week and a half, he too rallied. Neither of us sought or required medical attention. But I suspect that, come the day when the antibody tests are more reliable and available, we will find out that we actually had the Covid-19 virus.

On Tuesday, March 10th, I flew with extreme caution to Vancouver to see my son and his wife for three days before heading home to Toronto. The ominous noise that this virus was potentially a Pandemic had begun to surface. The plane was packed but I was armed with disinfectant wipes that had taken me several stores to find and a bottle of hand sanitizer. I was like a one-woman germ-fighting crusader. I was suspicious of everyone and everything. The judgment had begun… *Was that person looking flushed? Was that person a germ-carrying time bomb!* There was nothing that I didn't clean on and around my seat as well as the one next to me. I finally settled back, and took in the surf-tipped Pacific Ocean thousands of feet below me. I drifted off and awoke fifteen minutes before landing, in time to see the still visible volcanic crater of Mount Saint Helens.

Arriving in Vancouver I was met by my close friend, Tasha. She had booked us massages and lunch at a favorite restaurant. I experienced a sudden and unusual wave of anxiety. I told her that having a stranger lay their hands on me didn't sound like a good idea. She didn't understand. Tasha knows that no one loves a good laying on of hands more than I do. I tried to explain. It didn't seem to be an issue for her. Social distancing was a novel concept – not mandatory, just a suggestion. Having just sat on a plane with people coughing and compressed like sardines, I was now feeling the need for space and vigilance.

I had two lovely days with my son and his wife, accompanied by great weather and stunning views of snow capped mountains. By the third day, before I was to fly to Toronto, it seemed that everyone was experiencing a 'level one' feeling of unease about this creeping ever closer, highly infectious, viral disease. Having a farewell coffee with my son turned weirdly awkward when he began to parent me. He warned me that I needed to stop travelling and stay home, as I was in the target group for people likely to contract the disease. I was healthy and feeling pretty great after all that I had experienced in Los Angeles. I argued and told him I believed I had already had the virus. He shook his head disbelievingly, thinking I was making excuses rather than taking better care of myself. It was then I realized that my son was scared. As his mother, I was in a more vulnerable category and he didn't want me to die. As we parted ways, he refused to hug me, offering up an elbow bump and a toe kick instead. It might have been a proactive choice to protect me but I was left feeling empty.

The low-grade apprehension I had been witnessing was now full blown fear. Level five. The death toll in China was staggering, and the virus appeared to be expanding its reach into Europe. On Friday, March 13th, I was aware that it was a bad luck day to fly, if a person was superstitious. I'm not... *unless you count knocking on wood should I happen to say something that could turn into a curse accidentally landing on me, or someone I cared about. Or if I accidentally smite someone I don't know with one of my dark thoughts... is there a Hallmark, "I'm so sorry card" for that?*

I boarded the flight home to Toronto. Luck was with me. The flight was practically empty and I had been magically upgraded to business class. *I was suddenly liking this Friday the 13th thing.* I spent almost the entire flight chatting to the lovely flight

Oops! I Forgot to Save Money

attendant. We bonded over my slightly, fanatical wipe-down of my seat and the empty one next to me. She said even though the plane gets cleaned after every flight, she too has always erred on the side of caution. We shared some laughs over the gross bad habits of some passengers. She told me that in the good old days before the virus, she would be sitting in the jump seat, and when passengers went to the bathroom, she would hear the click of the lock and then a flush and the person would step right out. Now, she hears the click of the door, the flush and then water running as hand washing commences. She added that she had never needed to supply the bathroom with a second and even third stack of paper towels, until the news of this virus became so real.

On Saturday, March 14th, the weather was unusually warm and sunny. I had not seen my extended family and friends in the three months I had been in California. Everything felt normal. We had dinner with my sister, her grown kids and their kids. It was, as always, loud and funny, yet the conversations around the terrible toll the Corona Virus was taking in Italy was hard to shake. For us, the next two days, March 15 &16th, were about catching up with friends over laugh filled meals, until the talk invariably swung back to the serious situation that loomed over China and now Europe. The death tolls were mounting into the thousands. But it was over there...

Monday, March 16th was the day the world, as we knew it, vanished. The Corona Virus had been declared a full blown global Pandemic by the WHO on March 11. But here in North America they didn't start shutting things down until five days later and the reality that we were to be confined to our own homes wasn't yet penetrating our consciousness. We had rights. "You can't tell us what to do!" The denial was deeply dug in. We weren't ready to accept our new reality. Yet, Canada, the great

283

friend of refugees from all over the world, closed its borders to non-Canadians.

A week passed and the death count climbed higher but still not so much in Canada. We clung to the idea that by our quick response we could club this unseen enemy into submission. That notion disappeared by March 21st, as New York City became the epicenter of the global pandemic. Toronto was a scant five hundred miles away. We were wrong!! IT was here! IT was everywhere! But where was IT, this insidious, invisible mass murderer?

A level ten panic began to escalate. Fearmongering along with endless misinformation was coming at us with the velocity of a confetti gun.

I could feel dread coming from everywhere. I have always prided myself on having excellent coping skills but cracks in my armor were allowing fear to take hold.

We were suddenly prisoners in our homes – and not all our cells were spacious or private. Parents were pulling their hair out trying to find ways to corral their agitated, trapped children. Hospitals were under siege; families were separated, unable to reach out to give reassuring hugs. The dying were alone and isolated from family. No funerals for loved ones to commemorate. No wakes. No Shiva's. No weddings. No dinners. No company. No jobs! No money! Only the relentless hum of an ever-building panic as a rudderless global population drifted further and further from its moorings into a sea of unknowns.

So much for the best laid plans; all that 'coming to Jesus' about my finances. All plans were put on hold or cancelled outright, scared as to what the future may bring, or worse... not bring. No direction other than being confined to home.

The Quarantine Fifteen became a thing. Carbs calmed our frayed nerves. Sourdough bread and all kinds of baking united a skittish world. Flour and yeast became the contraband everyone was

Oops! I Forgot to Save Money

suddenly seeking. Those with access began to dole out small amounts to friends and family with the stealth of drug dealers. Hand sanitizer, much like the tulip wars of old, became auction worthy – only the highest bidders would remain sanitized. *Those hoarding massive amounts of toilet paper remain a mystery, as this was not a virus that caused diarrhea.*

Straightjacketed as we tried to tame our claustrophobia, when we broke free it was as if we were in an endless corn maze, walking 6' feet apart, desperately seeking a way out.

As always in times of trouble, there were rays of sunshine. We now realize there is a bigger definition of 'essential workers' - from the over-worked nurses, doctors, and garbage-collectors, to the transport truck drivers, delivery people and the hard working grocery store clerks who never missed a beat to keep most of us far too well fed. The unbridled family sing-a-longs and brilliantly choreographed parodies arrived on every streaming platform to make us laugh. Horn honking parades coursed through neighborhoods to brighten the days of those with birthdays and graduations, comforting those with dashed hopes and dreams, and bringing smiles to the lonely and isolated. They showed us that somehow we would find our way through this.

But economic recovery remains a bigger uncertainty. For many months all but essential businesses were ordered to close. So, how does one earn a living? The lucky ones have the skills and jobs that allow them to work remotely from home. But so many jobs don't. Restaurants that couldn't provide take-out meals were soon shuttered. All their staff, from cooks to wait staff were unemployed. Housekeepers and hairdressers suddenly had zero income. Drycleaners were done. No one needed his or her unworn clothes cleaned. Even dog walkers were sidelined. The devastation was so far-reaching; very few industries remained unscathed. Imagine an office where everyone must be 6 feet away from her co-worker. No wonder downtown office buildings were ghost towers. How do you distance people working on an assembly line? People the world over were scared. How were they going to put food on the table, let alone pay their rent?

In the words of Stanford economist Paul Romer: "A crisis is a terrible thing to waste." People from every corner of the world started to become problem solvers. Creativity and innovation flourished. Homemakers, film costumers and designers, my hubby included, began firing up their sewing machines, making masks for nurses and doctors along with all the other much needed PPE. Doctors in Boston ran out of virus-testing swabs, so they mobilized an army of 3-D printers to churn out new ones. Car companies retooled their machines to make Ventilators. Distilleries rejigged and made liquid sanitizer. A non-profit modified snorkel masks so doctors would have protection.

A seventeen-year-old created one of the most popular Coronavirus tracking websites in the world. A good friend of mine's son started a concierge testing business that would come to people's homes. The live streaming of everything from fitness classes to art classes was an instant success with financial opportunities for many. Streamlined grocery shopping apps proliferated. So many creative innovators became entrepreneurs over night. Tutoring companies from math to language skills filled a void for parents who were desperate to keep their children's education on track. All of these creative thinkers pushed a form of economic growth into being.

Not wanting to just eat cake to stave off panic – *although I admit there was a lot of that going on* – I knew that I too would have to pivot/reinvent myself. The entertainment industry in general will be one of the last to come back. My acting career was indefinitely on hold. Live speaking gigs, which had paid well, were also on hold. But, my constituency has always been women. If I couldn't speak to them from a stage or podium at this time, I could reach them virtually. I took some time – this time of stillness and being home – to foment an idea. I created a virtual platform called 'The Sisterhood Connection', in the hope I could reach perhaps an even larger global audience and bring together a bright, creative community of women to share ideas and promote each other's businesses.

This is the time when resilience is truly required. But what exactly is resilience? To my mind, it's about bouncing back. It's being able to shake it off, adjust, and take the next step forward. But like bobsledding or axe throwing, it's a skill that requires practice. Into every life there are troubles big and small. And as I write this, we are dealing with one of the biggest - a ravaging death stalker called Covid-19. Its tentacles are everywhere, but we can't see them, except in the body count that is still climbing every day. Of course we are scared. We don't know which way to point our sword. How can a little facemask and endless hand washing protect us? But it does! So does this uncomfortable, ill-fitting idea of distancing ourselves from our friends and family, the very people we lean on in times of trouble, only now we can't. We have to find our own way through this daunting time. But not alone, the entire planet is at war with this virus. We are all soldiers going into a battle that we have never fought before. How we handle these troubles is what can make us or break us.

For those who are stuck in a state of fear and panic, I believe that while in this holding pattern there is gold to be had. Writers can write resumes, biographies, birthday poems, eulogies – *sadly of which there are and will be so many needed.* Those who knit can make beautiful sweaters for adults, babies and for the

287

lucrative market that provides clothing for pets. Jewelry makers, painters, there are places galore for you to sell your wares. Etsy and E-bay are just a couple.

This is also the time to clean those closets of things you think you might wear sometime in the future. *You know you won't.* There's money to be made. Take pretty photos of your discards and put them on E-bay, Thread-Up or Posh Mark. Maybe this crisis will remind us how little we really need to be happy.

Become a virtual assistant. Help those boomers who desperately need computer help. Offer to take those boxes of photographs so many people have in their attics or basements and get them digitalized. *Cha Ching! (Just make sure that after you pick them up from OUTSIDE a door, that you sanitize!)*

Resilience. Creativity. Innovation. Possibility. Open-mindedness. Open heartedness. Community. Find someone to talk to, or laugh with, even if it's online… or pick some flowers and make them into a bouquet. It's always about making the best out of every situation. Those are the weapons that will get us through this. And I really believe faith is the unsung companion to make resilience whole.

We are not powerless. If we spin this pandemic into an opportunity we can learn from this dark time, brightening the blue ball that we all cluster together on. Take a moment to appreciate that our planet is breathing better, sparkling more; it's letting the fish stocks replenish; the dolphins and whales have a little more room to play without fear while every animal is finding its migration path and resting places in the sun. We humans can use this time to find our place as part of the community of species with which we share the Earth. There are new and better ways to share what we have with those in need. There is technology to unite us all in a common goal. Just look at how quickly we were able to develop vaccines to help us stave off this monster! We don't have to take to the street to make change happen. We can unite and demand that the inequality between rich and poor be narrowed. We have the power to change. It starts with us. The Coronavirus helped wake us up to these possibilities. Save! Hope! Plan! Diversify!

Now what? One foot in front of the other and don't look back. This is our reality. We cannot cling to what was. We must accept what is. Only then can we move forward. My wish and hope is that we will have all learned from this monstrous, life-sucking virus.

We need each other.

Recommended Medication: Anything and everything but... in moderation with a chaser of hope and possibility.

The Beginning

ACKNOWLEDGEMENTS

I have so many people to thank for their willingness to open the vault on that most taboo of subjects: money! I am forever grateful to all of you who answered my money questions with open hearts and open minds; for your candor and advice, patience, expertise, and support and above all else, your love.

A special thank you to my wonderful pal and very strict editor, the amazing Deborah Burgess.

The next thank you goes to my husband and partner in crime, Gilles, for always supporting me in everything I do. Thank you also to our son and daughter-in-law, Ezra and Lise, who enlighten me endlessly with their informed and committed relationship to saving and spending wisely. (Lessons not learned from me – But possibly because of me:) "You're welcome."

In no special order, huge thanks to: Margo Rapport, Michael Moore, Darlene Chan, Leah Komaiko, Barnet Bain, Sandi Stuart, Laura Robinson, Jean Smart, Karen Tanz, Julie Bristow, Wendy Crewson, Karen Breslin, Betty Gaertner, Maya North, Laurie Campbell, Adriana Molina, Gail Leija, Howard Simkins, Christie Andrus Nakano, Tami Fink, Heidi Von Palleske, Aaron Brown, Perry Goldberg, Nancey Silvers, Arlene Sarner, Trish Mennell, Noreen Halpern, Elizabeth Bradley, Caroline Neville, Carla Singer, William Forster, Linda Hart, Kimmie McPherson, Tonya Perkins, Diane Flacks, Wallis Nicita, Bonnie Bruckheimer, Jeanne Beker, Allison Dore, Frances Fisher, Christina Jennings, Gail Taylor, Joan Giamarco, Sonja Picard, Kerrie Keane, Alexandra and Lindsay Lorusso, and so many others I spoke to on this quest.

About the Author

Monica Parker is an actor, writer and producer in theatre, television, and film – most notably *All Dogs Go to Heaven*. She is the author of the much-loved book *OMG! How Children See God*. Her hugely successful one-woman show *Sex, Pies, and a Few White Lies* spawned her best-selling anti-diet memoir *Getting Waisted: A Survival Guide to Being Fat in a Society That Loves Thin*.

www.IamMonicaParker.com